92

NEW IMAGES OF
MEDIEVAL WOMEN

Essays Toward a Cultural Anthropology

NEW IMAGES OF
MEDIEVAL WOMEN

Essays Toward a Cultural Anthropology

Edited by
Edelgard E. DuBruck

Mediaeval Studies
Volume 1

The Edwin Mellen Press
Lewiston/Queenston
Lampeter

Library of Congress Cataloging-in-Publication Data

New images of medieval women : studies toward a cultural anthropology
    / Edelgard E. DuBruck , (ed.) .
        p. cm. -- (Mediaeval studies ; v. 1)
        ISBN 0-88946-265-8
        1. Women--History--Middle Ages, 500-1500. 2. Women--Social
conditions. 3. Women in literature. 4. Women in art. I. DuBruck,
Edelgard E. II. Series: Mediaeval studies (Lewiston, N.Y.) ; v. 1.
HQ1143.N49 1988
305.4'09'02--dc19   88-9351
                                                               CIP

This is volume 1 in the continuing series
Mediaeval Studies
Volume 1 ISBN 0-88946-265-8
MS Series ISBN 0-88946-264-X

The Edwin Mellen Press   The Edwin Mellen Press
Box 450   Box 67
Lewiston, New York   Queenston, Ontario
USA 14092   L0S 1L0 CANADA
                  The Edwin Mellen Press, Ltd.
                  Lampeter, Dyfed, Wales
                  UNITED KINGDOM SA48 7DY

Printed in the United States of America

NEW IMAGES OF
MEDIEVAL WOMEN

Essays Toward a Cultural Anthropology

TABLE OF CONTENTS

NEW IMAGES OF
MEDIEVAL WOMEN

Essays Toward a Cultural Anthropology

INTRODUCTION

The inner schizophrenia of the waning Middle
Ages is clearly shown up in the gulf between
prevailing theories and social reality. Women,
feared by monks and theologians and disdained
as the least valuable of all human material,
contributed largely by their labours to both
urban and rural economic life. Women worked in
the fields and sometimes, as among the Germans,
were responsible for the entire agricultural
routine. Townswomen were active in a wide
variety of trades and industries. The women of
Paris are known to have been engaged in more
than a hundred different occupations. The
decline of the towns in the late Middle Ages is
bound up with the suppression of flourishing
feminine industries and the replacement of
skilled women by men, which created a large
female proletariat. . . . There was no suitable
outlet for their great abilities and no satisfaction for their spiritual and intellectual
yearnings. . . . The Middle Ages had conspicuously failed to solve the problem of woman's
place in society; it was left as a heavy
mortgage on the future (Heer, 322-23).

Studies on women, monographs and collections on
medieval women begin to fill our bibliographies today, a
welcome sign that a hitherto neglected field is being
opened up to scholarly scrutiny. The present collection
tries to stay aloof of bias, overt feminism and market
consciousness alike. Our contributors are asking very
general, but candid, questions, such as: What is truly
male or female? How can femininity be defined other
than by opposing it to masculinity? Was the woman of
the Middle Ages able to transcend stereotypes? How
about individual differences? Was there one male vision
of the female which remained unchanged during several
centuries? Should we not seek a non-alienated expression of gender and sexual identity? Must women speak
from within patriarchal discourse? Is, on the other
hand, language the true equivalent of all forms of
expression which medieval women had at their disposal?

The essays presented here attempt to show new images
of medieval women worthy of the reader's attention. It
is possible that the latest wave of similar titles was
initiated by Postan's 1975 edition of Eileen Power,
Medieval Women. In fact, our collection touches--but
also elaborates--some of the topics treated by Power:
the social position of the lady and the working woman,
women's education, the phenomenology of women in daily
life, reconstructed carefully from the sources. We
bring new aspects, such as alternate life styles, the
very important reality of married daily life, and
clandestine marriages and their legal and clerical
implications. Above all, however, our essays ponder
images of the female in literature and art, which are
often somewhat different from women's position in real
life. Since we take for granted the reader's familiarity with the basic theoretical ideas about medieval

women, we shall add here a short survey only of these concepts. Our demonstration, together with the various contributions, may help to explain the "inner schizophrenia" observed by Friedrich Heer, ultimately a clash of ideology and reality.

Created by the nobility and the church, the two classes least familiar with women, the basic concepts of the female range from the courtly lady, the object of (adulterous) adoration, to Eve, woman temptress, corrupted by the snake, but corrupted a priori, because she was willing to be seduced; from the Virgin Mary, adored in courtly love songs, to the shrew of fabliaux misogyny. Of these stereotypes the oldest was doubtless the image of Eve. In medieval thought, inspired by Genesis and Pauline doctrine, the first woman became evil personified, whose temptation, whose very contact, were the origin of man's fall. Eve mythology, ultimately, is to be blamed for witch persecution and massive miscarriage of justice in Europe until the middle of the seventeenth century. Astonishingly, it was Thomas Aquinas who promulgated some of the most debasing opinions based on this mythology.

According to this eminent philosopher/theologian, of the two sexes, women are especially susceptible to the workings of the devil, who tempted Eve (rather than Adam) in the form of a serpent (Commentary to Lombard's "Sentences," IV). It must be said at this point that as a rule women are conspicuously absent in Thomas' monumental work; but in the few passages where he discusses them, his views are decidedly negative. In the chapter "The Production of the Woman" he muses:

> As regards the individual nature, woman
> is defective and misbegotten, for the

> active force in the male seed tends to
> the production of a perfect likeness in
> the masculine sex; while the production
> of woman comes from a defect in the
> active force or from some material
> indisposition, or even from some exter-
> nal influence; such as that of a south
> wind, which is moist, as the Philosopher
> observes (De Gener. Animal., IV, 2).

Woman is naturally subject to man, Thomas continues,
because in man the discretion of reason predominates.
Females serve only to supply the corporeal matter to
their children, which is, however, originally derived
from Adam (cf. Part I, qu. 119).

The application of this type of thought during the
Middle Ages and later could take the subtlest forms.
Thus, even matrimony was believed by some Fathers of the
Church to be an inferior state of being and ultimately
only good inasmuch as a woman might bear virgins. If
marriages remained without offspring, it was also
thought to be the woman's fault: in her the devil had
impeded conception, perhaps even by way of an incubus or
succubus, for facts about male impotence were unknown.
Needless to say, it is this stereotype which has had the
farthest reaching consequences for the position and
image of woman in the Western world, and it certainly
accelerated women's movements in the nineteenth century
and the plea for emancipation, equality and women's
studies in the twentieth.

Perhaps as a reaction to the Eve syndrome, the image
of the courtly lady was created by Western society, our
second conventional paradigm. She was, as a rule, a
married aristocratic woman, adored in poetry and song by

young noblemen most of whom were in feudal relationship
with either her husband or herself. The courtly troubadour society of twelfth-century Provence produced this
image for adoration, often not just platonic, doubtless
under the influence of Arab treatises on love, and historians have gone to great length to explain the phenomenon in terms of socio-economic developments (decrease in
wars, absence of husbands during crusades). The extraor-
dinary fortune of the courtly concept in the following
centuries is well known. Courtly society created a
great deal of literature, above all love poetry and
romances, and the courtly lady inspired chivalry, codes
of moral behavior and, ultimately, the rules of Western
polite society. Here, as a sample, is a stanza by
Bernart de Ventadorn (fl. 1150-1160), which shows the
cruel lady on a pedestal, as it were, but who has cap-
tured the lover's heart:

> Alas! how much I knew of love,
> I thought, but so little know of it!
> For now I cannot check my love
> For her, who'll give me little profit.
> She has my heart and all of me,
> Herself and all the world; and nothing
> Leaves to me, when thus she takes me,
> Except desire and heartfelt longing.

Artificial as this stereotype may be--its value for
literature, art and manners must not be underestimated.
It remains an aristocratic image, and while it was
either admired or ridiculed by the middle classes, it
was unknown to the peasants. The concept is questioned
early (The Châtelaine de Vergy, c. 1250) and again later
(Le Petit Jéhan de Saintré, 1459, and Les Arrêts

d'Amour, c. 1460), and ridiculed and parodied in such
works as Wittenwiler's Ring (c. 1400) and in farces and
carnival comedies. The didactic Ship of Fools (1494)
gives it no consideration, but features instead a long
chapter on adultery which is even longer in the French
version.

Transformed by the clergy, the courtly concept soon
generated the Cult of the Virgin Mary, our third stereotype which, like the others, has lasted to the present
day. It is a largely unacknowledged paradox that the
idea and function of the Virgin may cancel out the full
weight of Eve's guilt: while Mary was created to bear
the Redeemer, Eve was needed to give Christ a fallen
mankind to redeem. This type of logic is, of course, as
scholastic as the attempts of late-medieval fatistes
(authors and/or directors of mystery plays) to justify
the tortures and death of Christ by elaborate typolo-
gies, juxtaposing the New to the Old Testament, and by
inventing the diableries, whole empires and hierarchies
of devils and demons which parallel God's Heaven and the
realms of the Just.

The veneration of the Virgin inspired pilgrimages,
helped build and name cathedrals, created legends, and
Her miracles were immortalized in the dramatic genre.
It influenced mystic poetry and produced hymns and other
religious music. In the fifteenth century the Virgin
appeared more and more humanized on altar paintings and
as a statue, and the Christ child was the first infant
depicted in the visual arts. Villon's mother would
therefore pray to a Divine Lady humanized, an empress,
regent, and mistress (governess), thus giving Her the
highest titles in her anthropomorphic vocabulary:

Lady of Heav'n, God's Regent over man
And Empress over the infernal mere,
Receive Thou me, Thine humble Christian,
That I may dwell with them Thou holdest dear,
Though naught at all have I deserved here.
Such grace as Thine, Lady and Governess,
Doth far outweigh my human sinfulness;
That grace sans which (I know, and tell no lie)
No soul can e'er aspire to saintliness.
'Tis in this faith I mean to live and die.

More than the cult of the courtly lady, the veneration
of Mary could have served to redeem (and to relieve) the
Eve syndrome—which is, however, still much in evidence
in our fourth conventional paradigm, that of the shrew.

Appearing early in Chaucer, the shrew fills late-
medieval bourgeois literature, the _fabliaux_, farces,
Schwänke, and many a German shrovetide play. Advocates
of genre theory shy away from the study of mentalities,
but it still is indicative that so many similar genres
all containing the shrew should have been cultivated and
appreciated in the late Middle Ages. While subjected to
her husband, the shrew is ultimately superior to the
henpecked male, who becomes ridiculous by his very
helplessness or by his gullibility. Conformity to
traditional Christian morality is a variable in the
fabliaux. Women deceive, lie, and exploit situations,
and while the sympathy of the reader is at times with
the duped person (the husband), one must often acknowledge the shrew's ingenuity.

The urban society of the fifteenth century was,
physically, closely knit; living space was crowded for
the average man, and only patricians and wealthy master
craftsmen could afford mansions. It is therefore not

astonishing that the topic of human relationships should
arise in our literary sources. While marital problems
became a popular theme in the narrative genre as a
reaction against, and yet concomitant with, the courtly
topics, not all of the literary evidence is as outright
misogynist as the following text, which takes us to
Spain:

> SEMPRONIO:
> . . . Who could tell you their lies, their
> tricks, their changes, their fickleness,
> their sniveling, their bad temper, their
> impudence? Their deceits, their gos-
> siping, their ingratitude, their incon-
> stancy, their presumption, their boastful-
> ness, their false humility, their folly,
> their scorn, their servility, their glut-
> tony, their lust, their filth, their
> cowardice, their insolence, their sorcery,
> their gibes, their scolding, their want of
> shame, their whoring? Consider their
> giddy little brains concealed behind those
> long and delicate veils! Or within those
> fine and sumptuous gowns! What corrup-
> tion, what cesspools, beneath those gaudy
> temples! They are called limbs of Satan,
> the fountainhead of sin, and the des-
> troyers of Paradise.

This passage, which repeats a collection of common-
places on wicked women, was chosen from La Celestina
(1499) for several reasons. It shows 1) that the com-
monplaces occurring in our literary masterpieces have a
significant function in the work as a whole; 2) that

Sempronio's opinion of women, contrasted here (and
throughout La Celestina) with that of his (courtly)
master, Calisto, represents the intellectual level of
the common man who--in spite of the learned allusions
given to Sempronio by Fernando de Rojas--enjoys those
forms of literature which have made of woman a cesspool
of evil and of husbands cuckolds and laughingstocks
since the beginning of story telling in Asia Minor and
probably before; 3) that misogyny was possibly just as
strong in Spain as in other European countries, although
it should be understood that this trend formed only one
aspect of the complex Celestina. Similar passages could
indeed be cited from other contemporary literatures;
they abound in German carnival plays.

What were the reasons for this wave of misogyny at
this point in time? It is true that crowded living
quarters are to be blamed for some problems, but above
all, this tendency must be seen as a somewhat more
realistic differentiation from the veneration of courtly
women and the Mother of God, and literary influences are
certain. Misogyny speaks from many pages of the
thirteenth-century Roman de la Rose, II, by Jean de
Meung, which is removed by only fifty years from its
first part, entirely courtly, by Guillaume de Lorris.
It is well known that by his work Jean de Meung started
the Querelle des femmes, also called Querelle du Roman
de la Rose, in which Christine de Pisan participated.
In our opinion, however, the entire work could doubtless
be integrated and rewritten in the style of a debate.
According to recent findings, there is evidence that
even its first readers misunderstood the intention of
this seminal novel, as they began immediately to contrast the first part with the second. Jean Dufournet, a
recent critic, elaborates the traditional view by
quoting Gaston Paris:

"Guillaume praises and shows true love only and
condemns false lovers; Jean, in the mouth of
Reason, finds that the latter are smart alone
and that the others are foolish; Amor, in
Guillaume, forbids the use of gross expressions, Jean justifies them and demonstrates his
theory cynically; Amor recommends, above all,
in the first part, to respect women, while they
receive in the second the bloodiest insults
ever addressed to them; even the allegory of
the rose, delicate and graceful with Guillaume,
becomes flatly crude with Jean." Guillaume de
Lorris (Dufournet continues), devoted to the
woman, is supposed to have been the mouthpiece
of an aristocratic and courtly society, while
Jean de Meung, critical and virulent, would
have represented the bourgeois frame of mind,
triumphant after the decadence of chivalry,
courtliness and asceticism.

However this may be: the fact that the famous work was
misunderstood is still indicative of the pervasive
impact of misogynist attitudes in the late Middle Ages
and subsequently. Its second part was to influence many
literary works and to condone in advance certain societal attitudes for centuries to come.

The four theoretical views outlined above are
addressed in various ways throughout our essays which
highlight medieval women in literature and art, thus
opening up a perspective missing in Power's work. We
proceeded inductively on the premise that a very complex
reality can be assessed best by presenting its diverse
aspects. Since the role of medieval women in society,
in the church, and in politics has been well researched

by Herlihy (monograph), Rose and Berman (collections), we have concentrated on literary and artistic manifestations instead. We also felt that medieval women writers have been treated extremely well in the Wilson and Rose collections and in monographs such as Bornstein's. Besides, medieval authoresses remain a succinct, but atypical, group. While other titles published recently focus on one particular literature (Chance), we prefer to take a wide sampling: French, English, Cornish, German, Spanish. Most of our essays feature late-medieval women, which may be considered a disadvantage, but in view of the abundance of material on this period alone we decided to limit our reach and to provide in depth an exposure which would have been superficial otherwise. Finally, inasmuch as the origin, development, and typology of womankind, as well as the changing forms of its behavior toward its environment should be the subject of anthropology, which also might investigate the position of woman in the world and in history, we have decided to claim these studies to be essays toward a cultural anthropology.

What are the diverse aspects and themes treated in our collection? The following pages will give the reader an overview--and perhaps elicit preferences.

Christine de Pisan, the eminent French authoress, spoke up for women in the famed querelle des femmes, but Lynne R. Huffer finds that Christine's discourse is often masculine. How indeed are women, forced to act like men (as in Christine's case), able to communicate professionally, unless they inscribe themselves into the patriarchal order--be it in order to be understood! Writing in Latinate style, lacking a specifically feminine idiom, the astrologer's daughter, widowed too early, calls phallic modes into question, nevertheless.

In the _Dit de Poissy_, Christine proposes alternate life
styles for aristocratic women: the courtly and the
convent life, according to Kathleen E. Kells. The total
suppression of the feminine voice in the _Legend of Good_
Women is part of Chaucer's irony, as he defends himself
for having created Criseyde, according to Elizabeth D.
Harvey. Refusing to engage in Ovid's transvestite
ventriloquism (_Heroides_--Harvey's term), Chaucer has
thus--perhaps unwittingly--created a text ultimately as
debasing as an anti-feminist work.

The literary and artistic image of women in the
Middle Ages rarely transcended stereotypes, the foremost
being woman as object of courtly love. The lady to whom
a knight pledged his love and for whom he proved his
valor in battle or duel was an idealized woman placed on
a pedestal, as James R. Stamm explains. Sometimes she
remained without personal characteristics in the novels
of chivalry, almost as an abstraction. Cruel or
not--she was able to inspire courtly conduct and polite
manners, essential in a society no longer threatened by
massive military action, Christian or pagan.

Soon, the Virgin Mary seems to take the place of the
courtly lady, as the Mother of Christ appears in lyrics,
miracle plays and medieval tales, while her opposite,
Eve, turns out to be even richer in survival strategies,
as Evelyn S. Newlyn observes. In medieval Cornish
drama, Eve is a most interesting figure. Are spectators
more attracted by evil than by holiness? Humans tend to
identify with human weaknesses and may be reluctant to
follow a call to emulate the divine. Perhaps Eve, by
yielding to temptation after some agony, then by
seducing Adam, presents a more interesting spectrum of
psychological motivations and choices. Since the Fall,
female nudity has been associated with sexuality and is

ultimately not acceptable in medieval art. John A.
Nichols calls attention to the fact that woman's
procreative function seems to have been forgotten or
overshadowed: in art, medieval women are stereotyped
indeed, and nudity spells lasciviousness, even for
fairies and mermaids.

Can women transgress a stereotyped role? Martin B.
Shichtman denies the possibility for both of his
heroines, Elaine and Guinevere in Arthurian romance.
Elaine remains confined to her paradigmatic role: she
loves Lancelot and dies unsatisfied. Guinevere has a
place within history, but has ultimately no free
choice. A development toward women's individuality,
away from stereotypes, is observed by Judith B. Diner in
the Cent Nouvelles Nouvelles. In a style totally
unpredictable, the male author shows the full complexity
of fifteenth-century women: wives faithful to their
husbands, but who occasionally act "out of character,"
blurring the distinctions between serious and comic
style; young women in love with older men, young men
happy with oldsters--a whole gamut of very diverse
attitudes and feelings in the relationship between the
sexes.

Individual differences are noticeable in William E.
Jackson's study as well. The late twelfth-century
Austrian poet Reinmar der Alte shows women who, contrary
to courtly love behavior, evince the desire to lie next
to a man and who suffer from a frustration in unrecipro-
cated love, emotionally troubled women who are dominated
by men, have lost their power, and are therefore astereo-
typical.

In a very different tonality, our three studies on
marriage present an interesting triptych. Diane Scillia
has investigated Israhel von Meckenem's Alltagsleben

(_Everyday_ _Life_), twelve scenes by a relatively unknown
fifteenth-century artist, who has taken a rational
approach to marriage. His wife Ida was his business
partner. According to Meckenem, lechery is foolishness,
and wisdom in marriage brings happiness and prosperity.
Sebastian Brant would agree, but he is of course much
less confident that humans could be wise (_The_ _Ship_ _of_
Fools, chapter 33).

The wives of the _Quinze_ _Joyes_ _de_ _mariage_, shrewd,
awake, animal trainers of their husbands, receive the
reader's hearty approval. Often on the level of
fabliaux, the stories unmask the female unmasking of
men, according to Steven M. Taylor. Here, men are a
meek menagerie, often blackmailed in bed. There is no
doubt who has the upper hand in this tamed-tamer
paradigm.

Lest we forget, though, there were indeed loving
couples, who in spite of stereotypes and possible
paradigmatic situations wanted to get married. Like
today, parents were not always in agreement, and
sometimes, legalistic ramifications prevented the happy
union of the "right" persons. There was much controversy about the nature of marital consent, including
differences of opinion between the Paris School of Law
and the Roman Curia, assures Zacharias P. Thundy.
Before the Council of Trent declared clandestine
marriages illegal and invalid, quite a few of these
unions were allowed _post_ _factum_ by Courts of Law,
especially in the case of conflicting competencies.

Whether saint or sinner, stereotype or individual,
idol or victim, eloquent or silenced, the husband's
business partner or domestic scourge, the medieval woman
appears probably in as many varieties as her modern

counterpart. If our collection results in that conclusion, we have reason to be satisfied. More significant,
however, is the fact that here and there in these essays
the silhouette of the "real" woman begins to appear
against a background of stereotypes and paradigms.
Diner detects a desire for showing women's individuality, if not in the author, then at least in the
narrator/persona of the Cent Nouvelles nouvelles.
Huffer asserts that Christine de Pisan questioned the
stereotype early, while Newlyn suggests that the Eve
type is probably closer to reality than the Virgin
concept. Reinmar's courtly victims could be compared to
some of the good women in Chaucer's Legend, and yet
Jackson approaches realism when he speaks of pathologi-
cal symptoms in women whose unrequited love brings them
close to insanity. Scillia's married woman appears in
everyday life, reminding us both of the advice of the
Goodman of Paris to his future widow and of the lamentations of Saaz's Ackermann aus Böhmen for his deceased
wife Margarete. Finally, Thundy investigates the facts
behind and consequences after secret marriages. Even
Taylor concedes a sort of equality between the sexes (if
not a reversal of the power structure) in certain misogynistic works.

Our images provide as many approaches to an anthropology of the female during a time span which is slowly
opening up its recesses to patient research, the Middle
Ages. Historians assure us that still only one tenth is
known about the medieval millennium, for lack of
sources. Ergo, we hope to have contributed to this
research in a small way. Much remains to be done, for
medieval studies, alive and well since the early 1800's,
were up to now focused almost exclusively on men:
Heer's treatment of women (in the chapter named "Jews
and Women") comprises seven pages!

Lege, quaeso, benevolent reader! I would like to take the opportunity to thank the contributors for making this venture possible. We are indebted to Rita Edwards, who, with competence and patience, prepared our manuscript for publication, and to Professor Herbert Richardson and the Edwin Mellen Press. My special thanks go to three friends who have helped and encouraged me to undertake the collection: Renate Gerulaitis (Oakland University), Mireille G. Rydell (California State College--San Bernardino), and, above all, William C. McDonald (The University of Virginia). I dedicate this book to them.

Edelgard E. DuBruck

WORKS CITED

Berman, Constance H. et al. (eds.), The Worlds of
Medieval Women: Creativity, Influence and
Imagination. Morgantown, WV: West Virginia
University Press, 1985.

Bornstein, Diane. Ideals for Women in the Works of
Christine de Pizan. Detroit: Medieval and
Renaissance Monographs, 1981.

_____. "Women at Work in the Fifteenth Century,"
Fifteenth-Century Studies, 6 (1983), 33-40.

Chance, Jane. Woman as Hero in Old English Literature.
Rochester: Syracuse University Press, 1985.

DuBruck, Edelgard. Changes of Taste and Audience
Expectation in Fifteenth-Century Religious Drama,"
Fifteenth-Century Studies, 6 (1983), 59-91.

_____. "Death and the Peasant: A Testimony on
Fifteenth-Century Life and Thought by Johannes von
Saaz," Fifteenth-Century Studies, 3 (1980), 55-70.

_____. "The Emergence of the Common Man in
Fifteenth-Century Europe: A Probe of Literary
Evidence," Fifteenth-Century Studies, 1 (1978),
83-109.

_____. "Homo ludens--homo cogitans: Images of
Fifteenth-Century Man in German Carnival Plays,"
Fifteenth-Century Studies, 4 (1981), 61-78.

_____. "Thomas Aquinas and Medieval Demonology,"
Michigan Academician, 7 (1974), 167-83.

_____. "Time and Space in Wittenwiler's Ring,"
Fifteenth-Century Studies, 2 (1979), 73-81.

Dufournet, Jean. "Postface" à Guillaume de Lorris et
Jean de Meung. Le Roman de la Rose, trans. A.
Mary. Paris: Gallimard, 1984, 381. Translation is
mine.

Ecker, Gisela (ed.). Feminist Aesthetics. Boston:
Beacon Press, 1985.

Flores, Angel (ed.). Medieval Age. New York: Dell,
1963. Bernart de Ventadorn: p. 179 (trans. Muriel
Kittel); François Villon: p. 599 (trans. Norman
Cameron).

Gunn, Alan M. F. The Mirror of Love. A Reinterpreta-
tion of the Romance of the Rose. Lubbock, 1952.

Heer, Friedrich. The Medieval World. Trans. Janet
Sondheimer. New York: Mentor, 1963.

Herlihy, David. Women in Medieval Society. Houston,
1971.

Lafitte-Houssat, J. Troubadours et Cours d'Amour.
Paris: PUF, 1966.

Pearcy, Roy J. "Investigations into the Principles of
Fabliau Structure," in Versions of Medieval Comedy,
ed. P. G. Ruggiers. Norman: University of Oklahoma
Press, 1977, 67-100.

Power, Eileen. Medieval Women. Ed. M. M. Postan. Cambridge: Cambridge University Press, 1975.

Radcliff-Umstead, Douglas (ed.). The Roles and Images of
Women in the Middle Ages. Pittsburgh, 1975.

Rojas, Fernando de. La Celestina. Translation taken
from Lesley Byrd Simpson, The Celestina. Berkeley,
1955, pp. 7-8.

Rose, Mary Beth (ed.). Women in the Middle Ages and the
Renaissance. Rochester: Syracuse University Press,
1985.

Stuip, Rene (ed. and trans.). La Châtelaine de Vergy.
Paris, 1985.

Thomas Aquinas. Summa Theologica. Trans. by Fathers of
the English Dominican Province. London, 1922. I,
qu. 92, art. 1.

Ventadorn, Bernart de: see Flores.

Villon, François: see Flores.

Wilson, Katharina M. (ed.). Medieval Women Writers.
Athens: University of Georgia Press, 1984.

FILLING IN AND FLESHING OUT THE FEMININE FIGURE: INNOVATIVE REPRESENTATIONS OF WOMEN IN LES CENT NOUVELLES NOUVELLES*

by Judith Bruskin Diner**

By the middle of the fifteenth century in France, the currents of literary inspiration are shifting. The great swell of Arthurian, epic, and allegorical fictions is ebbing, although authors continue to satisfy the readers' taste for these traditional tales by moralizing them and translating them into contemporary French to please a public which prefers to read prose rather than listen to rhymed fiction (Doutrepont 1909; 1939).

However popular these traditional tales may have been in their own day, they do not have the modern appeal of a new current of anecdotal fiction, not formed entirely by the narrative molds of the past, works like the chivalric narrative Jehan de Saintré, and Les Cent nouvelles nouvelles, the first secular collection of prose tales in French, composed at the court of Philip the Good, Duke of Burgundy, sometime between 1456 and 1462.

Part of this modern appeal derives from the fact that, like the Chronicles of Georges Chastellain and Jean Molinet (poets and official historians of the Burgundian Courts), these narratives are not placed in a distant, idealized, fictional past. Nor are they situated in an invented Arthurian or allegorical setting.

Instead, the reader is invited to believe that the
inspiration for these fictional tales is drawn from the
fifteenth-century reader's historical world of events,
and that the domestic incidents which they represent
could have actually occurred in the fifteenth-century
reader's daily world (Regalado 1987).[1]

We notice that in several of these works written
outside the traditional genres, the female characters
behave in intriguing and unpredictable ways. Witness
the case of Belles Cousines, the courtly lady of Jehan
de Saintré. In the course of this chivalric narrative
(written in 1456), she changes from a teasing widow to a
moralizing benefactress, a long-winded pedagogue, and
finally to a wanton who betrays her lover with a sensuous, brawny abbot.

Some of the female figures of Les Cent nouvelles
nouvelles strike us with their similarly perplexing,
unpredictable behavior. How, for instance, are we to
understand the wife of the nineteenth nouvelle? In the
beginning of the tale, her relationship with her husband
is described in terms of mutual respect and reciprocal
affection. During a long absence, she remains faithful
to him, and even proves herself an astute business
woman, earning her the esteem and affection of her
spouse (19-23).[2] Subsequently, however, she behaves
like a sly, fabliau trickster. When her husband returns
from a second prolonged absence and questions her about
the paternity of the extra child he notices in the
household, she glibly lies to him, staunchly insisting
that the child was engendered by her eating snow in
their garden (59-95).

We should not attribute these sudden shifts of
character to our author's insufficiencies as a writer.
Rather, we should recognize that Les Cent nouvelles

nouvelles (and Jehan de Saintré) were written during a
period of shifting fictional forms, the breakdown of
established genres and styles. In his depiction of this
female figure, our author has combined narrative conventions from serious and comic style.

Elsewhere, we have argued that the author of Les
Cent nouvelles nouvelles transforms the twelfth- and
thirteenth-century system of stylistic distinctions,
which focus on the compatibility of subject, class of
characters, ethical systems, and the literary diction of
a text (Diner 1986; John of Garland 1974, pt. 2: pp.
38-41; pt. 5: pp. 86-89). Briefly stated, he establishes a new form of thematic and stylistic play between
courtly and comic styles.[3]

Thirteenth-century methods of combination (such as
those of the sottes chansons, or fabliaux which parody
courtly material) are characterized by contrastive techniques which demonstrate a keen awareness of these distinctions.[4] This awareness is prolonged into the
fifteenth century.[5] In striking contrast, our
fifteenth-century author participates in a stylistic
counter-current, towards the smudging of style distinctions, attenuating the distance between them.

The way in which the author mixes characters, narrative motifs, and lexical items from these two styles
opens up new stylistic areas within which he can challenge the relationship of style to subject, break long
standing thematic links, and modify traditional plot
developments.

The focus of this paper, then, is the implications
of this new method of mixing elements drawn from different styles and genres on the representation of female
figures' psychology, behavior, and experience in Les
Cent nouvelles nouvelles. We shall see that our

fifteenth-century author shifts the representation of
female characters drawn from the comic style towards the
courtly stylistic register; infuses new themes into the
representation of female character's psychology, emotions, and experience; and gives fuller, more integrated
representations of female characters (both at the level
of individual nouvelles and of the collection as a
whole) than traditional genres.

One of the thematic links which our fifteenth-
century author does not break is that between female
protagonists and narrative material which tends towards
the comic and the low (White 1982; Johnson 1983; Lacy
1985; Bowen 1964; Knight 1972). Like the thirteenth-
century fabliaux and the fifteenth-century farces
(short, dramatic pieces which prolong the comic vein of
the fabliaux) Les Cent nouvelles nouvelles gives a
preeminent place to female protagonists.6 Eighty-
eight of the one hundred tales have female characters
(those which do not are 5, 6, 10, 11, 62, 63, 64, 70,
79, 93, 96 and 100). Once again, like the fabliaux, the
narrative material of the individual tales is heavily
slanted towards trickery and skirmishes in the battle of
the sexes (Söderhjelm 1910, 122-23; Ferrier 1954, 15-16;
1966, 62-63).

The narrative material and controlling themes of our
nouvelles thus contrast sharply with those of Arthurian
romances or lais. In these, the heroine (often a young
girl on the verge of marriage), is a spectator to be
impressed, won, and kept through the performance of
military and chivalric exploits. Consequently, these
narratives are forced towards an interest in the male
protagonist.7 This same focus is maintained in
fifteenth-century chivalric biographies such as Le livre
des faits du bon Messire Jacques de Lalaing. Although

this Burgundian hero wears the sleeves of a succession
of ladies during his participation in ceremonial jousts
and pas d'armes, female characters are only a vehicle
for male interaction: the author never shows him in a
relationship with a woman.

As we mentioned earlier, the representation of
female figures in the traditional narrative genres is
strongly enmeshed in a system of thematic and lexical
constraints, as a discussion of two key areas of stylistic distinction--ethical and sexual topics--will
illustrate. These areas will also structure our subsequent discussion of selected, representative examples
from Les Cent nouvelles nouvelles.

The treatment of ethical topics in the representation of courtly heroines is strongly tied to the theme
of love. As the object of the hero's love, the heroine
must be seduced through a series of ritualized steps,
including: a first glance, conversation, the hero's
recognition of her as a worthy love object, an exchange
of letters, demonstrations of prowess, a declaration of
love, a plan to meet (which often requires the assistance of a confidante), and, finally, an assignation.
When the author represents the effects of love--which he
always denotes with exalted sentimental terms (for
instance, amour, joie: love, joy)--on the heroine, he
attributes feelings of self-doubt, timidity, and moral
conflicts to her. This love, then, thrives on obstacles,
both internal and external.

In striking contrast, obstacles in comic style are
only an occasion for displays of craftiness and ingenuity. Ethical topics in comic style are developed
through the theme of trickery: the female protagonists'
activities are unfettered from any moral constraints, or
fear of shame or reprisal.

Similar antitheses mark the treatment of sexual
topics in these two styles. The treatment of sexual
topics in courtly narrative is strongly linked to the
theme of female beauty, which is developed through the
courtly portrait, a discreetly erotic encomium with a
fairly stable set of traits (Colby 1965). Body parts
appropriate to the courtly style include faces, eyes,
heads, arms, and breasts, as well as colors and tint of
skin. These are often used in metaphoric combination to
ennoble the body by emphasizing its esthetic qualities
(Erec et Enide, 399-441).

Once again in striking contrast to courtly style,
sexual topics in comic style are tied to the theme of
woman's imperious sexual desires, well-illustrated by
the common fabliau equation: household minus husband
equals wife plus lover[8] (White 1982, 196). Furthermore, comic style could admit the anatomically low
noises, products, and parts of the body used in excretory and sexual functions.

These remarks suggest that these two stylistic
levels represent female experience from widely diver-
gent, narrow, fragmentary perspectives. Each of these
perspectives is broadened, and the distance between the
two is attenuated, in Les Cent nouvelles nouvelles.

The assimilation of non-courtly female characters to
the courtly ethical register will illustrate one way in
which the themes of comic narrative are broadened to
include courtly themes and narrative motifs. For
example, the twenty-fourth nouvelle is a comic tale
which recounts a debasing trick played on a knight by a
non-aristocratic young woman whom he surprises alone in
the woods, and tries to seduce. This plot, then, ad-
heres to one of the conventional narrative patterns of
thirteenth-century pastourelles, light, dramatic,

courtly lyrics, which took as their theme the meeting of representative characters from the courtly and non-courtly worlds (Jackson 1985, 68).

The women of the thirteenth-century pastourelles resist the knight's advances either out of preference for a rustic lover (as in Adam de la Halle's dramatization of pastourelle themes, Le Jeu de Robin et Marion), or out of fear of punishment (Rivière 1974, 14; 17; 13). In contrast, the woman of the twenty-fourth tale resists the knight's advances out of concern not to compromise her honor (43-46; 86-88; 109-10). Her actions are regulated by elevated sentiments, which are consistently designated with noble lexical items (such as honneur: honor), placing internal obstacles in the way of sexual satisfaction. Here this assimilation is given a narrative expansion: after the maid tricks the knight, he helps her to marry well (146), thus attenuating the distance between the courtly and non-courtly social levels by enabling her to transcend economic and social circumstance.

This same pattern of shifting the ethics of non-courtly females towards courtly social values is followed in the ninth, seventeenth, and eighteenth tales. In each of these tales (all of which prolong fabliaux themes of trickery, and battles of wits) a non-courtly woman--a servant (9, 17) or a prostitute (18)--is endowed with courtly ethical standards of behavior: concern not to compromise her honor (9, 17), or reputation (18).

The treatment of ethical topics is drawn even further towards the courtly style register in the thirty-seventh nouvelle (Diner 1986; 1984). On the one hand, this nouvelle resembles fabliaux in which a cunning woman tricks her husband in order to lie with her lover. For instance, the theme of the tale is feminine guile: an obsessively jealous husband studies misogynistic literature in order to forestall his wife's being unfaithful to him. Furthermore, the author's management of this narrative material emphasizes the lovers' underhanded cleverness, a trait of comic style.

On the other hand, however, the treatment of ethical topics in this tale shows a shift away from comic style towards courtly style. For example, the woman initially rejects her suitor's request for a rendezvous out of loyalty to her husband (83). Moreover, as in courtly style, her worthiness as a sexual object is underscored by the narrator's comment that the lover seeks her out because of her reputation (43). In addition, also as in courtly style, she must be seduced through a series of ritualized steps: a declaration of love (47-57); an exchange of letters (68-71; 80-83); a request for an assignation (79); an elaborate plan to meet which requires the help of a confidante (103-32).

This analysis of the treatment of selected ethical topics demonstrates that the author of Les Cent nouvelles nouvelles tones up the ethical characterization of non-courtly female characters in tales which prolong fabliau material, assimilating them to the courtly ethical register, shifting his representation of them towards social respectability. He thus challenges the twelfth- and thirteenth-century thematic links between subject, class of character, and ethical values.

The author also challenges assumptions about the relation of style to subject inherited from the twelfth and thirteenth centuries, opening up new stylistic areas within which he can treat in a serious manner subjects traditionally confined to comic style, or antifeminist invective, such as female sexual desire and needs.

In the twenty-first nouvelle, for instance, an abbess falls ill and is told that the only cure is to have sexual intercourse. If she does not follow this prescription, she will die.

The author treats this comic material--a playful thematization of the courtly motif of the curative powers of Love (see the twelfth-century courtly romance Enéas 7985-92)--in a serious style. For instance, the diagnosis and prescription put the abbess in an ethical dilemma. On the one hand, if she follows the doctor's prescription she will transgress her vow of chastity. If, on the other hand, she refuses, she will effectively commit suicide (117-21).

The abbess places internal obstacles in the way of following the doctor's prescription. Her actions are regulated by a code of sublime motivations which preclude her following the doctor's advice. These motivations are consistently designated with lexical items from theological and moral discourse: she is afraid of committing a mortal sin (126; 128); she wishes to preserve her honor and avoid shame (126-31; 149; 150-52; 183) or social ostracism; she fears she will be morally unworthy to govern the convent if she follows the prescription (134-35).

Her weeping (75-78), her readiness to die (56), and the efforts of her nuns to convince her to follow the doctor's orders all invite us to consider that her protestations are sincere. Indeed, it is striking that in a tale which takes its subject, female sexual needs, from the comic register, the heart is the only organ mentioned (96)! When the abbess finally lets herself be convinced, it is in a spirit of self-sacrifice, out of concern for her nuns, and with a great weight on her heart (174-78).[9]

By assimilating this comic theme to serious style,
the author has legitimized female sexuality as a serious
literary theme, suggesting that it might be an integral
component of the adult female personality.10 An even
more marked shift towards serious style is found in the
ninety-ninth tale, in which a woman whose husband is
absent is attracted to a clerk, and confesses this to
him, thus assuming a role in amorous affairs which is
considered improper in courtly style: Soredamors in
Cligès, for instance, refrains from declaring her love
(1008-12) (Ille et Galéron 796-98). Despite the non-
courtly nature of the heroine's declaration in the
ninety-ninth tale, the author nonetheless makes us feel
the worthiness and respectability of the woman's sexual
desire, by designating it with the exalted sentimental
term amour (417; 468; 537; 544).

This worthiness can also be extended to female
sexual parts (traditionally confined to comic style)
which in Les Cent nouvelles nouvelles are assimilated to
the courtly ideal of female beauty. In the forty-eighth
and forty-ninth tales, for instance, a lover admires his
mistress's beauty, gazing on her mouth, eyes, breasts
(all appropriate to courtly style), and taking in also
her stomach, thighs, sexual parts and buttocks. The
anatomically and stylistically low female sexual parts
and buttocks are, therefore, denuded of their excretory
associations and assimilated to portions of the female
anatomy considered attractive and sexually enticing,
ennobling them. By making low body parts integral com-
ponents of the female anatomy, the author fills in and
fleshes out the courtly corpus.

The representation given the theme of female sexual
desirability is also expanded in another direction, to
include older women. For one thing, our author breaks

the thematic link between youth and sexual attractiveness. In the Middle Ages, an old woman was considered a
ludicrous sexual object, as evidenced in the embarrassment of La Vieille (The Old Woman) in Le Roman de la
Rose when she is presented with a garland by Bel Accueil
(12730-39). In the fiftieth tale, however, a young man
sharing a bed with his grandmother tries to have intercourse with her. His actions thus contrast sharply with
those of a young man in the fabliau La Vieille Truande
(5:171), who is flabbergasted and disgusted by the mere
suggestion that he kiss, much less make love to, an old
woman.

In addition, our author expands his concept of
sexual attractiveness in another direction, to include
wives. Conjugal sexual relationships were considered
comic literary material in the Middle Ages: satires on
marriage and women consistently present wives as physically repugnant.

For instance, in the thirteenth-century comic play
Le Jeu de la feuillée, Adam de la Halle plays off a
nostalgic portrait of his wife's physical perfection--
before marriage had satisfied his sexual desire (174)--
against her present appearance. Love had made him think
that her hair was golden and shining (87), her forehead
white and smooth (92), her face and figure well propor-
tioned (108; 119). Now he sees that she has black, limp
hair (89), and a wrinkled forehead (93). Similarly, in
Rutebeuf's Le Mariage (composed in the second half of
the thirteenth century), the author depicts his wife as
the comic antithesis of a courtly lady: poor, old,
ugly, thin, and dry. She is altogether undesirable, and
the poet cannot conceive of her in a sexual role ("N'ai
pas paour qu'ele me treche": I have no fear that she'll
be unfaithful to me) (Rutebeuf 1960, 1: 548, 26-31).

In contrast, the twelfth tale of Les Cent nouvelles
nouvelles (a comic narrative in which a laborer surprises a couple making love), presents a peasant husband
who finds his wife sexually seductive, and takes pleasure in gazing on her naked body, admiring her buttocks
and sexual parts. The husband's desire is designated
with the serious lexical items dévotion (devotion: 35),
désir (desire: 65); the sexual act is designated with
the chivalric metaphor gracieuses armes (gracious arms:
63); and the wife's physical attributes are subsumed in
the courtly lexical item beauté (beauty: 73).

This depiction of the sexual attractiveness of a
peasant wife in a comic narrative thus contrasts sharply
with that in the fabliau Les Quatre Souhaits which
includes a grotesque description of a peasant wife's
sexual organs (5:   206).   The author of Les Cent nouvelles nouvelles integrates the peasant woman of the
twelfth tale into an elevated sexual register, just as
he integrates the non-aristocratic woman into a high
ethical register in the twenty-fourth tale, analyzed
previously.

There is, however, a contrary stylistic drift within
Les Cent nouvelles nouvelles, the toning down of serious
material, the assimilation of serious material to comic
style.   For instance, in the twenty-first tale, the
author draws moral material towards the comic style,
partly by attenuating the means by which serious style
makes us admire a character.   The exemplary virtues of
the abbess are not given a narrative expansion.   Rather,
she is described simply as being young, beautiful, and
in good health (5-6).   In addition, the moral code which
governs her actions is rather casual: she does in fact
consent to have sexual intercourse, rather than letting
herself die (in contrast to a woman in the ninety-eighth

tale, who commits suicide when threatened with rape).
Finally, our author does not transform the abbess's
dilemma into an occasion to exhort the reader to virtue. Instead, he trivializes ethical concerns by
applying them to traditionally comic material, female
sexuality.

This same pattern of drawing serious material
towards comic style is repeated in the treatment of
courtly ethical and sexual topics. In the twenty-fourth
tale, the non-aristocratic woman is endowed with integ-
rity, but the author does not make us admire her through
an exemplary moral portrait. The portrait of her thus
contrasts with that of Anathais in Gautier d'Arras's
twelfth-century courtly romance Eracle, who is chosen as
the emperor's wife because she is the most virtuous
woman in the land (2581-667). Furthermore, although the
author transforms low body parts into material appropriate for an encomium (48, 49), he does not make any
use of metaphoric combination to stress the esthetic
quality of the woman's body, or to veil its physical
nature, as do authors composing in courtly style. The
beauty of the mistress is, thus, debased by its association with low body parts.

Similarly, the author does not represent the sexual
desire for an old woman (50), or a wife (12) in elevated
terms, by calling them ardent or sublime love. Rather,
the obsessive sexual activity of the peasant (12-20),
and the young man's attempt to mount his grandmother in
the middle of the night (28-29), invite us to believe
that each is acting out of unrestrained lust.

Our above remarks strongly suggest that the author's
blurring of style distinctions by combining characters,
narrative motifs, ethical values, and lexical items from
different styles and genres means that a theme (such as

female sexual desire or desirability) does not dictate its literary treatment in tone and vocabulary. Nor does it dictate plot development and structure.

For instance, our author can treat the theme of May-September marriage by infusing it with sexual fidelity and conjugal affection. In medieval literature the union of a young girl and an older man was traditionally considered an inappropriate match, often culminating in the wife's infidelity. This pattern is followed both in comic fabliaux (such as Aubérée 5:110), as well as in courtly narratives. In Marie de France's twelfth-century courtly lai Yonec, for example, the desperately unhappy wife of a jealous old man takes a lover. In Huon le Roi's thirteenth-century courtly narrative Le Vair Palefroi, a young woman, betrothed against her will to an older man, is rescued by her lover before the marriage can take place. Furthermore, the lyric genre chanson de mal mariée (song of an unhappily-married woman) takes as its theme the contrast between a husband who is variously described as ugly, mean, low-born, and old, and a lover who is just the opposite (Bec 1977, 1: 68-90). In each of these examples, then, the author clearly affirms the values of extramarital love.

In striking contrast, when the author of Les Cent nouvelles nouvelles treats this narrative motif, he can either follow this traditional plot structure, or modify it. On the one hand, in tales thirteen and twenty-three, young wives participate in sexual deceptions to trick their older husbands. On the other hand, however, the author can also infuse the values of mutual esteem, conjugal affection, and sexual fidelity into his tale. In the fifty-third tale, for instance, a young woman is married to an older man by mistake, and is pleased to remain his wife (99-100). In addition, in the ninety-

ninth tale, a young wife whose older husband is absent
resists sexual temptation and remains faithful to her
spouse, for whom she feels deep affection and respect
(745-52).

Our analyses of these representative examples
strongly suggest that in Les Cent nouvelles nouvelles
the literary treatment of a subject (in vocabulary,
tone, and plot structure) is not controlled by inherited
literary convention. It is, rather, the emanation of an
individual conscience. Because the nouvelle was not
enmeshed in the same thematic and lexical constraints as
traditional narrative genres, the author was left more
latitude to develop his narrative material according to
his personal perception of the subject.

The genre of the tale collection, an extremely
elastic narrative form, bestowed an additional freedom
on him (Wetzel 1981; Cooper 1984, 72-90). Because a
tale collection consists of autonomous, self-contained
narratives, the author can integrate a wide spectrum of
narrative material, giving it an encyclopedic feel.
Indeed, the female figures in Les Cent nouvelles
nouvelles span broad chronological and sociological
spectra: from young adolescents on the verge of
marriage to elderly women; from prostitutes to noble-
women. They also span a broad range of social roles:
daughters, wives, mothers, and a grandmother.

In addition, the author includes tales which treat a
broad variety of themes relating to female experience:
female sexual desire (15, 20, 21, 46, 48, 49, 55, 65,
81, 90, 99); sexual attractiveness (12, 48, 49); pregnancy (8, 19, 22); childbirth (22, 29); motherhood (8,
14, 19, 20, 22, 51, 77, 86); rape (23, 24, 25, 50, 98);
and the larger subject of reciprocity in male-female
relationships (16, 19, 53, 57, 69, 99) and conjugal

sexual relationships (3, 12). The encyclopedic feel is enhanced by the author's giving each of these themes a wide spectrum of treatment throughout the collection, from the trivializing to the tragic.[11]

A similar wealth of characters and subjects related to female experience characterizes the fourteenth-century dramatic genre known as Les Miracles de Notre Dame, with which Les Cent nouvelles nouvelles shares many themes (such as female sexual desire, pregnancy, childbirth, and motherhood, for example). Again, like the Miracles, the author of Les Cent nouvelles nouvelles sometimes represents these themes in terms of familiar human emotions which are both plausible and contradic-tory.

Examples abound. A wife who has repeatedly given free rein to her libidinous urges decides on her death-bed that she does not wish her husband to be financially responsible for her many illegitimate children (51); a young wife who loves her older husband, but who is none-theless attracted to a younger man during her spouse's absence (99); a pregnant young woman, who is exiled from her home by her mother, suffers many vicissitudes to find her former lover, and finally rejects him, just when he is willing to marry her (8); the wife of the nineteenth tale (cited at the beginning of this discus-sion), who is both faithful helpmate and sly trickster, and whose infidelity the narrator pretends to explain by saying that she was a victim of her sexual desire during her husband's long absence ("elle fut contrainte de son demeurer" = she was forced to it because of his pro-longed absence, 34-35).

In the Miracles, however, interest centers on the divine intervention of the Virgin Mary and her compas-sion for sinners, however wicked, who have repented.

Consequently, in the **Miracles**, the realistic, creatural
treatment of characters' contradictory emotions and
motivations is integrated into a transcendent theological framework.

In contrast, **Les Cent nouvelles nouvelles** is un-
moored from any such transcendent framework. Rather,
the familiar, humble, creatural details which create an
impression of intimacy and psychological complexity are
an attempt to dress literature up as life, concealing
the fictional nature of the narratives.

Indeed, the author's multi-faceted representations
of individual women's unpredictable impulses, motivations, and emotions invite us to consider each a complex, self-conscious adult personality. In addition,
the breadth of characters and narrative material noted
above invites us to consider that each female figure is
integrated into a complex and variegated social fabric.
Furthermore, the varying perspectives on women's experiences opened by the broad stylistic range according to
which each of the themes enumerated above is treated
creates a cumulative impression that the author of **Les
Cent nouvelles nouvelles** has encompassed every species
of female character, every variety of feminine circumstance, within the boundaries of his collection.

This complexity of representation and the combined
effect of the two stylistic countercurrents--toning up
comic material and toning down courtly material--which
run through the work ensure that the reader's sympathies
are pulled in different directions. The nuances and
ambiguities the author thus creates establish the potential for differing interpretations by individual male
and female readers. An interpretation of a character's
actions and motivations depends to a certain extent on
personal inclination, as well as on the relative

importance each reader wishes to give each of these
facets of the character's personality.

Our analysis demonstrates, therefore, that the
author of Les Cent nouvelles nouvelles transcends the
limits of literary convention in his representation of
women. Our remarks further suggest that the author's
perception of a given subject is no longer determined by
the prefabricated thinking inherited from tradition.
His innovative perspective might, then, indicate an
attempt to resolve the latent tension between conventional, stereotyped, literary representations of women,
on the one hand, and his desire to represent his personal perception of the multifariousness and complexity
of female experience, on the other hand.[12] He thus
suggests an awareness of the problematic representation
of women's emotions, experiences, and motivations within
medieval literary traditions which are the product of
masculine imagination. In fact, Les Cent nouvelles
nouvelles fits into a historical context of debate about
this subject.

This awareness was clearly articulated by the
historical female voice of Christine de Pisan, who,
starting in 1402, participated in the debate over Le
Roman de La Rose. Christine provides the prototype for
a feminist re-reading of this text, underscoring the
role of gender in reading, for she objects to the
demeaning reduction of woman to a passive sexual object
(the Rose), an old whore (La Vieille) (12710- 14516) and
to the misogynistic speeches of Amis (7253-9972; especially 8531-9176) and Genius (19475-20637), with their
wholesale condemnation of women (Hicks 1977, 11-22; Huot
1985).

An equally eloquent female voice (a male fictional-
ization, this time) was raised by the lady of Alain

Chartier's Belle Dame sans merci (1424), a poem which
engendered a spate of imitations, refutations, and
condemnations (Piaget 1901). The lady of this lovers'
dialogue questions the sincerity of her supplicant
lover's courtly discourse (297-304), refutes his claims
of impending death with implacable logic (267-68; 380),
and asserts her sexual independence, by categorically
refusing to grant any man sovereignty over her: "Je suy
franche et franche vueil estre" (I am free, and wish to
remain so: 286).

The author of Les Cent nouvelles nouvelles does not
openly challenge the misogynistic literary tradition, as
does Christine de Pisan. Nor does he debunk the male
fantasy of the courtly love game, as does Alain Chartier.

The feminine voice emanating from this text is still
very much a voice from the margins, that of the author
probing and questioning the prefabricated thinking
implicit in stylized, masculine literary conventions.
He does this by creating innovative stylistic areas
within which to ring changes on the masculine mythology
of fictional female stereotypes, revitalizing and challenging these stereotypes by infusing them with greater
individuality, complexity, and scope (a procedure also
followed in Christine de Pisan's treatment of certain
mythological figures in her Epitre d'Othéa: Reno 1980).

It is impossible for the modern reader to assess
accurately the impact of these stylistic transformations
on the fifteenth-century audience, upon whom the notion
of stylistic distinctions and literary conventions had
been deeply impressed. Nor can we know if the representation of more individualized, unpredictable, complex
women challenged readers to revise deep-seated preju-
dices.

All we can affirm with any certainty is that the author of Les Cent nouvelles nouvelles begins to move away from conventionalized representations of women towards a modern sense of individualization. He does not, however, effect a disruptive break with tradition. Instead, he opens an innovative perspective on the literary tradition within which his work is inscribed.

This fifteenth-century author's replacement of the traditional stylistic poles with a variegated globe set between them reflects the broadened horizons of the male imagination, expanding (and hence transforming) the male perspective on women embodied in twelfth- and thirteenth-century ideas of style and genre.

NOTES

** A rough draft of this paper was read at the Twenty-first Conference on Medieval Studies at Kalamazoo, Michigan, in May 1986. It is a pleasure to acknowledge my great debt to Nancy Freeman Regalado, who has graciously provided me with copies of her own articles and talks. Most important, she understood instantly the ideas I was groping towards, and her many pertinent suggestions have greatly contributed to this paper. Grateful recognition and thanks are offered to the following friends who read successive drafts of this paper: William Huseman, Yvonne LeBlanc, Virginia Reinburg, and Jindrich Zezula.

References to <u>Les Cent nouvelles nouvelles</u> are from the edition of F. Sweetser (1966). Line numbers will be indicated parenthetically within the text. <u>Fabliaux</u> are cited according to Montaiglon and Raynaud's collection, still the most comprehensive. Volume and page numbers are noted parenthetically within the text. French has been paraphrased or translated within the text. Untranslated French quotations have been confined to the notes.

[1] The most striking example of this is the collection's onomastic realism. The author ascribes the narratives to courtiers of Philip the Good, whose names are found in contemporary archives and <u>Chronicles</u>, as well as to the Duke himself. In addition, he makes historical characters participants in the following fictional anecdotes: 5; 24; 25; 27; 47; 62; 63; 69; 74. He thus firmly anchors his fictional collection in the world of historical fact.

[2] ". . . sa bonne femme garde tresbien son corps, fist le prouffit de plusieurs marchandises, et tant et si tresbien le fist que son mary au bout des diz cinq ans retourne, beaucop la loa et plus que par avant l'ama" (19-23).

[3]As will become obvious in the course of this demonstration, I do not use the word style in a narrowly
rhetorical sense, to refer to figures of speech. I use
it, rather, in an extended sense, to refer to complexes
of characters, themes, motifs, and lexical items stylized by literary tradition, such as the registres
defined by Zumthor (1963, 123-61). Rough synonyms for
style as I use it here are literary mode, tone, and
stylistic register.

[4]The sottes chansons (silly songs), comic lyrics
popular starting in the thirteenth century, parody the
highly-stylized treatment of the sexual topic of female
beauty in the courtly love lyric (Dragonetti 1960,
248-78). They apply courtly lexical items (such as
plaisant, blanche, douce) to grotesque physiognomy (see
Langfors 1936, 1: 10, 19; 2: 7; 3: 14). Fabliaux which
parody the courtly stages of seduction are: De la
pucelle qui abreuva le polain (4: 199); De la demoiselle
qui n'ot parler de foutre qui n'eust mal au cuer (5:
24); La pucele qui voloit voler (4: 208); De la
damoiselle qui ne poot oir parler de foutre 3: 81).
Ritualized steps in these seductions consist of lovers
touching each other's sexual parts and asking "What is
this?" The man tricks the woman into having intercourse
by giving courtly names to the sexual organs and act,
thus parodying courtly treatments of these topics.

[5]Christine objects to Jean de Meung's flaunting the
literal vulgarism coilles within the serious philosophical discourse of Le Roman de la Rose (Hicks 1977,
11-28; Huot 1985).

[6]Here the term fabliau refers to a body of brief,
rhymed tales written from the early thirteenth to the
mid-fourteenth century in northern France. Since my
interpretation depends in part on the Old French vocabulary, I do not use the extended meaning to refer to a
medieval tale in a comic or obscene vein, as does
Dronke, 1973, 75.

[7]Marie de France's Lais are an obvious exception.
(Freeman 1984; 1985)

[8]The following fabliaux treat this theme explicitly.
In Le Vallet aux douze fames (3: 186), a young husband
is physically exhausted by his wife's sexual needs after
only a year of marriage. In Les Quatre Souhaits (5:
201) a woman tries to assuage a long-felt sexual dis-
satisfaction by wishing that her husband was covered
with penises. In Les Souhaits desviez (5: 184) a woman

whose husband falls asleep in bed has a dream designed
to relieve her feelings of sexual deprivation. In _Trois
femmes qui trouverent un vit_ (5: 32) the male sexual
organ is a prize coveted by three women who argue over
it, and submit their case to an abbess. She reveals
that it is the bolt from the convent door.

[9]". . . portant au cueur ung grand fardeau d'ennuy,
pour l'amour de ses seurs se laissa ferrer et s'accorda,
combien que ce fut a grant regret . . ." (174-78).

[10]An additional example of the legitimizing of sexuality is studied by Regalado (1981). In _Le Roman de la
Rose_ (ca. 1275), Jean de Meung formulates literary
structures within which sexuality could be treated as a
serious theme, in a literal manner. A close reading of
La Vieille's portrait (Beltran 1972) reveals an explora-
tion of reciprocity in gender relationships, suggesting
that _Le Roman de la Rose_ might be a model for these
ideas in _Les Cent nouvelles nouvelles_.

[11]I call a "trivializing" treatment a serious tale
which ends with a witticism. In the ninetieth tale, the
husband of a mortally ill woman begs forgiveness for any
pain he may have caused her. She responds that she can
never forgive him for not having sufficiently assuaged
her sexual needs. He immediately obliges, and a half
hour later she is up and about. Other examples of
trivializing treatment are: 8; 22; 50.

[12]The tension between conventional rhetorical poses
and the sense of personal identity is a pervasive theme
in fourteenth- and fifteenth-century courtly lyrics
(Poirion 1965, 23; 226). On Christine de Pisan's "femi-
nizing" of male literary conventions see Poirion (1965,
532-33).

WORKS CITED

Adam de la Halle. 1970. _Le Jeu de la feuillée_. E. Langlois, ed. 2nd rev. ed. Paris: Champion.

_____. 1960. _Le Jeu de Robin et de Marion_. K. Varty, ed. London: Harraps.

Bec, Pierre. 1977. _La Lyrique française au moyen age_. 2 vols. Paris: Picard.

Beltran, Luis. 1972. "La Vieille's Past." _Romanische Forschungen_ 84: 77-96.

Bowen, Barbara. 1964. _Les Caractéristiques essentielles de la farce française et leur survivance dans les années 1550-1620_. Urbana: University of Illinois Press.

Les Cent nouvelles nouvelles. 1966. F. Sweetser, ed. Genève: Droz.

Chartier, Alain. 1949. _La Belle Dame sans merci_. A. Piaget, ed. Genève: Droz. (TLF 1).

Chastellain, Georges. 1962-66. _Oeuvres complètes_. 9 vols. Kervyn de Lettenhove, ed. Bruxelles.

Chrétien de Troyes. 1978. _Cligès_. Alexandre Micha, ed. Paris: Champion. (CFMA 84).

_____. 1973. _Erec et Enide_. M. Roques, ed. Paris: Champion. (CFMA 80).

Colby, Alice. 1965. _The Portrait in Twelfth-century French Literature. An Examination of the Stylistic Originality of Chrétien de Troyes_. Paris: Droz.

Cooper, Helen. 1984. _The Structure of the Canterbury Tales_. Athens (GA); University of Georgia Press.

Diner, Judith. 1984. "Comedy and Courtliness: The Form and Style of _Les Cent nouvelles nouvelles_." Ph.D. dissertation, New York University.

_____. 1986. "The Courtly-Comic Style of _Les Cent nouvelles nouvelles_." Accepted for publication in _Romance Philology_. Tentatively scheduled for 1988.

Doutrepont, Georges. 1909. La Littérature française à la cour des Ducs de Bourgogne. Bruxelles.

_____. 1939. Les Mises en prose des épopées et des romans chevaleresques. Bruxelles.

Dragonetti, Roger. 1960. La Technique poétique des trouvères dans la chanson courtoise. Contribution à l'étude de la rhétorique médiévale. Paris.

Dronke, Peter. 1972. "The Rise of the Medieval Fabliau: The Latin and Vernacular Evidence." Romanische Forschungen. 85: 75-97.

Eneas. 1968-73. J-J Salvera de Grave, ed. 2 vols. Paris: Champion. (CFMA 44, 62).

Ferrier, Janet. 1954. Forerunners of the French Novel. Manchester: Manchester University Press.

_____. 1966. French Prose Writers of the Fourteenth and Fifteenth Centuries. Oxford: Oxford University Press.

Freeman, Michelle. 1984. "Marie de France's Poetics of Silence: The Implications for a Feminine Translation." PMLA 99: 8961-83.

_____. 1985. "Dual Natures and Subverted Glosses: Marie de France's Bisclavret." Romance Notes 25: 288-301.

Gautier d'Arras. 1976. Eracle. Guy Raynaud de Lage, ed. Paris: Champion. (CFMA 102).

_____. 1956. Ille et Galéron. Frederick Cowper, ed. Paris: Picard.

Guillaume de Lorris and Jean de Meung. 1965-70. Le Roman de la Rose. 3 vols. Felix Lecoy, ed. Paris: Champion. (CFMA 92, 95, 98).

Hicks, Eric, ed. and trans. 1977. Le Débat sur Le Roman de la Rose. Paris: Droz.

Huon le Roi. 1970. Le Vair Palefroi. A. Langfors, ed. Paris: Champion. (CFMA 8).

Huot, Sylvia. 1985. "Seduction and Sublimation: Christine de Pizan, Jean de Meung, and Dante." Romance Notes 25 (1985): 361-73.

Jackson, W.T.H. 1985. "The Medieval Pastourelle as a Satirical Genre." In The Challenge of the Medieval Text. Joan Ferrante and Robert Hanning, eds. New York: Columbia University Press. (Reprinted from Philological Quarterly (1952). 31: 256-70).

John of Garland. 1974. The Parisiana poetria of John of Garland. Traugott Lawler, ed. and trans. New Haven and London: Yale University Press.

Johnson, Lesley. 1983. "Women on Top: Antifeminism in the Fabliaux?" Modern Language Review 78, 1: 297-307.

Knight, Alan. 1972. "The Farce Wife: Myth, Parody, and Caricature." In A Medieval French Miscellany: Papers of the 1970 Kansas Conference on Medieval French Literature. Lawrence: University of Kansas Publications, 15-25.

Lacy, Norris J. 1985. "Fabliau Women." Romance Notes. 25: 318-27.

Langfors, A., ed. 1946. Deux recueils de sottes chansons. Helsinki.

La Sale, Antoine de. 1967. Jehan de Saintré. Jean Misrahi, ed. Genève: Droz.

Le Livre des faits du bon Messire Jacques de Lalaing. 1966. Kervyn de Lettenhove, ed. In Georges Chastellain, Oeuvres Complètes. Vol. 8. Bruxelles.

Marie de France. 1966. Les Lais. Jean Rychner, ed. Paris: Champion. (CFMA, 93).

Montaiglon, A. and G. Raynaud, eds. 1972. Recueil complet des fabliaux. 6 vols. Paris, 1972. (Reprint Slatkine, 1973).

Piaget, A. 1901-5. "La Belle Dame sans mercy et ses imitations." Romania. 30, 31, 33, 34.

Poirion, Daniel. 1965. Le Poète et le Prince: L'Evolution du lyrisme courtois de Guillaume de Machaut à Charles d'Orléans. Grenoble: Presses Universitaires de Grenoble.

Regalado, Nancy Freeman. 1976. "Choice and Uncertainty in Fifteenth-Century French Narrative." Paper presented at the French I division, Medieval Literature, MLA Convention.

Regalado, Nancy Freeman. 1981. "'Des contraires choses': La fonction poétique de la citation et des exempla dans Le Roman de la Rose de Jean de Meun." Litterature. 41 (Feb.): 62-81.

Reno, Christine. 1980. "Feminist Aspects of Christine de Pisan's Epitre d'Othéa à Hector." Studi francesi. 24: 271-76.

Riviere, J-C, ed. 1973. Pastourelles. 3 vols. Genève: Droz. (TLF, 213, 220, 232).

Rutebeuf. 1959-60. Oeuvres complètes. 2 vols. E. Faral and J. Bastin, eds. Paris.

Söderhjelm, Werner. 1910. La Nouvelle Française au quinzième siècle. Paris: Champion.

Wetzel, H. H. 1982. "Elements socio-historiques d'un genre littéraire: l'histoire de la nouvelle jusqu'à Cervantes." In La nouvelle française à la Renaissance. Lionello, Sozzi, ed. 41-78. Paris: Slatkine.

White, Sarah Melhado. 1982. "Sexual Language and Human Conflict in Old French Fabliaux." Comparative Studies in Society and History. 24(2): 185-210.

Zumthor, Paul. 1963. Langue et technique poétique à l'époque romane (XIe-XIIe siècles). Paris: Klinksieck.

SPEAKING OF TONGUES: THE POETICS OF THE FEMININE VOICE IN CHAUCER'S LEGEND OF GOOD WOMEN

by Elizabeth D. Harvey

When, in Troilus and Criseyde, the heroine laments that her reputation will be lost, that she will be "rolled" "on many a tonge" (V:1061), she encapsulates not only the demeaning familiarity that her tragedy will acquire in the mouths of those who retell it without understanding, but also the potent connection behind textuality and sexuality, a nexus that links the process of literary misunderstanding with Criseyde's transformation from lover to whore. The phrase betrays her acute awareness of the power that others, particularly male poets, will wield over her, possessing, as they do, the capacity to shape her textual representation. The narrator's own plea that his poem not be miswritten or mismetered "for defaute of tonge" (V:1796) obliquely aligns his voice with that of Criseyde, since the future of his poem is clearly inseparable from her fate, for both are at the mercy of subsequent interpreters. Despite the narrator's sensitivity to Criseyde's plight, he is--however reluctantly--also linked to Diomede, the first instrument of Criseyde's downfall. It is not incidental to this ligature of speech and dominance that Diomede is described as having a large tongue since it could be argued that both he and the narrator use their tongues to perpetrate the fame (or infamy) of Criseyde.

Fame, which is derived from the Greek "phanai," "to say" and the Latin "fari," "to speak," is depicted in literature (including Chaucer's House of Fame) as many-tongued.[1] Fame is also commonly represented as a woman, a monstrous exaggeration of what was conventionally considered to be a feminine quality: garrulity, the irrepressible compulsion to magnify sound and disseminate gossip.[2] Yet, despite this fabled feminine loquaciousness, women were as frequently the victims as the owners of wagging tongues, since fame for a woman usually meant ill-fame, a notoriety that almost always implied sexual licentiousness. To be "rolled" "on many a tonge," then, describes the erotic and discursive powerlessness of the subject to control the magnification and distortion of its own representation as it travels from tongue to tongue. My interest in the tongue thus derives from its status as a metonomy for voice, for the possibility women have to speak--and be spoken about--within a discursive structure, an issue that is, I argue, important in Troilus and Criseyde and central to the palinode that followed it, The Legend of Good Women.

The narrator in Troilus and Criseyde asserts ironically just before he introduces his translation of a Petrarchan sonnet that he will present the original exactly as it was except for the small matter of "tonges difference" (I:395), ostensibly the difference between Italian and English. But as the narrator demonstrates throughout the poem, particularly where he departs from his central source, Boccaccio's Filostrato, the tongue's difference is everything, and any linguistic translation is also always a re-creation. The narrator's control over his poetic material is most apparent where he re-writes his sources, and his power is most problematically

presented when he depicts Criseyde, since the "tonges
difference," that is, the sexual difference or gender of
the speaker, shapes and mis-shapes the poetic subject,
in this case, the representation of woman. In fact, it
is in the narrator's refusal to condemn Criseyde, his
depiction of her as a text that is hard to read, in the
numerous and contradictory allusions and citations that
cluster around her and that she herself speaks, and most
of all, in his acute awareness of the authority a male
poet possesses to shape the image of women in texts that
separates him from Boccaccio.

Despite Chaucer's self-consciousness about the power
he exercises in his representation of Criseyde and the
reluctance of the narrator to judge her, in The Legend
of Good Women we find Chaucer condemned for his defama-
tion of women because of his portrayal of Criseyde's
infidelity, subjected, that is, to the very censorious-
ness that he himself had refrained from indulging in.
The Prologue to the legends thus describes a trial scene
in which the poet is accused of defaming women, and, in
an inversion of the dynamics of power both in the Troilus and the legends themselves, the poet is silenced,
allowing a woman to speak on his behalf, to represent
him legally. (That Alceste also depicts Chaucer poeti-
cally--describing him in verse and listing the titles of
his works--accentuates this inversion of control, for
although Alceste's power over the poet is an illusion
created by the authorial Chaucer, this does not obviate
the extreme helplessness he represents himself as experiencing). When the God of Love provides an impassioned
indictment of the poet, enumerating all the sources he
might have drawn from and all the good women he might
have talked about instead of Criseyde, Alceste inter-
venes as intercessor for Chaucer, as advocate for the

accused poet. The etymology of advocate stems, of course, from the Latin vocare and is cognate with voice, so that when Alceste speaks for the silenced poet, she becomes, in effect, his voice. Alceste's appeal to the God of Love is based on a definition of the tyrant as a ruler who will not let his accused subjects speak before he condemns them: "He shal nat ryghtfully his yre wreke,/ Or he have herd the tother partye speke" (G:324-25). Later Alceste returns to the point when she tells the God of Love that "it is no maystrye for a lord/ To dempne a man without answere of word" (G:386-87), yet despite her emphasis on the necessity of hearing the accused speak, she insists on defending Chaucer in her own words, on substituting her voice for his. Her defense of the poet, moreover, turns out to be demeaning, for it rests on the assumption that the poet had no idea of what he was reading, that he simply gathered sources and translated them without fully understanding their import. This suggestion prompts the silent poet to attempt to speak for himself, to claim a defense that would not indict his poetic powers so completely, but Alceste, who has already proposed a penance for the poet and proleptically pronounced on his guilt, will hear none of it: "Lat be thyn arguynge," she tells him, "For Love ne wol nat counterpletyd be/ In ryght ne wrong" (G:465-66). His sentence is to spend the rest of his life composing a "gloryous legende" of good women, relating how they were true in love and were betrayed by false men.

Chaucer's poetic coercion by Alceste and the God of Love generically defines the legend of good women that he is forced to write as a palinode, and Chaucer's legends preserve their genealogical connection with the original palinode, a lyric composed by Stesichorus,

disavowing an earlier ode in which he had claimed that
Helen had caused the Trojan War. Struck blind by the
gods for this blasphemy, Stesichorus retracted his accusation, asserting in a second ode that is structured
around the trope of erasure, a palimpsest that reveals
the traces of an earlier, partially obliterated discourse, that Helen never went to Troy at all (Edmonds
1922, 39-45). For Stesichorus, the palinodial form and
the ode that engendered it function as a kind of poetic
trial in which what is at stake is feminine virtue and
at which the poet performs as both defense and prosecu-
tion. Since Criseyde is herself associated with Helen
in the Troilus,3 there is a neat logic to Chaucer's
use of the form. More importantly, the ode-palinode
diptych provides a model for the dichotomization of
woman into either totally depraved or wholly virtuous
images, a polarity that Chaucer attempts to dismantle in
his legends. Furthermore, the palinode is linked to
questions of authority and truth, since because a
palinode is commissioned by an audience dissatisfied
with an earlier poetic utterance, the status of the
retraction, whose production is clearly constrained by
its readers, must also remain suspect. The Stesichoran
palinode is not the only model to which Chaucer is
indebted; Ovid's ironic palinodes, the Remedia Amoris
and Book III of the Ars Amatoria pretend to furnish
remedies for the damage incurred in earlier poems but
they actually reinforce the original conceptions by
their transparently parodic gestures. The Ovidian palinode is the prototype from which Chaucer's Legend of
Good Women is most clearly descended, for in his blatant
mockery of his commission, Chaucer demonstrates the relative nature of poetic truth.

The central intertext for Chaucer's collection of legends--a text that subtends six of the nine legends and that was ironically suggested by the God of Love as a possible storehouse for tales about good women--is Ovid's Heroides, a collection of epistolary complaints that is specifically filiated with the legal model of the defense. That is, the fifteen epistolary complaints in the Heroides depend on earlier sources, many of them epic sources, in which the heroines are depicted in third-person discourse, their representation controlled by the shaping presence of the narrator.4 Ovid's letters of the heroines, on the other hand, unmoor the heroines from a narrative context, so that their story is seen through the eyes of the feminine speakers only, as if the epic had been swallowed and were being seen from the inside. In these letters, the women seem to speak for themselves, for, liberated as they appear to be from the constraining influence of a third-person narrator, they give explanations for their iniquity or seek redress for the wrongs they have suffered at the hands of the men who have seduced and betrayed them. Their defenses are set in opposition to the narratives from which they derive, and through the authority of the ostensibly autobiographical voice, these exercises in first-person discourse challenge the truth of the poets, substituting their own versions for received accounts.

But where Ovid's Heroides seem to seal off the epistles from their poetic antecedents, Chaucer reopens Ovid's text, reintroducing the clamorous voices of con-tradictory sources and making the Ovidian account simply another voice in the cacophony. The God of Love had attempted to preempt this problem by insisting that it is possible to choose only those texts (or parts of texts) that represent feminine goodness, but the Legends

argue persuasively against such univocality. They are
crowded with alternate versions of each of the women's
stories, so that the narrator appears to be exerting a
tyrannical but still tenuous control over his unruly
subtexts. But while he pretends to impose a unified
version on his disparate sources, he surreptitiously
advances all of their causes simultaneously. Where one
might expect to find only Ovid's account for the Legend
of Dido, for instance--since it is, after all, a more
sympathetic account of Dido than Virgil's--the double
invocation to the Legend reminds us of its double
source. Similarly, the Legend of Hypsipyle and Medea
relies on Guido delle Colonne, Ovid's Heroides and
Metamorphoses, Valerius Flaccus' Argonautica, and
perhaps Statius as well. The Legend of Ariadne depends
principally on Ovid's Heroides and Metamorphoses, although this description fails to represent adequately
the labyrinthine collection of related tales that
Chaucer has gathered together to subtend and subvert the
Legend proper.[5] The self-conscious use of multiple
sources, then, intensifies Chaucer's irony, for whenever
the narrator sends his eager readers back to the sources
for an ending the narrator has truncated too soon, as he
frequently does, he implicitly re-opens the question of
an authoritative source. Each time Chaucer seems to
offer the possibility of closure through a return to
origin, he also simultaneously denies the possibility of
that comfortable assurance. To return to a source con-
founds instead of provides an absolute truth, so that
the very possibility of locating a stable or definitive
version of a tale implicitly undermines the God of
Love's certitude.

   Much of the comedy in the legends is the result of
forcing the complaint form into the hagiographical mold,

a project that entails translating the Heroides from
first to third person. This transposition of voice
signals the wresting of control from the women and the
transmutation of the complaint into narrative. Further,
since the complaint has generic links to the legal plea,
and therefore seems to proclaim by its formal configura-
tion its right to be heard, the silencing of the women
acquires the symbolic significance of legal censorship.
But vestiges of the Heroides bear witness to this
textual violation; direct translations from the Ovidian
epistles appear as lyrical codas appended to six of the
legends, and the metrical form of the Legend (Chaucer's
first use of the heroic couplet and its initial appearance in English literature) testifies to the influence
of Ovid's elegiacs. Yet the opposition is not simply
between first-person and third-person discourse, between
speaking and spoken subject, because the Heroides are
really exercises in transvestite ventriloquism, ren-
derings of the feminine voice composed by a male author
and not actually uttered by women at all. Although the
Ovidian epistles seem to bestow rhetorical power on the
heroines, then, this control is only an illusion, since
their representation is ultimately controlled by an
invisible author. While Ovid's appropriation of the
feminine voice almost obliterates the traces of its
ventriloquistic status, Chaucer makes the question of
voice with its attendant conferral of authority and
power on the speaker central to his text. Within the
legends, the poet is ostensibly the women's advocate; he
is their voice and their champion, yet this role bestows
upon him the ability to distort and misshape the very
women he pretends to celebrate.

The distortion and censorship at work in the legends
is evidenced by the narrator's frequent use of the

occupatio, a figure that functions as a kind of textual
scar, marking the site where a source has been suppressed or where two sources have been spliced together. The legend that clearly images the question of
voice and its censorship is that of Philomela, the
heroine who is raped and has her tongue cut out so that
she cannot speak and reveal the wrong Tereus has inflicted upon her. In Ovid's Metamorphoses, Chaucer's
main source for the legend,6 the excision of the
tongue is incited by its manifest power to make public
the violation of its victim: after Philomela has been
raped, she begins to scourge Tereus verbally, calling
him a barbarian, a scoundrel, and a traitor. At the end
of her diatribe, she promises to get justice by proclaiming his deeds to the world: "si copia detur,/ in
populos veniam; si silvis clausa tenebor,/ inplebo
silvas et conscia saxa movebo;/ audiet haec aether et si
deus ullus in illo est!" ("If I should have the chance,
I will go where people throng and tell it; if I am kept
shut up in these woods, I will fill the woods with my
story and move the very rocks to pity. The air of
heaven shall hear it, and, if there is any god in
heaven, he shall hear it too.") (Ovid 1977, VI: 545-
48). Threatened by the disclosure that her speech
promises, Tereus cuts out Philomela's tongue, and, even
after it had been severed from its mistress' throat,
Ovid tells us "the mangled root quivers, while the
severed tongue lies palpitating on the dark earth,
faintly murmuring" ("radix micat ultima linguae, ipsa
iacet terraeque tremens inmurmurat atrae/ utque salire
solet mutilatae cauda colubrae,/ palpitat et moriens
domniae vestigia quaerit" [VI: 557-60]). If we recall
that the earliest meaning of the word "rape" was not
sexual assault but theft, then we can see that the

double violation to which Philomela is subjected is both
the loss of her virginity and, in a complicatedly analo-
gous way, the theft of her tongue or voice, a kind of
lingual rape. The extirpation of Philomela's tongue
becomes a metonym for the suppression of the feminine
voice in the Legend itself, since it is upon this metaphoric silence that Chaucer's narrator inscribes his
legends, ostensibly providing a surrogate voice through
which similarly victimized women can speak.

Yet the narrator is also aligned with the violated
and silenced woman for whom he seems to speak because of
the poetic coercion to which he is himself subject. The
narrator's speech is thus radically constrained, as if
his own voice had been censored and another voice super-
imposed upon that silence. The narrator, like Philomela, does not acquiesce easily to this violation.
Rather, like the Ovidian heroine he celebrates, he
fashions—or weaves—a text that bears witness to his
punishment and silencing. The Legend of Philomela is
itself one version of that testimony, thematizing as it
does the question of enforced silence or constrained
speech. But within that particular legend, the narrator
not only tells a tale of lingual violation but acts out
the trope of censorship in his own discourse, expur-
gating both the metamorphosis and the bloody revenge
that Procne and Philomela take on Tereus, namely, the
murder of Procne's son, Itys, whose dismembered body is
served to Tereus for dinner. The excision of this
ending effectively subverts the narrator's claim to
truth, for the revenge and subsequent metamorphosis
would have been familiar enough to his audience to
expose the truncated nature of the legend. When Procne
learns of the violence that Tereus has inflicted on her
sister, she is, Chaucer tells, struck dumb with the

horror of it: "No word she spak, for sorwe and ek for
rage" (2374). It is as if Philomela's condition had
infected the narrative with a contagion of muteness, and
we are left with a tableau, a literal dumb show, for
which the narrator furnishes the spoken interpretation,
telling us that the sisters make "wo" and "compleynt"
and "mone" (2379), but their voices are censored along
with the revenge. The legend can be seen, then, as a
kind of hysterical text (in the Freudian sense), where
the text or body must act out what the tongue cannot
tell.[7]

In the place of the Ovidian ending, the narrator
inserts a warning addressed to women to beware of men,
who may not all be as savage as Tereus, but who are,
nevertheless, not to be trusted. Superinscribed over
the sisters' expurgated revenge, the caveat betrays the
narrator's irony towards his subject, but it also under-
lines the problem that lies at the heart of the Legend:
to assume the voice of a silenced woman or to act as
advocate for a group of women unable or unwilling to
speak on their own behalf entails a power that can
easily become despotic. The male narrator, by his own
admission, is no more trustworthy than the treacherous
men he supposedly castigates. As in Troilus and
Criseyde, the narrator is here simultaneously identified
with the women and their oppressors, at once censor and
censored. In his exposure of the role that discourse
and its control play in the representation of truth,
Chaucer defends rather than condemns his interpretation
of Criseyde in the Troilus by demonstrating that the
legends and the tyrannical control that they exert over
the supposed celebration of women's virtue are as ultimately debasing and despotic as the most virulent of
anti-feminist texts.

NOTES

[1]The tradition of fame is discussed both in general and in its relation to Chaucer's House of Fame in Boitani (1984).

[2]Feminine garrulousness as a rhetorical strategy has been comprehensively and brilliantly treated by Patterson (1983).

[3]Kittredge suggested that Benoît de Sainte-Maure may have had Helen in mind for his portrait of Briseida ([1905] 1969, 72), and Edgar Finley Shannon points out numerous echoes between Chaucer's Criseyde and the Ovidian epistle from Helen in the Heroides (1929, 157-68). More recently, Mary-Jo Arn has explored the relationship between Helen and Criseyde in "Three Ovidian Women in Chaucer's Troilus: Medea, Helen, Oenone" (1980, 1-10).

[4]The best discussion of Ovid's use of sources is Jacobson (1974).

[5]Chaucer's use of sources in The Legend of Good Women has been well documented by Leach (1963) and by Fyler (1979). Both Leach and Fyler argue that Chaucer's self-consciousness about his sources in the legends is ironic.

[6]Robert Worth Frank compares Chaucer's version of the Philomela story with Chrétien de Troyes's Philomena and Gower's "Tale of Tereus" in the Confessio Amantis, claiming that Chaucer's excision of the sisters' revenge and the final metamorphosis represents his "shying away from violence" (1972, 138). I argue, however, that Chaucer not only does not censure the violence, but he actually enacts Tereus' terrible silencing of Philomela in his suppression of the Ovidian ending.

[7]The link between censorship and hysteria has been worked out by Higgins (1986) in the context of French film. See also Kahn (1986), who discusses the history of hysteria as a concept and its relationship to Freud's "talking cure."

WORKS CITED

Arn, Mary-Jo. "Three Ovidian Women in Chaucer's
Troilus: Medea, Helen, Oënone." The Chaucer Review
15 (1980): 1-10.

Boitani, Piero. Chaucer and the Imaginary World of
Fame. Totowa, NJ: Barnes and Noble, 1984.

Chaucer, Geoffrey. Works. Ed. F. N. Robinson. 2nd
ed. Boston: Houghton Mifflin, 1957.

Edmonds, J. M., trans. Lyra Graeca, vol. 2. London:
William Heinemann, 1922.

Frank, Robert Worth. Chaucer and "The Legend of Good
Women." Cambridge: Harvard University Press, 1972.

Fyler, John M. Chaucer and Ovid. New Haven: Yale
University Press, 1979.

Higgins, Lynn. "Historical Woman/Hysterical Text:
Gender, History and Their Dynamics of Representation." Paper presented at conference, Literature
and History, Dartmouth College, Hanover, NH, April
11-13, 1986.

Jacobson, Howard. Ovid's "Heroides." Princeton:
Princeton University Press, 1974.

Kahn, Coppelia. "The Absent Mother in King Lear." In
Rewriting the Renaissance: The Discourses of Sexual
Difference in Early Modern Europe. Edited by
Margaret W. Ferguson, Maureen Quilligan, and Nancy
J. Vickers, 33-49. Chicago: University of Chicago
Press, 1986.

Kittredge, G. L. The Date of Chaucer's "Troilus" and
Other Chaucer Matters. 1905. Reprint. New York:
Russell and Russell, 1969.

Leach, Eleanor Winsor. "A Study of the Sources and
Rhetoric of Chaucer's Legend of Good Women." Ph.D.
dissertation, Yale University, 1963.

Ovid. Metamorphoses. Trans. Frank Justus Miller, 3rd
ed. Cambridge: Harvard University Press, 1977.

Patterson, Lee. "'For the Wyves love of Bathe': Femi-
    nine Rhetoric and Poetic Resolution in the Roman de
    la Rose and The Canterbury Tales." Speculum 58
    (1983): 656-95

Shannon, Edgar Finley. Chaucer and the Roman Poets.
    Cambridge: Harvard University Press, 1929.

CHRISTINE DE PISAN:
SPEAKING LIKE A WOMAN/SPEAKING LIKE A MAN

by Lynne Huffer

Where lies the power of female discourse? How do we characterize woman's voice? as a polemic? didacticism? an angry, strident cry? silence, the unsaid? In the first "feminist" text of the French canon, The Book of the City of Ladies by Christine de Pisan, these questions of textual and sexual politics emerge. This work from the early fifteenth century is a courageous defense of the female sex in the face of centuries of misogynist writings. The text attracts our attention, in part, because it is a woman who is speaking; Christine is one of the first women to find herself, as Nancy Miller puts it, "poised at the violent intersection of sexuality and textuality."1 But despite the evident feminism of the text, the issue of its femininity is less clear. Is this truly a female voice? Why is it that, historically as well as today, the sexuality of a work is as important as its textuality? And where the textual and sexual axes overlap, what meanings appear behind and between the words?

My analysis attempts to answer these questions. By reading The Book of the City of Ladies through a grid of textual figures, I have found these figures arranged in configurations of tension. First, textual tension appears through a series of oppositions which could be described, rather simplistically, as a conflict between

the masculine and the feminine. Second, the text,
because it generates these tensions, becomes a model of
textual and sexual alienation.

Tension first appears in Christine's treatment of
the body. In view of my opening questions concerning
the sexuality of the text, the relationship between body
and text is essential. Further, since the only cri-
terion which ultimately determines femaleness is biological, Christine's treatment of the body is important.
Curiously, in Christine's feminist text, one is aware of
a denial or flight away from the body; the body is subli-
mated and appears as an abstraction. This movement away
from the body is apparent from the first pages of the
book. For example, just before the appearance of the
three ladies who will direct the construction of the
city of ladies, Christine states:

> in my body I considered myself most
> unfortunate because God had made me
> inhabit a female body in this world.[2]

Subsequently, the three ladies reveal to Christine
the folly of this belief. However, Christine, here and
in other passages, is at the same time defending and
denying her femininity by rejecting her body. In fact,
Christine defends "woman" by presenting herself as an
essentially masculine being. The words of the first
lady to appear, addressed to Christine, reveal this
paradox:

> You resemble the fool in the prank who
> was dressed in women's clothes while he
> slept: because those who were making
> fun of him repeatedly told him he was a

woman, he believed their false testimony
more readily than the certainty of his
own identity (p. 6).

If Christine is like the fool who mistakes "the
certainty of his own identity" because of his feminine
apparel, the implication is clear: Christine's femininity is no more than "clothing"; the "certainty of her
identity" is masculine, like that of the fool.

On one level, this denial of the body is convincing
and reinforces Christine's principal argument, that
women are as intelligent and virtuous as any man. The
argument is a tool Christine uses to promote the notion
that man and woman are essentially equal. Underlying
this belief in sexual equality is the religious conception of the soul, a soul created by God and existing in
both male and female bodies. Christine says:

> God created the soul and placed wholly
> similar souls, equally good and noble,
> in the feminine and in the masculine
> bodies (p. 23).

The initial conflict between body and spirit, however, remains unresolved. Without a body, woman is,
like man, the spiritual work of God. Paradoxically,
this bodiless woman, according to the most reductive
definition, is no longer a woman, but an asexual being.
Christine therefore finds herself faced with an irre-
solvable conflict: she can either defend woman as body,
and thus admit sexual difference; or she can defend the
bodiless, masculine woman, admit sexual equality, but at
the same time deny woman any sexual specificity.

Tension also appears beyond the body at the level of
imagery and metaphorical language. My exegetic reading
is justified, I believe, by the allegorical nature of

the text. I have found that the work's major metaphors
and symbols reinforce the basic tension between masculinity and femininity. For example, Christine says to
the three women:

> Who could give fitting thanks for such a
> boon? With the rain and dew of your
> sweet words, you have penetrated and
> moistened the dryness of my mind, so
> that it now feels ready to germinate and
> send forth new branches capable of
> bearing fruits of profitable virtue and
> sweet savor (p. 15).

The preceding description is built primarily upon
"female" metaphors: the majority of the images describe
fertility and reproduction, a female domain. But, within the same passage, images of sweetness and feminine
fecundity are modified by those of male insemination.
Christine says: you "penetrated and moistened the dry-
ness of my mind." How are we to interpret, then, the
role played by the three ladies? How do we characterize
their pedagogical gesture—as "rain and dew" or as
sexual penetration? Is this a masculine or feminine
translatio studii? In this particular passage, the
conflict remains unresolved.

Elsewhere, Lady Reason explains to Christine the
construction of the city, which "will be founded on a
flat and fertile plain" (p. 16). The image, flat and
fertile, implies the hope of a new beginning which will
come about through the destruction of the masculine
fields of discourse and the construction of a new city
upon the fields of female fertility. However, the image
is nuanced by the name given to the plain: the "Field

of Letters" (p. 16). In the fifteenth century this
field, the field of letters, could only be a masculine
one, a field of the male auctoritas. So, is the city,
like the book, founded on male writings, or "on a flat
and fertile [female] plain?" Is Christine, as architect
and as writer, placing herself within a masculine lineage,3 or is she proposing a new feminine translatio,
represented by the three ladies and by images of fertility and birth?

Tension finally exists at a third level, that of
language. First, the act of naming is a gesture privileged by the text, especially in the allegorical
context, where the significance of any given character
resides entirely in the name. The moments where the
three ladies name themselves are important and are
privileged by the delay which separates the initial
appearance of the ladies and the moment of their
naming: I am called Rectitude" (p. 12); and "I am
Justice" (p. 13). Modern psychoanalysis tells us that
to name means, in Lacanian terms, to inscribe oneself in
the symbolic order, and corresponds to the separation of
the infant from the order of the Imaginary, from maternal corporality. When we name ourselves, we designate
ourselves through the Name-of-the-Father; we are forever
dominated, defined by the Other, by the place of the
law. In the case of the three ladies, their names link
them to a patriarchal heritage which valorizes reason
and logocentrism.

However, the text creates a tension between this
nominal inscription in the symbolic order and the subversion of the name. These subversive effects are
subtle, but they nevertheless create a distinct textual
tension. Christine places herself within a lineage of
masculine authorities, auctoritates who are specifically

designated by their proper name. But at times Christine subverts this traditional topos: she forgets the name. For example, she writes: "just like the man--I cannot remember which one . . ." (p. 19); or again, "some pope--I don't know which one . . ." (p. 22); and again, "this proverb says (which someone, I don't know who, invented . . .)" (p. 28). This nominal amnesia is subversive, given the context of naming and identity and their link to the symbolic order.

The ambiguity of the name is perhaps the most visible where Christine narrates the story of her own patron saint, Saint Christine. This passage is important because of its length, its place in the text just before the end, and the importance of naming in the allegorical and religious context. On the one hand, the bestowal of the female name--Christine--of one woman onto another could be interpreted as existing outside of patriarchy, outside of the domain of the male patronymic. Christine says to her saint:

> O blessed Christine, worthy virgin
> favored by God, most elect and glorious
> martyr, in the holiness with which God
> has made you worthy, pray for me, a
> sinner, named with your name, and be my
> kind and merciful guardian. [In the
> original Old French, guardian is "mar-
> raine" or godmother, which, we will see,
> is significant.] Behold my joy at being
> able to make use of your holy legend and
> to include it in my writings, which I
> have recorded here at such length out of
> reverence for you. May this be ever
> pleasing to you! Pray for all women,

for whom your holy life may serve as an
example for ending their lives well. Amen
(p. 240).

Christine here suggests a matriarchal lineage
through the phrase "named with your name" and the word
"marraine." Further, this passing on of the name from
woman to woman parellels a passing on of stories to be
put into writing. Christine expresses her joy at being
able to "make use of [her saint's] holy legend and . . .
include it in [her] writings" (p. 240). But, one must
admit, behind this female lineage hides the masculine
power of the Church and Christianity; behind the name
"Christine" hides Christ, le "Christ," the son who
inherits from God the Father. Christine herself emphasizes this patriarchal lineage in another passage:
"whereupon Jesus Christ descended in His own person with
a large company of angels and baptized her and named her
Christine, from His own name . . ." (p. 236). The two
conflicting aspects—the masculine tradition and the
feminine subversion—coexist, remain in tension, and
reinforce the ambiguity of the text's sexuality.

Christine's choice of the vernacular instead of
Latin creates another linguistic tension in the text.
The masculine lineage of which Christine is a part
includes a large number of men who wrote in Latin. As
Earl Jeffrey Richards explains:

Christine was strongly committed to
writing in the vernacular, a conviction
which placed her in the unenviable
position of also having to use the
vernacular to best her predecessors who
had written in Latin. Thus, she faced

the double task of proving herself both
as a woman writer AND as a vernacular
writer.[4]

The choice of the vernacular is a decision to write
using the language of birth, the maternal language or
mother tongue.[5] This "feminine" aspect of the text is
important. Walter Ong explains that

> [t]he concept of "mother" tongue regis-
> ters deeply the human feeling that the
> language in which we grow up, the
> language which introduces us as human
> beings to the human lifeworld, not only
> comes primarily from our mother but
> belongs to some degree intrinsically to
> our mother's feminine world.[6]

Latin, on the other hand, is the paternal language,
without any attachment at all to the oral world of child-
hood. Latin is one of the "sex-linked male languages"
(Ong 25) which "depend on writing rather than on oral
speech for their existence" (Ong 25). Further, Latin
was, at the time that Christine wrote, taught and
learned almost exclusively by men, and as Ong explains,
"the admission of women to academic education and the
decline of Latin moved pari passu" (Ong 26). In light
of the sexual significance of Latin and the vernacular,
the obvious conclusion is that Christine's choice to
write in the vernacular is a key aspect of the text's
femininity.

But such a portrait of Christine's writing would be
overly simplistic. Although Christine chose the vernacular for her work, her style is "Latinate," what Richards

calls her "'high style'" (Richards 18), and states categorically: "[Her] style could not be more Latinate"
(Richards 19). This critic points out specific stylistic and grammatical features such as the Latin ablative
absolute construction, the Latin cum clause with the
imperfect subjunctive, the Latinate syntax, and the diction (Richards 19). Further, Richards considers this
"hypotaxic" style to be the sign of a "feminist" rhetoric, but my own interpretation is different: Christine's Latinate style is more masculine than feminist.
In order to display her erudition, Christine writes as
if she were writing in Latin. The maternal language,
the mother tongue, the female heritage, is in constant
tension with the Latinate style, the masculine translatio.

The underlying conflict between masculine and feminine brings us again to my opening question: where lies
the power of female discourse? What is its function:
to reclaim a lost female ·territory, or to inscribe
itself in a masculine order? Christine, it appears,
attempts to do both, thus maintaining sexual and textual
tension.

Tension results, however, in alienation, or specifically the alienation of the feminine voice, and a
primary manifestation of textual alienation is the
allegorical form of the text. Of course, allegory is a
conventional medieval form, but in Christine's work its
use is significant because the feminine "I" is doubly
alienated. She creates herself, first, like every other
allegorical "I," through the discourse of another; the
second or double aspect of her alienation is due to the
fact that this "other" discourse is masculine. Through
the mediation of the three ladies, Christine learns to
speak the word of God. Given the Christian allegorical

context, God becomes then the Lacanian Other, the Name-of-the-Father; it is the word which inhabits the speaking woman. Christine says: "God endowed women with the faculty of speech" (p. 28); and later, "God has demonstrated that He has truly placed language in women's mouths so that He might thereby be served" (p. 30). The allegorical "I," then, through this double transmission of the word of the Other is a model of the alienation of the female voice: "I" (as woman) speak the Other. Ironically, this textual alienation is Christine's source of power as a writer and a sign of her own auctoritas.

Lacan has said: "the la of woman [la femme] . . . cannot be written."[7] Femininity, the la of woman, exists only as not-man, the non-phallic, the not-all in relation to the phallic all. Symbolically, woman does not exist: "Woman's sex tells man nothing," says Lacan (Lacan 13). Thus, if woman wishes to speak, if she chooses to write, if she wants to exist for man, she must adopt a masculine discourse, the discourse of the phallic all. As Larysa Mykyta says in an article on Lacan, "since as not-all woman is outside of discourse, her speech must by definition be a co-optation, an assumption of the masculine position."[8]

This symbolic nonexistence of feminine discourse helps us to explain the phenomena I have uncovered in Christine's text. The feminine voice is in constant tension with its phallic inscription in a masculine order precisely because the feminine voice cannot speak itself. Woman's discourse is alienated because it exists only in relation to the phallic signifier, the One, the Other, God. Christine, as a woman writer, as a woman who speaks, must reject the la of la femme, of her own identity, and recognize like "the fool . . . dressed

in women's clothes" that the "certainty of [her] identity" is masculine. To defend women as she does against
misogynist attacks, Christine is obligated to speak
man's language. As Mykyta says, "females that speak,
that occupy positions of power . . . occupy these positions in the phallic mode" (Mykyta 56).

To reverse this symbolic structure, so that the
female voice is more than silence, the phallic mode of
discourse must be put into question. And this Christine
does, at least for us as modern readers, simply by
speaking as a woman: by reclaiming a lost heritage, a
female translatio, and at the same time gaining political and historical legitimacy by inscribing herself in a
masculine symbolic order. More importantly, by forcing
us, as readers, to consider questions concerning the
power and function of woman's discourse, Christine
transcends woman as silence and, as a historical and
literary figure, remains an important foremother of the
feminist canon.

NOTES

[1] Nancy Miller, "Arachnologies: The Woman, The Text, and The Critic," forthcoming in _Poetics of Gender_ (New York: Columbia University Press, 1986), ed. Nancy Miller, p. 284.

[2] Christine de Pisan, _The Book of the City of Ladies_, trans. Earl Jeffrey Richards (New York: Persea), p. 5. Trans. of _Le Livre de la cite des dames_, Maureen Curnow, a critical edition, Ph.D., Vanderbilt University, 1975. All further references to Christine's work will be taken from this translation, unless otherwise specified.

[3] The sources for Christine's examples include: _De Claris Mulieribus_ by Boccaccio, _Livre de Leesce_ by Jean Le Fèvre, _Speculum Historiale_ by Vincent de Beauvais, St. Augustine's _The City of God_, among others.

[4] Earl Jeffrey Richards, "Christine de Pizan and the Question of Feminist Rhetoric," _Teaching Language Through Literature_ XII, 2 (1983): 16.

[5] Christine de Pisan was born in Italy, but French can nevertheless be considered her mother tongue in relation to Latin.

[6] Walter Ong, "Transformations of the Word and Alienation," _Interface of the Word: Studies in the Evolution of Consciousness and Culture_ (Ithaca: Cornell University Press, 1977), p. 23.

[7] Jacques Lacan, _Le Seminaire XX_, "Encore" (Paris: Seuil, 1975), p. 75 (my translation).

[8] Larysa Mykyta, "Lacan, Literature and the Look," _Substances_ 39 (1983): 51.

REINMAR DER ALTE AND THE
WOMAN AS COURTLY VICTIM

by William E. Jackson

The Frauenlieder and Frauenstrophen (women's songs
and women's stanzas) of the late twelfth-century
Austrian poet Reinmar der Alte belong to the outstanding
achievements of medieval German literature.1 Toward
the end of this article I shall explain and attempt to
substantiate this statement in a brief discussion of
poems which I consider to be Reinmar's best efforts in
this vein. Before doing that, however, I shall try in
this first section to establish something of a context
by noting some features which Reinmar's Frauenlieder and
Frauenstrophen have in common with women's songs and
stanzas both in the German language and in other literatures of his age.

Reinmar's Frauenlieder and Frauenstrophen owe much
to the so-called Danubian Minnesang of earlier twelfth-
century Austria and eastern Bavaria. Helmut de Boor,
the author of one of the standard handbooks on medieval
German literature, refers to Reinmar's indebtedness to
this older tradition expressly as an inheritance ("Aus
ererbten donauländischen Motiven").2 De Boor sees
that inheritance reflected most clearly in poems--
including mainly Frauenlieder and Frauenstrophen--which
he considers to be creations of Reinmar's early
years.3 In so doing, de Boor draws on a long tradition which attempts to relegate a number of Reinmar's

Frauenlieder and Frauenstrophen, which portray clearly
woman's erotic longing for man, to an allegedly wild
period of Reinmar's youth.[4] Later on, as the tradition goes, Reinmar is supposed to have found himself and
to have become the lachrymose poet of high courtly love
familiar to most of the scholars who have heard of
Reinmar at all.[5]

De Boor follows the same scholarly tradition in
seeing Reinmar as a native Alsatian.[6] He pictures
Reinmar arriving in Vienna as a mature poet from the
West, bringing with him the most refined brand of
courtly love. In so doing, Reinmar allegedly caused
considerable consternation and aroused intense hostility
in the very Danubian circles from which he is supposed
to have inherited the basic stock of motives for his
Frauenlieder and Frauenstrophen. Like his predecessors
(and a number of successors) de Boor makes no attempt to
resolve this contradiction and apparently did not become
aware of it. He therewith assumes (and leaves outstanding) their indebtedness to explain how the same
Reinmar who supposedly grew up in far-away Alsatia and
only later came to Austria, should have also grown up
inheriting from the same Austrian tradition which he is
assumed to have opposed and threatened subsequently.

In the absence of an explanation for (or any sound
reason for assuming) such a curious development, I shall
in the following abide by my contention that Reinmar der
Alte at least grew up in Austria and was probably born
there.[7] I shall thus assume that whatever contact he
may have had with the literary traditions with which I
shall compare his own efforts was that of an Austrian.

1. Reinmar and the European Woman's Song

De Boor is less dependent on scholarly tradition in his interpretation of Reinmar's so-called youthful Danubian poems, most of which either take the form of Frauenlieder or include Frauenstrophen.8 And indeed the common features noted by de Boor between Reinmar and poets of this older tradition could indeed suggest very plausibly the passing on of an inheritance.9

First of all, as already indicated, it is typical of these poems for the woman to woo the man. Frequently, this wooing takes the indirect form of an attack upon potential opposition to the courtship. In MF 151,1-8 by Reinmar (RW 2-3), for instance, the speaker decries the presence of those "who would do better to stay at home," while suggesting pointedly that if her "ritter" were better at considering her wishes, he would be with her all the time.

These lines echo several extant poems from the older Austrian Minnesang where one can frequently hear a woman complain that her beloved man is absent because of third parties.10 In MF 7,1-9 by Kürenberg, the offending group, identified as people ("diu liute"), is named only in the accompanying stanza where the speaker is the beloved man. The two stanzas, in which the speech of man and woman is related but does not form a dialogue, constitute the poetic structure called the Wechsel.11 In MF 9,13-20 by Kürenberg, the detractors are called liars ("lügenaere"). In MF 16,8-14 by the Burggraf von Regensburg and MF 18,1-8 by the Burggraf von Rietenburg, we hear only a pronominal reference to the offenders as they/them ("si"). In 36,5-13 by Dietmar von Eist, the vexing third party is the world ("Diu welt").

MF 35,24-31 by Dietmar brings us closer to Reinmar.
For here we hear the speaker complain about the beloved
man himself, asking how he can go on allowing her to
suffer longing for him:

> 35,24 Wie tuot der besten einer sô
> daz er mîn senen mac vertragen?

A few lines later, she expresses great distress that
her grief should stem from someone who has become so
dear to her heart. Here we find ourselves approaching
the "courtly" age of Reinmar where the hindrance to the
love relationship is no longer attributable to third
parties, but to tensions between the lovers themselves,
and specifically to a curious lack of interest and
support on the part of the man. If the beloved man
himself were, as Reinmar's speaker puts it (MF 151,4),
more considerate of her will, there would presumably no
longer be any pain of longing, or in any case much less.
The wooing of man by woman in the Danubian Minnesang
can also become quite aggressive. The same poem by
Reinmar, MF 151,1 (RW 2-3),--actually a Wechsel of four
stanzas--also contains an example of this aggressive
wooing. Responding to the man's claim (151,17-18) to be
seeking grace in return for his service, the woman
answers that she will gladly bestow grace on the one who
does her will, and indeed will place him so close to
herself that it would seem as if the emperor were lying
there:

> 151,23 ich sage im lieubiu maere,
> daz ich in gelege alsô,
> mich dûchte vil, ob ez der keiser
> waere.

These lines are similar to passages in several
extant poems from the Bavarian-Austrian region which
Reinmar presumably could have known and thus may be
echoing here. One is the anonymous stanza MF 3,7-11
from the **Carmina Burana** manuscript where, in the earlier
of two versions, we hear a woman say that she would give
up all the world from the ocean to the Rhine to have the
King of England lie in her arms.12 Another is the
lines MF 14,34-35 by Meinloh von Sevelingen where a
woman expresses her wish to lie in bed with her lover in
a formulation very similar to that used by Reinmar:

> 14,34 Ich gelege mir in wol nâhe,
> den selben kindeschen man.

Other uses of the same motif (i.e., "woman talks of
placing her lover beside her in bed") in medieval German
literature take us farther afield, as, for example, in
MF 17,1-4 by Der Burggraf von Regensburg or MR 34,11-18
by Dietmar von Eist where the same thought is projected
into the past.

Much closer to Reinmar's use of the motif is that of
the Provencal _trobairitz_ known as the Countess of Dia.
In her poem "Estat ai en greu cossirier," the Countess
twice expresses the wish to lie beside her lover, once
in terms of holding him some evening in her bare arms
("tener un ser en mos bratz nut"), the other time in
terms of holding him beside her in her embrace ("e que
jagues ab vos un ser/ e qu'ie, us des un bais
amoros").13

This very striking similarity between poems by the
Countess of Dia and Reinmar der Alte brings up the first
of two very general points which I want to make during
the course of this article. It has to do with this very

similarity between passages composed by a woman poet on
the one hand and, on the other, by a man composing in
the persona of a woman. James M. Nichols has recently
pointed out the need to study this situation, proposing
in his case comparison of the Hispanic woman's song
(jarcha), presumably composed by men, with the compositions of Andalusian women poets.[14] In this regard,
some of my reservations about Meg Bogin's fine book on
women poets in Provence have to do with the fact that
features which Bogin is inclined to attribute to realities of the woman's situation also turn up in women's
songs composed by men. Her claims that the poetry of
the trobairitz is distinctive because they "wrote for
personal rather than professional reasons" or that they
"wrote about their own intimate feelings,"[15] seem to
hold up pretty well in contrast to the poetry of the
male troubadours--with which Bogin compares them--but
such assumptions become quite problematic when one
compares the compositions of trobairitz with women's
songs composed by men. Studies of the kind called for
by Nichols may some day give us a basis for differen-
tiating between the two, but until they do, viable
distinctions may be very difficult to demonstrate.

In this regard, the Countess of Dia and Reinmar der
Alte are a telling case in point. Among all the
passages quoted here showing the motif of the woman
expressing her desire to lie beside the man, those
quoted from the Countess and Reinmar are remarkably
similar in several regards. In both cases, the lover is
pointedly identified as a knight ("cavallier," "ritter"), a designation which, according to de Boor, occurs
in Reinmar's case only in his "early poems."[16] Both
the Countess and Reinmar portray situations in which the
problem in the love relationship is clearly between the

woman and the man themselves, not externally caused as
it is generally in the older Austrian lyric. We have
already noted Dietmar von Eist as another exception in
this regard, and it is interesting to note that Dietmar's poetry also shows striking similarities to that of
the Countess of Dia. For example, the motif--unusual
for medieval German poetry--of the woman calling her
lover's attention to her own physical attractiveness in
MF 37,26-28 by Dietmar also occurs in the first and
fifth stanzas of the Countess de Dia's "A chantar m'er
de so qu'ieu non volria."[17] Given the importance of
Dietmar's influence on Reinmar--MF 156,25 repeats ver-
batim MF 35,20 by Dietmar[18]--, it is interesting
indeed that their poetry should share features with that
of the Countess of Dia which are not found in the works
of their fellow-poets from the Austrian area.

One final similarity between Reinmar and the
Countess of Dia is the emphasis on the woman's will.
Twice in the final stanza of the Countess's "Estat ai en
greu cossirier," the speaker stresses her desire to have
her way. First she asks when she will have her "Bels
amics" in her power ("poder"). Then, at the end of the
poem, she offers him her husband's place beside her on
the condition that he will do what she wishes ("far so
qu'ieu volria").[19] This theme--one is reminded of the
old woman in Chaucer's Wife of Bath Prologue who "knows
what women want most: authority"[20]--occurs twice in
Reinmar's poem (MF 151,4 and 151,26) and recurs quite
frequently elsewhere in his Frauenlieder and Frauenstrophen.[21]

This insistence of the woman on her "willen" in the
sense of exercising authority over her lover seems to be
connected with the problematization of the relationship
between woman and man which Reinmar's poetry shares with

that of the Countess of Dia and, in part, with Dietmar
von Eist. No longer does Reinmar have her lash out at
third parties or go after her lover aggressively as she
did in the older Austrian Minnesang--Kürenberg, Regensburg, Rietenburg, Meinloh--, but instead he portrays her
musing rather passively about her treatment at the hands
of others (including her lover) and fixing just as passively on the "willen" that she cannot have. The old
aggressiveness has become a strikingly listless struggle
for an elusive means of exercising pressure.

It would be very difficult if not impossible to
prove that the similarities between the poetry of
Reinmar der Alte and the Countess of Dia, though very
striking, are not coincidental. In the case of Latin
poetry, however, we are on safer ground since a few of
Reinmar's poems appear in a Latin setting, namely in the
famous Carmina Burana manuscript, mentioned above, which
probably originates from Benediktbeuren in eastern
Bavaria near the Austrian border. That collection contains individual stanzas from three compositions by
Reinmar and, as Jeffrey Ashcroft has pointed out, this
makes Reinmar the "most frequently represented" of all
the German poets whose works appear in the Carmina
Burana.22 This may come as a surprise to some readers
familiar only with the widely held conception of Reinmar
as the quintessential poet of unrequited courtly love.
For the Latin love lyrics of this thirteenth-century
collection, in the words of Anne Howland Schotter,
"follow the older stereotype of being at best good-
naturedly, and at worst cruelly, sensual."23

As we shall soon note, Reinmar's Frauenlieder and
Frauenstrophen have much less in common with the Latin
woman's song--and Latin poetry in general--than with
those in other vernacular literatures. There are, of

course, valid reasons for this fact. The poems of the
Carmina Burana belong to the sphere of the medieval
educational establishment. The Latin language of the
poems "was seldom taught to women" and (thus) "effectively excluded medieval women from the audience."24
It was a poetry "written not only by men but for men, to
be performed before a male audience," and could thus
"express antifeminism with impunity."25 By contrast,
Reinmar's poetry was composed for a sphere where women
seem to have exerted considerable influence, for the
vernacular German language of his poetry seems to have
been read more widely by women than men and at times
even written specifically for women.26

On the other hand, the three stanzas of Reinmar
found in the Carmina Burana are by no means completely
out of place. For instance, his poem CB 143a, in
Ashcroft's words, "celebrates joy in the recollection of
erotic pleasures."27 It is the "recollection" of a
woman (Ashcroft does not note this fact), or actually
the first stanza of a "recollection" which, in the
version published as MF 203,10-23, consists of two
stanzas.28 In the first, the speaker responds to the
pleasure which her ritter has afforded her by promising
that she will always cherish him more than any of her
kin:

> 203,14 Ich wil im iemer holder sîn
> denne keinem mâge mîn.

The second stanza, which does not appear in the Carmina
Burana manuscript, continues what is actually a single
outburst of overflowing joy, and one which ends with a
rousing farewell to sadness and welcome to a week (?) of
joy:

203,21 Sô ist mîn trûren gar zergàn
und bin al die wochen wol getân.
ei, waz ich denne vröuden hân.

Thus, while the eroticism of the poem stops far short of
the obscenity found in a number of songs from the Carmina Burana, it is clearly direct enough to justify its
inclusion in this collection. The main difference is
that Reinmar does not ridicule or belittle the woman as
a "victim of male predation,"29 but rather portrays
her in a manner similar to the older "idealistic tradition of woman's song" in Latin from which, in Schotter's
view, the Carmina Burana poems have departed for the
worse.

CB 147a by Reinmar is also both like and unlike the
Latin poems which surround it. Here, however, I must
disagree strongly with a suggestion of Ashcroft.
Lumping the poem together with the third, CB 166a--
which, as a "Mannesstrophe," we will not discuss,--
Ashcroft characterizes the two as "songs which
demonstrate a code of behavior in love unsurpassed in
Minnesang for its uncompromising insistence on the
sublimation of passion as the true value of love."30
I consider this interpretation patently wrong and perhaps for both poems, but certainly for the one that will
now concern us.

CB 147a is--again--only the first stanza of a longer
poem published as MF 177,10-39, a poem which definitely
does not fit Ashcroft's description.31 The poem
actually portrays a conversation between a woman and the
messenger of a suitor with whom she has apparently had a
relationship of some duration. That relationship is now
clearly strained. Curiously, although she attributes
the problem to misbehavior on the suitor's part (second

stanza), it is she who seems to be trying to patch up the damage. Just as curious is the circumstance that she is attempting this delicate feat by soliciting the assistance of a messenger who is clearly representing her suitor's interests.

The behavior of the messenger is--strikingly--an excellent demonstration of ideal messenger qualities as prescribed in the following words of the eleventh-century Andalusian author Ibn Hazm:

> The messenger should be presentable, quick-witted, able to take a hint and to read between the lines, possessed of initiative and the ability to supply out of his own understanding things which may have been overlooked by his principal; he must also convey to his employer all that he observes with complete accuracy; he ought to be able to keep secrets and preserve trusts; he must be loyal, cheerful and a sincere well-wisher.32

The situation in Reinmar's poem will not support comment on all these fine attributes, but his messenger does demonstrate enough of them to make one wonder if the similarity is coincidental. The messenger is, for instance, "quick-witted" enough to see through immediately the woman's attempt to enlist his support by stealth. To her question about the lover's whereabouts, the messenger answers straightforwardly, but in a manner which puts the lover in an advantageous light: he is happy (she apparently is not), and if she commands (?), his (= the suitor's) heart will always be high (?)

(177,14-15). By the end of the second stanza (of five), the messenger is already in control of the situation to the point where he can admonish the woman (as a mere messenger!) to watch her tongue ("nû verredent iuch niht," 177,20). In addition, the messenger is so "possessed of initiative and the ability to supply out of his own understanding" that his improvised answers on the lover's behalf completely dismantle the woman's campaign: by the end of the poem she has lost all control and is babbling disparate and incoherent threats. And we can be sure that the messenger will "convey to his employer all that he observes with complete accuracy," a prospect which, we hope, will mercifully not occur to the woman herself.

Important for our theme is, again, Reinmar's departure from the depiction of the woman in the older Austrian Minnesang as an aggressive, forceful defender of her concerns to one which portrays her as a vulnerable, impotent, and clumsy prisoner of unclear but obviously troubling complexities. With this portrayal we approach the vicinity of Reinmar's courtly victims.

The two **Frauenstrophen** of Reinmar appearing in the **Carmina Burana** thus both turn out to be quite appropriate to their surroundings, but only in part. The one, CB 143a, belongs to a poem which portrays the ecstasy of erotic pleasure, not of the male predator as in the Latin poems, but of the gratified woman. The other, CB 147a, comes from a poem which portrays love as warfare, however not as the "virtual rape" or the "cynical seduction" found in the Latin poems, but as subtle psychological warfare suitable to the most refined of conspiratorial courtly circles, a warfare whose indirectness is symbolized by the function of a messenger as go-between.

To complete this attempt at establishing a context
for Reinmar's particular brand of woman's song, we now
turn to the poetry of Northern France. And, whereas any
suggestion about possible links between Reinmar and
either the Countess of Dia or Ibn Hazm would be purest
speculation, there are concrete reasons for assuming
that the similarities we shall note between Reinmar's
Frauenlieder and Frauenstrophen and Northern French
Poetry may reflect actual connections between Reinmar
and that area.

First of all, there is the use in Reinmar's poem
"Ein wîser man sol niht ze vil" (MF 162,7) of the poem
"Bien cuidai toute ma vie" by the trouvère Gace Brule.
It is the only link that has so far been established
between Reinmar and any poet outside the German-speaking
area. And that link is "so close between the first
strophe of Reinmar's poem and the second of Gace Brulé
as to make the imitation certain."[33] The stanzas of
both poets warn against investigating (Reinmar: testing
and accusing) a woman (Gace: a wife or lover) whom one
wishes to keep. Both Gace and Reinmar add the related
warning that one should not seek after information that
one would rather not know. This is a warning against
surveillance, German houte, which is spelled out
pointedly and thoroughly in Gottfried von Strassburg's
Tristan.[34] Nevertheless, while Gottfried's use of the
motif indicates possibly widespread familiarity, the
similarity between its (double) formulation in the poems
of Gace and Reinmar make coincidence seem unlikely:
this is a case of direct influence. And given the fact
that French literature usually influenced German in this
period, there are no grounds for challenging Sayce's
implicit assumption that Gace influenced Reinmar. However, since our knowledge about Reinmar is so limited

(as about Gace, for that matter), we have no way of
accounting for either his familiarity with contemporary
literature in general or for the influence of Gace Brule
in particular.

On the other hand, there are links between Austria
and Northern France from Reinmar's age which indicate
that literary influence between these two areas need not
surprise us. First, there is the fact that men of power
and influence in Austria, like those in other parts of
the German-speaking area, often sent their sons and
young male relatives to study in France. One notable
and particularly relevant example is the historian and
bishop Otto of Freising,[35] uncle of Duke Leopold V of
Austria, the "Liutpolt" of Reinmar's best-known woman's
song, the unusual Widow's Lament (MF 167,31-168,
29).[36] Also, there is the French influence on Austria
in the area of the arts, such as the adopting of French
melodies in Austrian church music,[37] or the obvious
familiarity of an artist active in Carinthia around 1200
with French sculpture of the late twelfth century.[38]

Given this background, we should not be surprised
that the poetry of Reinmar seems strongly influenced by
the woman's song of Northern France. And that influence
seems to have been quite pervasive, as we shall hear
shortly in reference to Reinmar's portrayals of troubled
women. For in the Northern French chansons de femme,
chansons d'ami, chansons de toile, and chansons de mal-
mariée, we find depictions of women in love so similar
to poems by Reinmar--in general tone as well as specific
formulation--that, in my view, it is hardly doubtful
that Reinmar knew and used examples of these genres as
his models.[39]

In the Northern French woman's song, as in vernacular women's songs generally, it is the woman who "seems

more in love with a man than the man with her."[40] Not
so general and of greater importance for our subject is
the (indirect) portrayal, particularly prominent in the
chanson de femme, of the "ami inhumain,"[41] the callous
lover who seems so indifferent to the sufferings of the
woman which, in many cases, clearly he himself has (at
least partly) caused. Most important for Reinmar, however, is the rendering of the thoughts, attitudes and
emotions of the woman--one thinks of the Northern French
woman writer Marie de France's focus on the "inner man
and woman"[42]--as she confronts various stages of a
complex and trying relationship. The woman in the anonymous poem "Lasse, por quoi refusai"[43] asks herself why
she has refused her lover since he has doted on her
("muse") for such a long time without finding mercy;
Reinmar treats the same theme in MF 186,19-187,30 where,
characteristically for the "courtly" tendencies we have
already noted, the woman in Reinmar's poem explains her
refusal in terms of concern for her reputation ("lîbes
êre," 186,28). In the fourth stanza of the same poem,
we hear the woman curse any who have offended her lover,
wishing them loss of ears and eyes; and in the fifth and
final stanza we hear her announce her intention to place
herself in her lover's mercy. Both these motifs receive
rather unsettling treatment in poems by Reinmar which we
will discuss shortly. And, finally, in the third stanza
of the poem "La froidor ne la jalee,"[44] we hear a
woman, who has made a total commitment to a questionable
relationship, confess that she should not have done so
("D'ameir lai ou je ne doi"). Such statements of regret
will also be heard below in the portrayals of Reinmar's
courtly victims.

I sum up. Reinmar der Alte was most directly
influenced by the poetry of twelfth-century Austria

where he grew up and where he was probably born. At
some point he became familiar with the poetry of
Northern France. He may also have encountered the
poetry of Provence and of Spain. His _Frauenlieder_ and
Frauenstrophen have much in common with the woman's song
of all these vernacular traditions, and also with the
poetry of at least one woman poet, the Countess of Dia.
They are also similar to the woman's song in Latin
poetry in some respects, but differ from it noticeably
in that, while the Latin woman's song--like Latin poetry
generally--focuses on the man's pursuit of the reluctant
woman, the woman's song of Reinmar and of the European
vernacular traditions focuses on the woman's love for an
often reluctant man.

Reinmar's portrayal of the woman in his _Frauenlieder_
goes beyond that of his Austrian predecessors in two
connected regards. First, the aggressive, combative
woman of the older poetry becomes in Reinmar's poems the
passive woman encumbered by complexities and apparent
restrictions. Along with this passiveness there is also
noticeable a progressive limitation of the woman's
focus: while in the older poetry the woman directed her
attention to outside forces which impinged upon her love
relationship, in Reinmar's poem she concentrates, first,
on the relationship with her lover itself and, secondly,
even more narrowly on her own inner thoughts, feelings,
and wishes.

This progressive passivity of the woman and the
related constriction of her sphere reminds one of the
development which Thilo Vogelsang notes in the position
of the woman ruler in medieval Germany: from the active
(co-)ruler of the tenth century,[45] the princely wife
sees herself progressively restricted until she becomes
the socially exalted but politically impotent woman of

the later twelfth century (Reinmar's age!), the age of
the "frouwe," the "domina," and the "dame."[46] The
similar development in Reinmar's poetry is highlighted
by the fact that the portrayal of the man undergoes no
such change. The reluctant, indifferent, and often
cruel lover, whom the woman in the older poetry could
openly pursue and attack, is the same lover with whom
the courtly women of the later development must find new
ways to deal and cope.

2. Reinmar's Courtly Victims

Reinmar der Alte's poems portraying women figures
whom I have been calling courtly victims are actually
depictions of women who have not found an effective way
of dealing with this unchanged lover in a situation that
has changed substantially. I shall focus here briefly
on three poems in Reinmar's opus which I consider the
best, most startling, and most interesting examples of
this new constellation. In all three cases the diffi-
culty seems to be an internal one: the failure of the
woman to cope with her situation wisely and effectively
has exacted a psychological price of formidable proportions. We are thus dealing, in a very real sense,
with poetic depictions of a psycho-emotionally troubled
woman.

In the first, MF 192,15-192,21,[47] Reinmar makes
use in the very first stanza of motifs which, I am
convinced, he derived from the woman's song of Northern
France. The speaker in this poem confesses right away
that she is totally at her lover's mercy: he forces her
("twinget") to do whatever he wishes. She then looks
back upon a time when she was stable ("hât ie vil
staeten muot") and contrasts it with the unsettling

present in which she lives and loves in fear ("angest-
lîchen"). The second stanza opens with the speaker's
startling suggestion that it is high time for someone to
exercise surveillance over her: "Der mîn huote, des
waere zît" (192,32). "Huote" we have encountered above
as that bane of lovers--its European origins, interestingly enough, go back to the Muslim Spain of Ibn
Hazm[48]--which lovers and their sympathetic poet-
creators tend to decry in the harshest terms.[49] That
the speaker views "huote" positively as a possibility of
rescue, is thus a measure of her clear recognition that
she lacks the inner strength to cope with the dis-
tressing situation in which she finds herself. The
remaining three stanzas of the poem consist of statements explaining how that situation came about, and of
references to pre-enslavement days when she would not
have believed that it was possible for her to end up in
her present predicament.

The second of our portrayals, MF 195,37-196, 35,[50]
is a particularly unusual poem on two counts. The
opening stanza of the poem turns out to be words of an
anonymous and unidentified speaker, functioning as a
kind of announcer/interviewer, who, meeting the "star"
of the poem after some time, inquires about her obviously deteriorated appearance: What has happened to
your beautiful body--you were such a beautiful woman;
now you have lost your color,--who did this to you? The
last words of this anonymous sympathizer constitute a
vehement curse upon whoever was responsible for this
ravaging of her former beauty. Her explanation of her
appearance constitutes the remaining five stanzas of the
poem.

Both this use of the announcer figure and the fact
that the woman is depicted as physically affected by

love--the woman in medieval German literature is
notoriously perfect in physical appearance--are unusual
in the extreme for poetry of this period. The former is
a device unprecedented in medieval literature to my
knowledge, and thus seems an original Reinmarian technique. The latter, on the other hand, is not totally
unheard of, and indeed two possible sources come to
mind. First, adverse affects of love on physical appearance constitute a theme that is treated at some length
by Ibn Hazm, whom we have now had several occasions to
mention.[51] Secondly, one is also reminded of the
figure of Sigune in Wolfram von Eschenbach's _Parzival_
and particularly of her first meeting with the titular
hero of that work. On this occasion Parzival, like the
anonymous speaker in Reinmar's poem, refers to Sigune's
loss of color, inquires about the cause of her misfortune, and pronounces a verbal attack on the perpe-
trator.[52] The similarity is all the more interesting
since this passage in _Parzival_ occurs a few pages after
a statement which has usually been interpreted as refer-
ring to Reinmar himself.[53]

The woman's explanation of her condition seems on
the surface to be clear and straightforward. On closer
observation, however, that explanation turns out to be
less than satisfactory and even a little suspicious. In
the second stanza (her first), we hear that her distress
is caused by the animosity ("nîde") of unnamed persons
who accuse her (?) and make her avoid a certain knight.
In the third, however, we hear that her beloved knight
has promised to come to her and that if she knew that
this were true, it would be the best news she has ever
heard. This prospect is formulated without any apparent
consideration of her envying detractors--will they not
cause trouble? Or are they perchance not the real

reason for her doubt whether the visit will actually come to pass?

The fourth stanza conveys her joyous reaction to the prospect of his visit and a brief insight into her plans to make her lover glad he has come, if indeed he does: she is ecstatic at the prospect ("vor liebe, daz mir alsô wol geschiht") and is already formulating her invitation to him to accompany her to pick flowers on the heath (196,22). However, this stanza seems to have been only a diverting interlude, for in the fifth stanza we hear her contemplating the opposite prospect: if it happens, she proclaims, that he does not come to lie next to her ("nâhen lît"), then alas for her beauty ("Owê danne schoenes wîbes!"). Never before will she have come in greater fear of her life (196,28). Is she contemplating doing (further) harm to herself (suicide?) if his visit does not come to pass? One is reminded of the "strategy of affliction" which, according to Schulenburg, numerous generations of European religious women from the early Middle Ages used to defend their virginity against the danger of enforced marriage, a strategy of "public exploitation of adversity and afflictions"--often taking the form of threats to do themselves bodily harm--which provided an "effective vehicle to manipulate their family or society."[54] In Reinmar's poem, however, the woman seems to be using her own "exploitation of adversity and afflictions" as part of what seems to be a campaign for sexual freedom. Could Reinmar be drawing on this tradition while reversing its intent and spirit?

In the sixth and final stanza, the poems take yet another curious and ominous turn. The speaker tells us that her intimates--"vriunde" can mean friends or relatives--have written her off as a hopeless case

("niemer werde rât"). She attacks them heatedly as
liars, but do we not have to wonder if their suspicions
are not justified? Certainly her somewhat incoherent
closing words are not designed to instill confidence in
her stability and capability to cope with her situation. The outburst begins with rejoicing that her
friends consider her hopeless: bless them for lamenting
me, she screams, how dear to their heart is my suffering! Is this tone of sarcasm not seriously out of
place? In any case, for her the concern of the
"vriunde" is not a thankworthy sentiment. Her only
concern is the beloved knight. If only he alone
comforts her ("getroestet"), she says in the closing
lines of the poem, then one will seldom (= never?) ever
see her crying again. Must we not wonder if there is
really any basis for this optimism?

Our third and final "troubled woman" portrayal, MF
199,15-201,11,55 features a woman who has come under
the sway of her "geselle" (199,36) to such an extent
that her infatuation has taken on religious overtones.
He has conditioned her ("gewent," 199,30) to total depen-
dence upon himself. Whatever he wants with her has to
happen (199,36-38). Furthermore, whoever honors him and
gives him joy, does so to her (200,11-13). She will
gladly relinquish whatever he wants her to give up
(200,14-16) and will happily suffer the envy of evil
people for his name's sake (200,17-18). If he breaks
off with her, she will relinquish her salvation (200,
22-24), but she will also be faithful to him whatever he
does (200, 30-32). At this point our speaker offers the
not clearly connected proposal that a woman ought to
guard her honor (!) at all times and not fight against
her friend ("friunt"). And thus will she await him with
honor (200,36-40). Do such sentiments not rival
Eloise's devotion to Abaelard?

Interspersed between these pronouncements of devotion are references, fully worthy of the **Carmina Burana**, to times which she and this very gifted lover enjoyed together (his gift is expressly praised in 199,29; 199,39-201,5; 200,19-21; 200,33-35). However, alas! at the end of the poem we hear a troubling undertone to this enjoyment of a relationship which otherwise seems to be pleasurable indeed. In words which could probably serve as a motto to a number of poems treated in this discussion, she leaves us with a disturbing confession: the very fact, we hear her say, that she knows so much about the "êre" (honor? reputation?) of this man, is the very cause of her pain of heart ("herzesêre").

To sum up, we have here three portrayals of women experiencing psychological domination by men whose attitude toward them seems ambiguous at best and, to judge by a few statements, frankly quite ominous. The women themselves show, on balance, little confidence that they have placed themselves in good hands and even indicate at times clear acknowledgment that their commitments have been mistaken or ill-fated. Thus, Reinmar's depiction of the woman in love has, in a sense, come full cycle: whereas we earlier saw him create women figures who longed and strove for power over their lovers, here we encounter women who have become frighteningly subject to the man's power over them.

Conclusion

I would like to begin this conclusion with the second of my very general observations. It concerns the fact that medieval love poetry and especially the poetry

of courtly love--they are commonly discussed as one and
the same--are still usually written from the point of
view of the man. The uninformed reader can--still
today--gain the impression that medieval love poetry
always portrays an unrequited male lover unreservedly
devoted to an exalted courtly lady from whom he can
expect to derive some educational value, but not the
pleasure that he obviously seeks (and that his devoted
service allegedly deserves).

The one-sidedness of this view, to which Bogin's
book stands as eloquent testimony,[56] becomes all the
more troubling when one realizes that--and this is the
insight which Bogin does not provide--a fairly large
number of medieval love poems composed by men depict the
love of woman for man. These men include some of the
better known poets in several medieval traditions, poets
who, like Reinmar, portrayed expressions of love both of
woman for man and man for woman. One could name the
Provencal poets Marcabru--his "A la fontana del vergier"
is not unsimilar to MF 195,37 by Reinmar--and Raimbaut
de Vaqueyras,[57] the trouvère Guiot de Dijon ("Chan-
terai por maon courage") and his countrymen, anonymous
and named, whose poems appear in Pierre Bec's edition.
And, among Reinmar's fellow-poets in the German language, one could mention such notable figures as Friedrich von Hausen, Heinrich von Morungen, Heinrich von
Veldeke, Walther von der Vogelweide--in a word, just
about all of the "name" poets active in the so-called
flowering of literature in Germany around 1200.[58]

It is thus not unusual that Reinmar should have
become interested in portraying the sentiments of the
loving woman. Such interest seems to have been fairly
widespread among lyrical poets in several European traditions, not to mention epic poetry with its Herzeloydes,

Lavinias, and Isoldes. What does set Reinmar apart is
his attempt, in a few poems, to capture a peculiar kind
of psychological endangerment threatening the courtly
woman who, having ventured into a _liaison dangereuse_,
can neither muster up the inner strength to escape nor
conceal pronounced discomfort over her state of subjec-
tion. I know of no poems which could have served
Reinmar as models for these beautiful but disturbing
pieces.

NOTES

[1]The standard edition of Reinmar der Alte's poems can be found in Hugo Moser and Helmut Tervooren, eds., Des Minnesangs Frühling, 36th ed. (Stuttgart, 1977), 285-403. Texts and English translations of eighteen Frauenlieder by Reinmar can be found in William E. Jackson, Reinmar's Women (Amsterdam, 1981), 1-42. These two books will serve as the basis for my discussion and will be referred to, respectively, as MF and RW. In references to the former, I shall use the numbering in the right hand margins of MF, which goes back to the original edition of 1857 and is still the most convenient.

[2]Helmut de Boor, Die höfische Literatur, 8th ed. (Munich, 1969), 291 (hereafter referred to as HL).

[3]HL, 289-90.

[4]This tendency to relegate poems by Reinmar which depict the erotic longing of woman for man to a supposed youthful period in Reinmar's career originates with Erich Schmidt, Reinmar von Hagenau and Heinrich von Rugge (Strassburg, 1974), 32; its appeal for de Boor is surely attributable mainly to Carl von Kraus, Die Lieder Reinmars des Alten, 3 parts (Munich, 1919), 1:42-43.

[5]See Schmidt, 5, where he expressly espouses the procedure of establishing the poet's image first, and judging the authenticity of poems in the light of this preconceived image. The fact that the poems transmitted under Reinmar's name are our main source of information about him gives Schmidt no pause in proclaiming this procedure.

[6]Again, the first important source for this idea is Schmidt, 1-4.

[7]For a discussion of this issue, including my criticism of Günther Schweikle's travelling minstrel idea, see RW, 54-194.

[8]HL, 290.

[9]Cf. William E. Jackson, "The Woman's Song in Medieval German Poetry," in John F. Plummer, ed., Vox Feminae: Studies in Medieval Woman's Song (Kalamazoo, 1981), 77.

[10]See Jackson, "The Woman's Song," 57-67 and 75-77, which provides content summaries and references to English translations.

[11]See Adolar Angermann, Der Wechsel in der mittelhochdeutschen Lyrik, Diss. Marburg (Bielefeld, 1910), 7-8 and 74; Olive Sayce, The Medieval German Lyric 1150-1300 (Oxford, 1982), 85-88.

[12]See Max Wehrli, "'Diu künegin von Engellant': Zu Minnesangs Frühling 3, 7-16," Germanic Review 31 (1956):5.

[13]Text and English translation of this poem can be found in Meg Bogin, The Women Troubadours (New York, 1976), 88-89.

[14]James M. Nichols, "Arabic Women Poets in al-Andalus," The Maghreb Review 4 (1979):114.

[15]Bogin, 67-68.

[16]HL, 190.

[17]Bogin, 84-87.

[18]Cf. HL 289-90; Gerhard A. Vogt, "Die Technik der Reimpaarverklammerung in 'Minnesangs Frühling,'" in 'Getempert und gemischet' für Wolfgang Mohr zum 65. Geburtstag, ed. Franz Hundsnurscher and Ulrich Müller (Göppingen, 1972), 76.

[19]Bogin, 88-89.

[20]Robert S. Sturgess, "The Canterbury Tales' Women Narrators," Modern Language Studies 13 (1983):45; cf. Lee Patterson, "'For the Wyves love of Bath," Speculum 58 (1983):691-93.

[21]Namely, MF 152,19; 177,22-24; 196,7-10; 203,12.

[22]Jeffrey Ashcroft, "'Venus Clerke': Reinmar in the 'Carmina Burana,'" Modern Language Review 77 (1982):619.

[23]Anne Howland Schotter, "Woman's Song in Medieval Latin," Vox Feminae, ed. John F. Plummer (Kalamazoo, 1981), 21.

[24]Schotter, 19 and 30; cf. David Herlihy, Women in Medieval Society (Houston, 1971), 9; cf. also Sara Lehrman, "The Education of Women in the Middle Ages," in

The Roles and Images of Women in the Middle Ages, ed.
Douglas Radcliff-Umstead (Pittsburgh, 1975), 134-35.

[25] Schotter, 19.

[26] See Herbert Grundmann, "Die Frauen und die Literatur
im Mittelalter," Archiv fur Kulturgeschichte 26 (1936):
133 and 149; Peter Ketsch, Frauen im Mittelalter, ed.
Annette Kuhn, 2 vols. (Dusseldorf, 1983-84), 2:215.

[27] Ashcroft, 619. The standard version of the poem can
be found in Alfons Hilka and Otto Schumann, eds.,
Carmina Burana, 2 vols. (Heidelberg, 1930-70), vol. 1,
pt. 2, p. 243.

[28] Hilka-Schumann, 251. For a translation and interpretation of the poem, see RW, 31 and 300-305.

[29] Schotter, 21-22.

[30] Ashcroft, 619.

[31] For a translation and more extensive interpretation,
see RW, 15 and 251-61.

[32] Ibn Hazm, The Ring of the Dove, trans. A. J. Anberry
(London: Luzac, 1953), 73.

[33] Sayce, 146. Texts with French translations of both
poems can be found in Istvan Frank, Trouveres et Minnesanger (Saarbrucken, 1952), 120-25. I have not yet been
able to locate an English translation of either poem.
An English translation of Gace Brule by Samuel N. Rosen-
berg and Samuel Danon has been announced by the Garland
Press.

[34] Gottfried von Strassburg, Tristan, trans. A. T.
Hatto (Baltimore, 1960), 176-79.

[35] See A.W.A. Leeper, A History of Medieval Austria
(Oxford, 1941), 229-30.

[36] RW, 10-11 and 241-48; cf. Jeffrey Ashcroft, "Der
Minnesanger und die Freude des Hofes," in Poesie und
Gebrauchsliteratur, ed. Volker Honeman et al. (Tubingen,
1979), 220 and 228.

[37] Rudolf Flotzinger and Gernot Gruber, Musikgeschichte
Osterreichs, 2 vols. (Graz, 1977), 1:79.

[38]Gerhard Schmidt, "Die bildende Kunst der babenber-
gischen Epoche," in Das babenbergische Österreich, ed.
Erich Zöllner (Vienna, 1978), 120.

[39]Pierre Bec, La Lyrique Française au Moyen Age, 2
vols. (Paris, 1977-78), 2:7-11, 165-66, and 172-75.

[40]Patricia Cummins, "The Chanson de Toile," Romance
Notes 21 (1980):117.

[41]Bec. 1:58.

[42]See Joan M. Ferrante, "The French Courtly Poet:
Marie de France," in Medieval Women Writers, ed.
Katharina M. Wilson (Athens: University of Georgia
Press, 1984), 66.

[43]Bec, 2:7-8.

[44]Bec, 2:9.

[45]Thilo Vogelsang, Die Frau als Herrscherin im hohen
Mittelalter (Gottingen, 1954), 30.

[46]Vogelsang, 61.

[47]RW, 20-21 and 274-80.

[48]Cf. Ibn Hazm, 102-17.

[49]Cf. Lilli Seibold, Studien über die Huote (Berlin,
1932), 24; Hugo Steger, Askese und 'amour courtois'
(Cuernevaca, 1971), 123; Winfried Hofmann, Die Minne-
feinde in der deutschen Liebesdichtung (Coburg, 1974),
28, 34, and 48; Glynnis M. Cropp, Le Vocabulaire
courtois des troubadours (Geneva, 1975), 235-36.

[50]RW, 22-23 and 280-83.

[51]Ibn Hazm, 42-43 and 197-201 (the latter entitled:
"Of Wasting Away").

[52]Wolfram von Eschenbach, Parzival, trans. Helen M.
Mustard and Charles E. Passage (New York, 1961), 77.

[53]Mustard and Passage, p. 64 and footnote 32; cf. HL,
91.

[54]Jane Tibbetts Schulenburg, "The Heroics of Virginity: Brides of Christ and Sacrificial Mutilation,"
in Mary Beth Rose, ed., Women in the Middle Ages and the
Renaissance (Syracuse, 1986), 53.

[55] RW, 26-29 and 286-300.

[56] Bogin, 8-13 and 66-70.

[57] Bec, 2:12.

[58] See Jackson, "The Woman's Song," 69-74, 77-81, and 102-17.

CHRISTINE DE PISAN'S LE DIT DE POISSY: AN EXPLORATION OF AN ALTERNATE LIFE-STYLE FOR ARISTOCRATIC WOMEN IN FIFTEENTH-CENTURY FRANCE

by Kathleen E. Kells

The literary reputation of Christine de Pisan in fifteenth-century France is well established despite deprecating critics such as Gustave Lanson who wondered if she were not "un des plus authentiques bas-bleus qu'il y ait dans notre littérature, la première de cette insupportable lignée de femmes-auteurs, à qui nul ouvrage sur aucun sujet ne coûte, et qui, pendant toute la vie que Dieu leur prête, n'ont affaire que de multi-plier les preuves de leur infatigable facilité, égale à leur universelle médiocrité."[1] In so far at least as these particular comments are concerned, G. Lanson strikes one as a kind of nineteenth-century reincarna-tion of that well-known medieval misogynist cleric, Jean de Meung, whose thirteenth-century continuation of Guillaume de Lorris' Le Roman de la rose had served to crystallize stereotyped, anti-feminist attitudes in the minds of the majority of Christine's male contem-poraries. However, before situating Christine's le Dit de Poissy within the current of fifteenth-century misogyny against which Christine was reacting, it must be remembered that the de Meung brand of mistrust and aversion to women was nothing more than the natural if unfortunate byproduct of a virulent strain of European anti-feminism which had first appeared in the Roman

Empire at least 500 years before the birth of Christ and was subsequently fortified by Judeo-Christian teachings and beliefs.[2]

In Roman society, the fear and oppression of women seem to have been motivated by political considerations more than by religious ones.[3] Lucretius in *De rerum natura* (c. 57 B.C.) condemned the sexual passion or "luxuria" which women aroused in men as the potential cause of the overthrow of the state due to the unbridled lusting of men after women which supposedly suppressed the male's ability to reason and could lead to the moral degeneration of society. As an antidote to this pre-dominantly male disease of "luxuria," both Lucretius and later Ovid (c. 3 A.D.) drew up a list of female faults intended to debunk any idealized notions a man might entertain with respect to a particular woman. In moments then of potential weakness, a man of the Roman Empire needed only to reach for Ovid, Lucretius (and later Juvenal [c. 116 A.D.]) to counteract lethal feminine charms.

In the Judeo-Christian tradition, blatantly anti-feminist passages contained in both biblical sources and the writings of the church fathers have consistently been used in order to justify the continued subordina-tion of women to men, woman having been cast in the role of the devil's instrument ever since Eve's reputed collaboration with Satan in bringing about the fall of Adam (and the entire human race) from God's grace in chapter three of Genesis. Accordingly, from the Christian era on, theological authority could be summoned up to reinforce political reasons for the oppression of women.

By the time Christine began to write at the beginning of the fifteenth century, Jean de Meung had already
synthesized in Le Roman de la rose the Latin writers'
politically provoked prejudice against women as the
source of "luxuria" with the theological bias of the
Christian church fathers against women whom they had
conveniently chosen as scapegoats and instigators of
original sin. In particular, de Meung appears to have
shared with Christian patriarchs such as Saint Jerome an
unfavorable attitude towards marriage over which virginity was favored, since it was felt that the love
shared between married people turned them away from
loving God. In particular, sexual intercourse, although
in principle sanctioned by the sacrament of matrimony
for reproductive purposes alone, was deemed nonetheless
destructive of man's relationship with God since it
fostered lusting after women who, aside from being the
presumed cause of man's exile from Eden, were also
considered to be insatiable in their desire for sex.
Clearly then, a married man was constantly diverted from
his true duty to love and serve God while he attempted
to satisfy his wife's concupiscence.

It was accordingly de Meung's apparent condemnation
of marriage in Le Roman de la rose which led to Christine's ongoing defense of women and matrimony in what
became known as the debate on Le Roman de la rose. This
famous quarrel, sometimes patronizingly named "la
querelle des femmes,"[4] began with Christine's Epistre
au dieu d'amour of 1399. By April of 1400, when she
composed Le Dit de Poissy, Christine had also been
involved in the establishment of two "courts of love"
founded for the purpose of upholding the honor of ladies
in the face of the new wave of anti-feminism generated
by the controversy concerning Le Roman de la rose.

Subsequently, in her *Cité des dames* of 1405, Christine continued to rehabilitate the reputation of many women who had been traditionally maligned by male authors throughout history. Nonetheless, it is curious that, despite Christine's manifest concern for the situation of women at the time of writing *Le Dit de Poissy*, critics have consistently failed to notice the obvious connection between her defense of women at the time of the quarrel over *Le Roman de la rose* and her concern for women in *Le Dit de Poissy*.

When critics do discuss *Le Dit de Poissy*, they neglect to treat it as a unified, thematic entity. Edith Yenal, for example, in her bibliography of 1982 on Christine de Pisan describes the work as an "evocative poem comprising two unrelated parts."[5] Yenal is not however alone in missing the connection between the first descriptive segment of the poem and its second dramatic portion or lovers' debate, since in so doing she appears to be following the critical trail already blazed by Maurice Roy, the first editor of Christine's *Oeuvres poétiques* published in 1891, and by Marie-Josephe Pinet, author of a seminal critical biography. Both Roy and Pinet in fact overlook any possible relationship between the two parts of the poem and treat the descriptions of the journey from Paris to Poissy, the convent of Saint Louis de Poissy and the life-style of the nuns who resided there quite independently from the lovers' debate of the second segment. A more recent commentary on *Le Dit de Poissy* deals only with the first half of the poem which is considered to be an interesting medieval documentary on nuns.[6]

What of course unifies the two parts of the poem is Christine's obvious concern for the place of women in fifteenth-century French society. Christine's purpose,

then, in writing Le Dit de Poissy in the midst of her
involvement in the dispute over Le Roman de la rose
could well have been to present two radically contrasting life-styles open to aristocratic women of her
time. Viewed in this way, Le Dit de Poissy becomes a
meaningful diptych containing two panels in which
religious and courtly societies are portrayed. On the
left, the female is depicted as strong, energetic and
independent as she goes about her daily tasks against
the serenely secure and matriarchal backdrop of Poissy.
On the right, we see her in the turbulent context of the
patriarchal court in which her reputation and well-being
are constantly threatened by domestic misfortunes,
waning favoritism, court intrigues, political upheavals,
wasteful wars and crusades.

My purpose in discussing Le Dit de Poissy will be
first of all to show how Christine reveals her attraction to the conventual life of the Poissy nuns in the
first segment of the poem. Secondly, I propose to
demonstrate how Christine wins the reader's support for
the court lady in the lovers' debate of the second part,
thereby leading the reader to conclude that this lady is
indeed more unfortunate in love than her male opponent.
However, one must remember that a judgment in favor of
the lady in the debate really indicates that she was the
loser in courtly society, the implication being that the
way of life of the cloistered ladies pictured in the
first panel of the diptych is preferable to that of the
lady in the second.

The first part of the poem, which includes the
description of the journey to Poissy, does more than
provide an occasion for the exchange of stories among
travellers along the lines of Chaucer's Canterbury
Tales[7] or Boccaccio's The Decameron. Christine

herself states at the beginning of the poem that she is
going expressly to visit her daughter (lines 39-52),
thus showing that she had a very personal interest in
the convent. Moreover, whereas she uses only slightly
under 200 lines to render the pastoral springtime
setting in which the trip to Poissy takes place, she
devotes almost 500 lines to relating her impressions of
the convent. In a "dit amoureux" such as Le Dit de
Poissy, the unique subject of which would normally be
courtly love, it is therefore structurally significant
that Christine apportions one quarter of the poem to
describing the life of nuns with whom, as she tells us,
she felt the need to show constraint in discussing
mundane affairs, especially love and courtly amuse-
ments: ". . . de choses mondaines / Pou devisames, /
N'y parlames d'amour ne ne dancames" (663-65).8

Although Pinet suggests that the Poissy sequence was
composed either to commend royal patrons who had established the abbey or to counter misogynist criticism of
women's religious orders,9 Christine's treatment of
Poissy indicates other underlying motivations: her need
to reassure herself of her daughter's comfort and safety
and her wish to celebrate the energy and determination
of women living and working together and caring for
themselves and each other independently of men. Christine reveals her affection for her daughter when she
arrives at Poissy (233-38) and toward the end of her
visit when they must part: ". . . Lors failli mon
plaisir / Si que des yeulx convint larmes yssir / Quant
je laissay celle ou est mon desir, / Qui m'est pro-
chaine" (702-704).10 Accordingly, when Christine is
leaving her daughter, the emotion she is experiencing is
in fact one of separation and loss more than concern for
her daughter's well being. Indeed, most of Christine's

observations concerning the cloister show that she had
become convinced that Poissy was a veritable utopia.
First of all, she directs her attention mainly to those
aspects of the physical environment which conspire to
produce the material and spiritual euphoria of its
inhabitants. Starting from the cloister itself, moving
on to the refectory, the chapter room, the dormitory and
finally the Gothic church, Christine finds nothing to
reprove in the architectural layout of the abbey;
instead, she marvels at the overall beauty of the
buildings. Similarly, she notes that the nuns have an
abundance of every vital supply they require: an
endless source of fresh, clean water flowing to all the
important areas of the convent to support such necessary
activities as wine-making and cooking; beautiful natural
surroundings rich in all types of fruit trees and
abounding in fish and game. In brief, as Christine
states, ". . . ce semble estre un trés doulz paradis"
(557).11 Moreover, as Christine delights in pointing
out, it is the sisters themselves who provide for their
own needs in almost complete isolation from men and the
secular world outside: "Si nous plut moult a veoir la
maniere / . . . qui leans yere, / Toutes dames, car en
nulle maniere / N'i entreroit / Pour les servir nul
homme, on n'i lairoit" (297-301).12

Thus it is that Christine's praise of Poissy cannot
simply be construed as flattery directed toward its
royal patrons. Nor should we conclude that the Poissy
sequence can be explained as a defense of devotional
life, since Christine's references to the religious
practices of the Poissy nuns are too scant to support
such an apology.13 Furthermore, Christine's unreserved admiration of the comfort enjoyed by the sisters
belies any effort to reply to those who might have

wished to reproach the nuns with failing to live by the
monastic rules of poverty. What the Poissy sequence
does display is Christine's esteem for women capable of
thriving on their own, apart from men, as well as her
inherent attraction to this serene and harmonious way of
life.

Contrasting with this first religious panel of the
diptych, Christine's second panel portrays a graphic
scene from court life as she and her retinue return from
Poissy to Paris. Central to the journey is a debate
between a young court dandy who has apparently been
rejected for no reason by the woman of his desire, and a
court lady whose lover has been incarcerated for almost
five years in a Turkish prison following the Nicopolis
crusade. The squire of course contends that he has
suffered more because of love than his female opponent,
but she legitimately objects, demanding that their case
be submitted for judgment to a third party. Christine
thereupon agrees to send the debate, in the form of Le
Dit de Poissy, by messenger to an external, anonymous
arbiter. Christine's choice of a judge who is conveniently away in a distant land serves to defer the
formal resolution of the debate and, in the meantime,
puts the onus on individual readers to decide for
themselves. By so involving readers in the debate and
by then disposing its probable outcome in favor of the
lady, Christine seeks to solicit our support for her
cause.

In fact, Christine's portrayal of the lady is much
more sympathetic than her treatment of the squire. To
convince readers of the lady's sincerity in her devotion
to her knight, Christine completely breaks with tradition and takes full advantage of dialogue to allow the
distinctly female sensitivity and psychological state of

the woman to break through the trite and highly formu-
laic male-generated discourse of contemporary lovers'
debates. In so doing, Christine provides us with a
unique portrait of a male lover from a thoroughly
feminine perspective. Never before, as Jeanine Moulin
has suggested,[14] had a woman participant in a lovers'
debate been permitted to give such a blatantly physical
appreciation of her lover. The novelty of this description becomes all the more apparent by the otherwise
conventional and impersonal blazon which the squire
offers of his lady. A comparison of the debate in Le
Dit de Poissy with Machaut's Le Jugement du roy de
Behaigne, for example, further shows the extent to which
Christine had broken with tradition. Whereas Christine's portrait of the female (as recounted by the
squire in the debate) is longer and more elaborate than
Machaut's, the two descriptions are nonetheless comparable in so far as Christine repeats Machaut's already
stock descriptions of, for example, the lady's nose
which is typically neither too big nor too small[15] and
her hands which are characteristically white with long
fingers.[16] However, when Christine depicts the lady's
knight from the female's point of view, she allots some
seventy-four lines to describing twenty-eight salient
male features in lively, sensuous language. In
contrast, Machaut grudgingly permits the lady in his
debate one line to outline briefly the physical traits
of her lover in hackneyed, conventional terms: "Gent
corps faites, cointe, opert et joli" (141).[17] One
need only compare this single line with Christine's
highly personalized and voluptuous description of the
male lover's eyes to understand why her portrayal of the
male would be more convincing to a reader than
Machaut's:

Car oncques homs ne porta plus doulz oeil
Brunet, riant, persant, de doulz accueil,
Qui ont occis mon cuer, mais son entreoil
   Fu large et plain,
Et son regart tant fu de doulcour plain
qu'il m'a donné le mal dont je me plain,
   Je vous dy bien,
Contenance n'avoie ne maintien,
Car a mon cuer sembloit qu'il deist: "ca vien"
(1105-14).18

Although Christine chooses to represent the lady's
falling in love in terms reminiscent of the traditionally masculine erotic language originally borrowed
from the hunt in, for example, Le Roman de la rose,19
it is the lady, not the man, who is shot by love's arrow
in the form of the man's piercing eyes. Thus, even when
Christine does borrow from the customary discourse of
male-identified "fin amor," she appropriates this
language in order to assert the female's right to
sensuality and physical pleasure: ". . . car maintes
fois recue / Par amour fine! / G'y ay esté, car sa belle
poittrine / Large, longue, bien faitte en tout termine /
Passe toutes de beaulté, . . ." (1147-51).20 Thus, we
see that whereas Christine shrewdly assigns conventional, courtly discourse to the squire to make his
situation appear as humdrum as the language he uses to
describe it, she allows the outspoken lady to subvert
this same, customary linguistic code, thereby dis-
tinguishing the authentic love she feels for her knight
from the puppy love of the squire.

    Christine similarly shocks readers used to the
traditionally passive, male-generated and supposedly
feminine idiom of the day by allowing her lady to speak

of the completely unreserved suffering and anger she experiences over the loss of her lover. The lady clearly, outspokenly and courageously condemns a specific event, the Nicopolis crusade, as well as those responsible for it and for the resulting imprisonment of her knight:

> Lasse! doulente! or fault dire l'amer
> Qui mon dolent triste cuer faist pasmer
> Et qui me fait tant de larmes semer
>   Pleine de rage!
> Ce fu le mal et doloreux voiage
> De Honguerie, ou trop ot grant dommage,
> Qui me tolli le bel et bon et sage
>   Que tant amoye.
> . . . .
> Ha! voyage mauvais de Honguerie,
> La ou peri tant de chevalrie!
> Et Turquie, puisses estre perie
>   Long et travers!
> Qui fis aler Monseigneur de Nevers
> En ton païs desloyal et divers,
> A qui Fortune ala trop a revers
>   A celle fois,
> Ou moururent tant de vaillans François
> Et d'autre gent bons, gentilz et courtois,
> Dont le dommage est et fu de grief pois
>   Et trop grevable
> (1207-80).21

The fact that Christine gives no such particulars to distinguish the squire's misfortune consequently makes it pale in contrast with the lady's; his is one more tedious example of courtly love gone amiss.

What of course underlies Christine's ability to use
language so as to sway the probable outcome of the
debate in favor of the lady is Christine's own female
sensitivity.[22] The unmistakable empathy which Christine has for the lady finds its source in Christine's
own personal grief and anger at the death of her husband
when she was only twenty-five.[23] Thus, when the lady
in Le Dit de Poissy cries out that she is "full of
rage," she is echoing the same sentiment of frustrated
deprivation expressed by Christine herself in an earlier
ballad: "Deuil angoisseux, rage démesurée."[24]
Similarly, Christine's wish to die in order to escape
the loneliness and despair caused by her husband's death
expressed in the "envoi" concluding the same ballad[25]
is repeated by the lady in Le Dit de Poissy when she
asserts that she would willingly sacrifice herself to
obtain her knight's release from prison rather than
endure without him: "Et se la mort me prenoit au
voyage, . . . / Ainsi seroit mon desir assovis . . .
Qu'il n'en craindroit peine, je vous plevis, / Pour
prendre mort" (1319-32).[26] Although the squire
complains that he almost committed suicide because of
his lady's harsh treatment of him (1844-52), one feels
that he is merely uttering another stock expression from
the repertory of "fin amor." One need only compare the
lady's determination to die, if necessary, while engaged
in the meaningful activity of procuring her lover's
freedom, with the totally unproductive, selfish and
attention-getting death wish of her male opponent to
realize the depth of the lady's sincerity.

So it is that the semiotic code of "fin amor" (which
the squire had no doubt acquired from André le Chape-
lain's The Art of Courtly Love and Le Roman de la rose)
is revealed by Christine for what it had become: a

meaningless collection of gallant verbiage in which the
signifier no longer represented the signified but rather
obscured the true desire and intent of the user. Seen
from this point of view, the squire's unhappy love
affair--aptly termed by his female opponent as "roses
eslites" (1367)27--can be directly attributed to the
failure of courtly discourse to communicate. It is
after all because the squire mistakes the lady's initial
friendliness and warmth for love and then refuses to
interpret her subsequent reactive coldness and indiffer-
ence as a signal to him that he was deceiving himself,
that she is finally forced to tell him in plain language
to leave her alone (1828-37). Even then, however, he
does not give up his pursuit of her, thinking no doubt
that she is merely being coy and thereby exposing himself to the sweet torment of unrequited love from which
he hopes death will release him.

The malfunctioning of the semiotic code is however
merely symptomatic of the more serious moral bankruptcy
of the society which had produced and progressively
banalized that code into sterility. At the source of
the ill from which the squire suffers is a fundamental
confusion in fifteenth-century France between the per-
petual need of the male to assert his dominance through
sexual conquest of the female and his desire to wage war
supposedly to prove his worthiness as a suitor able to
defend her. This confounding of "fin amor" and war,
which Daniel Poirion has called "le culte de la prou-
esse,"28 had been responsible for the resurgence of
chivalry at the beginning of Charles VI's reign and had,
as Poirion also suggests, been largely to blame for the
Nicopolis disaster of 1396. Thus, we see that both the
lady and the squire are participants in and victims of
the same frenzied and wasteful chivalry. Surely,

however, the lady is the more cheated since the squire
after all consented to play the courtly game. His loss
is then simply that--a loss, and he should learn to be a
better loser! The lady, on the other hand, has been
powerless to date having had no influence on the course
of events which have separated her from her lover. Moreover, one feels that despite her brave words she will
probably fail in her attempt to rescue her knight. For
her, chivalry is no game; its repercussions are far-
reaching, irreversible and tragic. There can be no
doubt who the "winner" of the debate should be.

To conclude, then, Le Dit de Poissy is a unified
thematic entity dealing with the situation of aristocratic women in fifteenth-century France, each of its
two segments presenting contrasting views of women. The
first panel of the diptych depicts the tranquil, harmonious and productive life of women living together and
supporting themselves in isolation from the male-
dominated society. In the second panel, we are led to
conclude that the woman portrayed is a victim of that
same courtly society from which the Poissy nuns of the
first part are happily removed. Christine's implicit
propensity toward the Poissy way-of-life is confirmed,
in the first place, by the fact that she had placed her
own daughter in Poissy and, secondly, by Christine's own
subsequent retreat to Poissy in 1418 to escape the
ravages of the civil war then devastating France.
Francoise du Castel believes that it was during Christine's last few years at Poissy that she worked on a
later manuscript of La Cité des dames.[29] There is no
doubt that during Christine's visit to Poissy in April
of 1400 the seeds were planted which would later germi-
nate and produce that extremely important feminist work.

NOTES

[1]Gustave Lanson, Histoire de la littérature française (Paris: Hachette, 1952), pp. 166-67.

[2]See Mary Daly, The Church and the Second Sex (New York: Harper and Row, 1968).

[3]See Robert P. Miller, Chaucer: Sources and Backgrounds (New York: Oxford University Press, 1977), in particular pp. 399-473, "The Antifeminist Tradition."

[4]For more detail on the quarrel over Le Roman de la rose, see Eric Hicks, Le Débat sur "Le Roman de la rose" (Paris: Champion, 1977).

[5]Edith Yenal, Christine de Pisan: A Bibliography of Writings by Her and about Her (New York and London: Metuchen, 1982), p. 32.

[6]Shulamith Shahar, The Fourth Estate: A History of Women in the Middle Ages (London and New York: Methuen, 1983), pp. 47-48.

[7]See Ronald Sutherland, "The Romaunt of the Rose" and "Le Roman de la rose" (Berkeley and Los Angeles: University of California Press, 1968), for a detailed analysis of the extent to which Chaucer may have translated parts of Le Roman de la rose into English as The Romaunt of the Rose. In any case, Chaucer's works like those of Christine de Pisan and other French writers of the fourteenth and fifteenth centuries continue to intertext Le Roman de la rose which had been copied and recopied due to its immense popularity.

[8]Christine de Pisan, Le Dit de Poissy in Oeuvres poétiques, ed. Maurice Roy (1891, rept. New York: Johnson, 1965), II, pp. 159-222, lines 663-65: ". . . of worldly matters / Little conversation had we, / Nor did we speak of love nor did we dance" (my translation). All subsequent references to Le Dit de Poissy are based on the above edition. Likewise all quotations from Guillaume de Machaut's Le Jugement du roy de Behaigne conform to the text of Oeuvres poétiques de Guillaume de Machaut (Paris: Librairie Firmin-Didot, 1908), I, pp. 57-135. References to the poetry of either of these texts are given in parentheses immediately following the original lines quoted in French. My translation into English of these lines is given in an accompanying note.

[9] Maris-Josephe Pinet, *Christine de Pisan* (Paris: Champion, 1927; rept. Genève: Slatkine, 1974), p. 56.

[10] "Then it was that my pleasure gave way / So much so that from my eyes tears started to come / When I had to leave her for whom I care so much, / Who is so close to me."

[11] ". . . it seems to be a very pleasant paradise."

[12] "And it pleased us very much to see the way of life / . . . that rules there, / (over) All the ladies, since for no reason whatsoever / Would any man enter therein / To serve them; it would not be permitted."

[13] See in particular p. 179, lines 666-72 where Christine abruptly changes the subject.

[14] Jeanine Moulin, *Christine de Pisan* (Paris: Seghers, 1962), p. 21. Moulin says: "un portrait aussi cocasse qu'inattendu, car, en règle générale, le lyrisme féminin n'exalte guère le corps de l'homme."

[15] *Le Dit de Poissy*, line 1501; *Le Jugement du roy de Behaigne*, line 339.

[16] *Le Dit de Poissy*, line 1558; *Le Jugement du roy de Behaigne*, line 367.

[17] "He had a noble body, full of grace, healthy and attractive."

[18] "For no man ever sported a more tender glance. / Brown eyes had he, laughing, penetrating with sweet invitation / So that they pierced my heart. And his forehead / Was smooth and flawless / And his gaze so full of sweetness / That he gave me the affliction from which I suffer,/ And in truth I tell you, / I could neither contain myself or help myself / For to my heart he seemed to say: 'Come here.'"

[19] Guillaume de Lorris and Jean de Meung, *The Romance of the Rose*, Trans. Harry W. Robbins (New York: E. P. Dutton & Co., Inc., 1962). See in particular: "The God of Love pursues the Dreamer," pp. 26-29.

[20] "For countless times greeted / By tender love / Was I, and his handsome chest / Broad, long, well-made to sum it all up / Surpassed all notion of beauty."

[21]"Alas! How I suffer! And I must tell of the bitterness / Which causes my poor heart to become faint / And
which makes me shed so many tears / Full of rage! / It
was the ill-fated and tragic expedition / To Hungary,
where too many suffered great losses, / Which took away
from me the handsome, kind, good man / Whom I love so
much. / . . . Oh! evil journey into Hungary, / There
where so many chivalrous men perished! / And as for you,
Turkey, may you be devastated / From one end to the
other! / You who caused the departure of our duke of
Nevers / Into your treacherous, inconstant land, /
Against whom Fortune turned too much adversity / On this
occasion, / And where death met so many valiant French-
men / And other courageous soldiers of noble and gracious birth, / Whose loss was and remains of serious
consequence / The cause of endless grief."

[22]Daniel Poirion, Le Poète et le prince (Paris:
Presses Universitaires de France, 1965), p. 551.
Poirion states: "une résonance pathétique . . . la
femme étant plus sensible, par sa condition même, à la
souffrance causée par le départ de l'aimé."

[23]Suzanne Solente, "Christine de Pisan," in Histoire
littéraire de la France (Paris: Imprimerie Nationale,
1973), XL, p. 340.

[24]Jeanine Moulin, p. 43, "Anguish and mourning, rage
without limits" (my translation).

[25]Jeanine Moulin, p. 44.

[26]"And if death should await me on the trip . . . / So
will my desire be calmed . . . And it would not frighten
me in the least, I swear to you, / To have to die."

[27]"elitist (implying rare and delicate) roses."

[28]Daniel Poirion, p. 33.

[29]Françoise du Castel, Damoiselle Christine de Pizan:
Veuve de M. Etienne de Castel (Paris: Editions A. et J.
Picard, 1972), pp. 85-86.

BETWEEN THE PIT AND THE PEDESTAL:
IMAGES OF EVE AND MARY IN MEDIEVAL CORNISH DRAMA

by Evelyn S. Newlyn

Two of the most pervasive and influential images for
women in western culture have been the bipolar figures
of Eve and Mary.[1] Female literary characterization,
inevitably a product of its cultural matrix, has therefore been very much shaped by this traditional Christian
dichotomy[2] so that, as Eileen Power has noted, women
in medieval literature are presented most often as evil
and lascivious residents of the pit or as pure and
virtuous paragons atop the pedestal (401). Of that
literature, medieval drama in particular may provide
especially useful testimony to the pervasiveness of
these two primary models in the culture (Auerbach
1598-59), and the medieval Cornish drama is no exception.

The extant Cornish drama from the Middle Ages
consists of four works: The Ordinalia is Cornwall's
three-day version of the cycle drama; Gwryans an Bys or
The Creacion of the World is the remaining initial portion of a larger cycle play with similarities to The
Ordinalia's first part; Beunans Meriasek is a Cornish
saint's play; and "The Charter Fragment" is a small bit
of dramatic dialogue from a lost source. Because these
plays were written in Middle Cornish and because good
editions and translations have only recently begun to be
available, they have not as yet received the critical

attention accorded other medieval drama. Yet, these
plays that developed in an out-of-the-way corner of
Britain can tell us much about the transmission and the
pervasiveness of medieval ideas, literary practices, and
dramatic conventions. Moreover, because they rely so
thoroughly on the traditional figures of Eve and Mary,
these plays can testify particularly to the dramatic
possibilities and limitations of the popular character
types for women.

While amply demonstrating the strength of the
Eve-Mary models in medieval culture, the Cornish drama
also betrays the disparate generic potential of the two
figures, since they offer significantly unequal possibilities for dramatic development. Not only must the
daughters of Mary be sacrificial, nurturing, self-
effacing, and asexual, but they must be unwavering and
therefore ultimately one-dimensional and static in their
goodness. If a female character is a type of Mary,
there is little room in her for personal doubt, weakness, or mixed behavior, and in consequence few possibilities for dramatic conflict or tension. No matter
how honored the figure of Mary is intended to be in the
culture, the rigid limitations on her characterization
ordinarily make her a relatively lifeless figure for the
drama; even her excesses, being all on the side of
unquestioned goodness, yield few dramatic rewards for
the playwright.

In contrast to Mary, the daughters of Eve are assertive, self-interested, independent, and sexual. Eve is,
in essence, the very stuff of drama: a character with
infinite capacity for complexity; with inherent audience
appeal, since every human alive experiences temptation;
and with innate conflicting impulses that ideally suit
her to dramatic situations. Hence, even though she must

be viewed, in the last analysis, as evil, medieval
audiences and writers alike seem willing to suspend
judgment at least until the play's conclusion, for the
interest and pleasure she inevitably creates. In fact,
the very nature of drama favors the Eve type, since the
genre, as the etymology of the word indicates, requires
action, or at least tension.

Consequently, Mary's one-dimensional and typically
passive goodness renders her inherently unsuited to the
drama, which may explain her vanishing from the stage in
the Renaissance. The Mary-model continues in medieval
and later poetry, especially in lyric, perhaps because
she can there represent the ideal but without any need
for action. In lyric she can simply "be," whereas the
drama requires her to "do." Not surprisingly, then, the
Cornish dramatists conform to cultural expectations by
including types of Mary as desirable models, but they
lavish their attention and their imaginations on
exploring and developing the far more interesting
daughters of Eve.

Nonetheless, even though Mary may lack dramatic possibilities, she still functions as a standard for real
women's lives. For this reason it is important to
remember that Eve and Mary are cultural and not simply
literary creations, and that they serve in their
polarity important cultural ends.

The antithesis that developed in western culture
between these two figures of Eve and Mary seems to have
resulted in large part from a fear of woman uncontrolled
and a fear especially of uncontrolled female sexuality.
In the creation story in Genesis, Eve disrupts the para-
disiacal order by her disobedience in taking the fruit,
and she overturns the divinely established hierarchy by
influencing Adam to sin as well. For her disobedience,

God punishes Eve by placing her under her husband's
control, and for listening to the snake's encouragement,
God sets Eve as woman in permanent enmity with the snake
(Lerner 197). The snake, of course, is a recognized
sexual symbol, and in Genesis, because of its
association with the ancient goddesses, it also perhaps
represents the free exercise of female sexuality.3 As
a result of Eve's punishment, then, her sexuality in
future time is to be governed by her husband; her
expression of that sexuality will result in the pain of
childbirth; and she, and all women to come, are forever
tainted by her deed and thus deserving of her
punishments.

Firmly rooted in the culture as the projection and
embodiment of male sexual desire and fantasies of power,
Eve thus offers a warning to women of what they may all
too easily become. The only available alternative,
represented by Mary, is at once impossible for women to
achieve and yet the standard against which they are
inevitably judged. While it is true that Mary has some
virtues and attributes traditionally associated with
women, Gold reminds us that "she has them to a much
greater degree than other women, and in a combination
(motherhood and virginity) impossible for anyone else"
(70). Moreover, Mary is depicted in scripture, legend,
and patristic writings as a woman who denies her own
needs and desires absolutely so as to devote herself
solely and unselfishly to her son. Finally, she is a
woman whose privileged role required the complete
surrender of her sexuality. An impossible model to
emulate, Mary is nevertheless held up as the only way
women have to "transcend their unfortunate sexuality and
free themselves from their corporeal shackles [by] a
life of sexless perfection" (Schulenburg 31). Sexual
and therefore evil, or sexless and impossibly perfect--

these are the alternatives posed to women by the Eve-
Mary ideals.4

Working within the received tradition, the Cornish
dramatists draw heavily upon the familiar taxonomic
system which limited women's role to virgin or seduc-
tress/shrew.5 In consequence, the plays not only
demonstrate the strength of the Eve-Mary models in our
literature and culture, but they also provide an analysis of the dramatic potential of these two traditional
models.

* * * * *

The earliest of the plays in Middle Cornish, in
chronological order of the existing manuscripts, is The
Ordinalia,6 which is also Cornwall's major extant
dramatic work. While the date of composition cannot be
definitely fixed, the play was probably composed between
1300 and 1400, perhaps in Penryn by someone associated
with the Glasney Collegiate Church. Although the
Cornish play is similar in kind to the medieval English
cycle plays in presenting a narrative of scriptural and
human history, it differs from the English cycles in its
narrower focus on Christ's passion and the legend of the
oil of mercy.7 Intended, like the English cycles,
both to entertain and to edify, The Ordinalia is divided
into three parts: "Ordinale de Origine Mundi" (The
Beginning of the World); "Passio Domini Nostri Jhesu
Christi" (The Passion of Our Lord Jesus Christ); and
"Ordinale de Resurrexione Domini Nostri Jhesu Christi"
(The Resurrection of Our Lord Jesus Christ). These
three parts were apparently intended to be performed
over a three-day period, as indicated by three stage
diagrams in the manuscript.8

Most of the female characters in The Ordinalia
cluster around the two poles of the Eve-Mary dichotomy.
Prominent among the daughters of Eve is Bathsheba, whose
character as presented in Samuel's account is transmo-
grified by the Ordinalia author into that of a totally
wicked seducer with no redeeming human qualities. In
the Biblical account, Bathsheba plays an entirely passive role as sex object: David sees her, desires her,
summons her to the palace to sleep with him, and
arranges for her husband, Uriah, to be killed in battle
(II Samuel 11-12). In The Ordinalia, however, Bathsheba
is cast as a "femme fatale,"[9] a woman who is not just
alluring but actively evil. For example, when David
approaches her and requests her love, Bathsheba
exclaims, "How pleasurable it would be," if only it
could be kept secret from her husband (PPH 241:2115).
Then, when David announces that he will arrange for
Uriah to be killed in battle, Bathsheba vigorously
encourages him to do so. Perhaps most harmful to Bathsheba's character, however, and certainly very powerful
dramatically, is her farewell conversation with her
husband, wherein she reveals her truly shocking hypocrisy. Begging Uriah not to go, wildly threatening to
starve herself if he leaves, she laments to him that she
was born; however, the instant he has departed, she
reveals her true wish, that he never return.

The Ordinalia author has clearly gone far beyond the
Biblical account in portraying Bathsheba as actively
bad; he takes the opportunity to develop her as an eager
adulterer, a conspirator in her husband's murder,[10]
and a hypocrite of appalling dimensions. The author in
consequence assigns large portions of Bathsheba's evil
to her eager sexuality[11] and her lack of feeling for
her husband, qualities associated with Eve and anti-

thetical to Mary. The author's reshaping of Bathsheba from her Biblical role as simply a woman who is sexual into a woman whose sexuality is the source and emblem of her evil is in keeping with the traditional polarity for women and the tradition of misogyny which permeates Christian thought.[12]

Yet, while the author's blackening of Bathsheba's character stresses her connection to Eve, her expansion of Bathsheba's Eve-like qualities serves an important doctrinal purpose as well, since part of David's atonement for his sin with Bathsheba is to begin building the temple. The notion of _felix culpa_, the "fortunate fall," may well have been in the author's mind as he establishes the link between the evil of David's sin with Bathsheba (comparable to Adam's sin with Eve) and the resulting good of David's expiation by building the temple (comparable to the good of Christ's birth). The primordial pattern of sin and recovery is thus reenacted; Bathsheba, depicted in The Ordinalia as a clear type of Eve, serves, as did Eve, an important germinal function by personifying an evil that spurs or makes necessary an ultimate good. Bathsheba's characterization also, of course, contributes further material to the misogynistic tradition.

An elemental quality associated with Eve, the quality the Ordinalia author most stresses in Bathsheba, is sexuality. Another conventional female attribute, which becomes a favorite medieval stereotype, is shrewishness. This quality, too, may be traceable to Eve, who established a precedent for disobedient and disagreeable wives by giving the forbidden fruit to Adam, thereby violating the divine hierarchy and inappropriately exercising control over her husband. In medieval literature the stereotypical shrew was very

popular, such outstanding examples of the type as Gill
and Noah's wife in the Towneley cycle13 coming immediately to mind.

An equally powerful image of the shrew exists in The
Ordinalia, in the Smith's Wife, the woman who, when her
husband refuses to make nails for the crucifixion, makes
them herself. Although the legend of the nails is widespread, the Ordinalia uniquely develops the Wife's
stereotypical role by exaggerating her shrewishness and
adding to it a dimension of crude and unsavory sexuality. In these ways the author again seems to go far
beyond the possible sources.14 In The Northern Passion, for example, when the Smith refuses to make the
nails and the wife volunteers to do so, she does not
berate her husband, and no sexual badinage occurs
between the wife and the Torturers.15 In The Ordinalia, however, when the Smith by way of excuse claims
falsely that his hands are sore and he cannot therefore
make nails, his wife accuses him of lying, orders him to
show his hands, and shouts that he deserves to be
hanged; she is thus portrayed as disloyal, unloving,
domineering, and vicious. When the Smith is forced to
show his hands and they have, indeed, suddenly become
sore, his wife then accuses him of having worshipped the
false god, Christ, who must have performed some magic
for the Smith. In an arrestingly dramatic juxtaposi-
tioning, her cruel and hateful speeches frame and contrast the speech of the Smith as he, staring wonderingly
at his hands, prayerfully acknowledges his faith in the
god whose help has just been proven ever-ready. The
Wife, engaged in obscene badinage with the First Torturer as she works eagerly to make the crucifixion
nails, is thus sharply and dramatically contrasted to
the Smith, who has become a believer. Further testi-

fying to her shrewish nature, the Wife verbally abuses
the First Torturer as well, even as they exchange sexual
banter. Perhaps most shocking, however, is her utter
lack of compassion; she expresses great pleasure at the
roughness of the nails she is making, since they will
feel that much worse to Christ. This disturbingly
sadistic streak in the Smith's Wife surely results in
part from an authorial desire to pander to the audience,
which was not only all too ready to accept evil in women
but which also enjoyed such cruel entertainments as
bear-baiting, bull-baiting, and cockfighting.

Nonetheless, by intensifying certain qualities of
the character he inherited and by adding others, the
author strengthens the reflections of Eve in the Smith's
Wife. He stresses the Wife's Eve-like sexuality[16] and
her nasty, shrewish behavior towards both her husband
and her prospective sexual partner. Yet, these unfavorable expansions of the Wife's character help to
serve important thematic ends. In her persona and in
her behavior the Smith's Wife intensifies the horrifying
brutality of the crucifixion, thus reinforcing two
central doctrinal points: the magnitude of Christ's
sacrifice, and the great need wicked humans had for it.
And, even as she attempts to belittle and vilify Christ,
she also testifies unwittingly to his power by acknowledging his ability miraculously to afflict the Smith's
hands.

Since the Smith's Wife is so thoroughly developed as
a whore and a shrew, and since Bathsheba's character is
so intensively besmirched, one may well wonder what
treatment the Ordinalia author accords Eve herself.
Surprisingly, however, Eve is not presented as the
one-dimensional seducer or shrew one might expect.
Amplified so as to serve both dramatic and didactic

ends, Eve's characterization is both broad and dynamic,
revealing a concerted authorial effort to move beyond
the stereotype towards complexity and individuality.
Nevertheless, even as he develops Eve's character in an
atypical way, he uses her to illustrate integral tenets
in medieval Christian doctrine, especially the tenet
that only grave danger could result from disturbing the
divine hierarchy.

In the establishment of that hierarchy in the second
Biblical account of creation (Genesis 2:4-2:25), and in
such legendary versions of the creation as Cursor Mundi
(Horrall 53), after Adam names the animals, Eve is made
for him and he then names her. In The Ordinalia, which
collapses the two creation accounts in Genesis, Eve is
made and Adam then names her and the animals at the same
time, thus indicating very precisely that Eve's place in
the hierarchy is below Adam and of course below God, but
close to the birds and the animals. The play thus
stresses at the outset that Eve, like the animals, is a
creature whom Adam controls and to whom he is superior.
Further demonstrating his superior status, Adam cites
the purpose and utility for himself of each creature God
brings to be named, including the beasts, the birds, the
fish, and Eve. Adam explains that just as the horse is
for him to use and the goose for him to eat so is Eve
created as a mate and companion, for his benefit. By
emphasizing that Eve's purpose is utilitarian and her
status subordinate, the play casts in sharper relief her
later independence and disobedience.

Although Eve is depicted at the time of her creation
and her naming as docile, obedient, and reverent, the
author reveals in her encounter with the devil additional facets of her personality as well as a surprising
capacity for growth and change. When the serpent offers

a secret which would delight her and make her a goddess,
Eve, eager for knowledge, clamors to be told at once.
In a psychologically clever maneuver the serpent demurs,
for fear, he says, that Eve will denounce him. Apparently unaware of the tradition that women cannot keep
secrets, or perhaps in the prelapsarian world they
could, Eve assures the serpent that he can share the
secret with her because she is a woman and will not
betray him.

This scene particularly well typifies a conflict in
the author's mind between admiration for the character
he carefully creates and the need to conform to scriptural conventions and audience expectations. On the one
hand, Eve's statement attributes to her a sympathetic
and inquiring mind and a strong sense of identity as a
loyal and trustworthy person precisely because she is a
woman and she therefore possesses those qualities. On
one level the scene asks to be read this way, given the
author's evident interest in this character and the way
he goes on to develop her. On the other hand, the
statement can also function as comedic, and at Eve's
expense, as an indication that she is unable to recognize the faults inherent in her as a woman. To the
audience in Cornwall, who knew that she would, in fact,
ultimately betray the serpent, her statement would
probably be seen as ironic and considered an opportunity
to heap scorn upon her. At the same time, however, the
scene encouraged members of the audience to identify
themselves with the character and the play, and to
recognize their commonality as creatures who must think
well of themselves in order to live in the world, even
as their flaws, like Eve's, incline them inevitably to
error.

The author further reveals his ambivalence toward
the character of Eve when the devil then discloses a
motivation not at all in accord with Genesis; he explains, "From heaven I have come down, / Sweet Eve, to
improve thy spirits" (PPH 61:165-66). One can hardly
help wondering at the implication that Eve was not
perfectly happy in the Garden. Perhaps the author here
acknowledges the burden of completely submissive
behavior, even if one is in paradise. Or, more likely,
he may be reflecting the idea promulgated by such
writers as Hugh of St. Victor[17] that Eve is funda-
mentally tainted--here, with dissatisfaction--even
before the fall. This latter idea may be reinforced
later when both Adam and God accuse Eve of having acted
"without reason" (PPH 69: 252; and 72: 278), both
thereby implying that Eve willfully and deliberately
attempted to deceive for its own sake, out of a predis-
position to evil.

Nonetheless, in response to the devil's suggestion
that she eat the fruit, Eve first cites the need to obey
God's command; the serpent then explains, very cleverly,
that God's reasons for the prohibition are jealousy and
a fear of being equalled. Confused and unsure, Eve
considers what to do, weighing her desire for knowledge
against her entirely sensible fear of trickery by the
serpent. Certainly meant to be seen as intelligent and
thoughtful, Eve assesses the situation, wondering at
Satan's motives and the possible results of disobedience. Again very cleverly, the serpent ignores her
deliberations and her questions and, like any good "con"
man, tells lies that force an immediate decision.
Finally, he urges her to go ahead and pluck the apple at
his peril, implying that he himself could and would
assume any blame or consequence.

Succumbing to his stratagem, Eve makes an instant
decision to take the fruit but, interestingly, commands
the serpent to bend down the branch so that she can
reach it. One wonders if the author recalls the legend
of the cherry tree bent down for Mary, and hereby makes
a connection between the loss of paradise through this
woman, Eve, and the winning of salvation through the
later woman, Mary. In any event, Eve's command to the
serpent, which seems to exist only in the Ordinalia's
version of the fall, further illuminates her character;
by that command she shrewdly obliges the devil to participate more fully in the transgression but, more
importantly, she also assumes control over him. While
the serpent may have begun by manipulating Eve, she ends
by manipulating him. Thus, even though Eve is the first
woman to sin, her characterization is not limited to
that fact; she is clearly conceived by the author as
intelligent, ambitious, and thoughtful, and as a
character who learns and grows.

The author expands Eve's characterization and her
significance in yet another, singular way by having the
results of the fall commence immediately after she,
alone, has eaten the apple. In most other versions of
the fall, whether scriptural or legendary, Eve's prior
tasting seems to cause no effect, since only after Adam
eats do they both experience sin and know that they are
naked. Not Eve's actual eating of the apple, but her
tempting Adam to eat it, is the cause of the fall, which
construction and interpretation of the event keeps Eve
in the subservient role at the same time as blaming
her. Departing from this convention and at the same
time giving added weight to Eve's role, the author be-
tokens significant disharmony in paradise immediately
after Eve alone eats. Obviously manifesting a hier-

archical disruption, Eve, approaching Adam with the
apple, conveys to him a series of explicit instructions:

> Adam, extend to me thy hand;
> Take that from me.
> Quietly, without blowing thy horn,
> At once do eat it (PPH 65: 205-08).

Although Adam was created to be her superior, Eve not
only tells Adam what to do but also behaves disrespect-
fully and insultingly to him in the process, commenting
negatively on his behavior by implying that Adam could
be arrogant and pompous. Adam responds in a similarly
unloving fashion, also before he has eaten the apple,
coldly addressing Eve as "thou woman." The author thus
exposes not only a disturbance of the hierarchy, since
Eve is commanding Adam, but also the presence of irri-
table and unloving temperament in both Adam and Eve,
prior to Adam's tasting.

Most convincingly demonstrating the immediate chaos
in paradise, however, is the exchange following Adam's
initial refusal. Eve succinctly announces that since he
does not believe her about the fruit's effect and will
not taste it then he will lose her love and never see
her again, an action Rosemary Woolf has labelled "crude
blackmail" (117). All his resolve collapsing on the
instant, Adam meekly acquiesces; rather than suffer the
terrible consequences of Eve's displeasure he will do as
she wishes, and he takes the apple. The author clearly
indicates their different motivations in eating: Eve
takes the apple because she believes the serpent's
story, whereas Adam disbelieves the story altogether but
takes the apple anyway, to avoid losing Eve's love.

This motivation for Adam, his unwillingness to risk
losing Eve's love, which Milton popularized in **Paradise
Lost**,[18] is not found in Genesis nor in the other
medieval cycles. In the York play, for example, Adam
takes the fruit in order to "wynne" the name of god
(Smith 25: 100-04), as in the parallel Towneley play.
In the N-town cycle, Adam eats so as to share God's
wisdom and to be God's peer in "kunnyng" (Block 24:
243-44). And in the Chester cycle Adam, with no de-
murral, seems to take the fruit simply because it is
"sweete and fayre in feere" (Deimling 30: 254). Although the **Ordinalia** author's decision to provide Adam a
different motivation concerned with the couple's relationship is unusual, he still indicates, in accord with
tradition, both Eve's assumption of power and the degree
of upheaval in God's hierarchy. Equally significant,
however, is that providing this motivation is in
striking accord with the author's attention to the
humanness of his two characters.

This motivation can be seen to function in at least
two ways. In one regard, the interchange Woolf so much
disliked serves importantly to reveal the author's psychological insight and his understanding of the elemental need humankind has for connectedness, at virtually
any cost, to other human beings. At the same time,
however, Adam's sacrifice of paradise for love, and his
giving control to Eve, has to be acknowledged by the
audience as foolish and, in accord with scripture,
sinful. This scene thus functions as another important
point of audience identification with the play, since it
encourages the audience to recognize their commonality
with Adam, whose human weakness causes him to put his
human needs first.

Obviously, Adam's emotional vulnerability helps make
it possible for Eve to assume control over him. Yet,
just as Eve becomes more powerful, she also becomes more
wise. If her perceptivity and understanding were less
than Adam's when she succumbed to the serpent's wiles
and believed his tale, these qualities have developed
considerably by the time God confronts them with their
disobedience. As is traditional, Adam blames Eve, who
brought him the apple, and by implication he blames God
as well, since God made Eve for him. Adam is not being
entirely straightforward in his accusation, though,
since in The Ordinalia it is Adam's own idea that God
make him a mate. Eve, in accord with scripture, states
that the serpent deceived her, but she then goes on to
analyze those aspects of her character that allowed this
to happen; she admits to having been covetous and to
having desired a higher status. In performing this
self-analysis and in accepting responsibility for her
deed, she sharply contrasts Adam. He, in conventional
fashion, simply transfers the blame to Eve, while she
examines herself with considerable honesty and takes
responsibility.

In the course of her interchange with God, Eve
suggests to the deity that he cut the serpent down with
his sword.19 God chooses not to follow Eve's suggestion, and in fact ignores her remark altogether, as if
she had not spoken; in contrast, Adam is allowed to
dicker with God and to make suggestions, as when he
argues with God, after the expulsion, for more land than
the spade-length originally granted. God's complete
inattention to Eve thus underscores her increased in-
feriority after the fall, in contrast to Adam's position. Nonetheless, Eve's courage and self-confidence in
presuming to advise the deity indicates a significant

transformation from the meek and pliant maiden first encountered. The author has shaped Eve as a character who, before our very eyes, learns and grows.

Although the Ordinalia author carefully develops a full and complex character for Eve, he nonetheless wishes to demonstrate that those very aspects of her character that he has innovatively chosen to develop—intelligence, curiosity, cleverness, and ambition—contributed to the disruption of hierarchy and thus to the fall. The author permits no doubt as to the cause or the consequences of taking the apple. Not only does God note thunderously that because Adam did "hearken to her, / A thousand mothers' sons shall be damned" (PPH 75: 323-24), but the deity later emphasizes more than once that Adam's major error was in allowing himself to be governed by Eve. For example, after giving Adam the earth to cultivate, God expresses his great regret that he ever made a man, since the man, "by listening to a woman," had lost paradise (PPH 85: 419). Eve's assumption of power and Adam's surrender of power to Eve, that mutual violation of the hierarchy, is thus reinforced as the ultimate cause of the fall, and those aspects of Eve's character which have been so carefully crafted and which we have been led to admire are nonetheless shown to have caused the loss of paradise.[20]

Thus the character of Eve, departing in some important ways from traditional medieval stereotypes, is created as complex and vital. Eve's transcendence of the stereotypes, and her possession of intelligence, curiosity, ambition, and vitality, make her interesting, credible, and multifaceted, but those same qualities also make her a character who could, and did, violate the hierarchy and cause the fall. Employing his innovations in characterization to convey doctrine, the author develops a fascinating and engaging Eve.

As one might expect, the daughters of Mary in The
Ordinalia serve doctrine without engaging our minds or
feelings to any significant extent. Mary Magdalene,
Mary the mother of James, and Mary Salome all represent
in their brief roles ideals embodied in the Virgin, as
does Maximilla, the first Christian martyr. While all
four of these Mary-types are relatively one-dimensional,
the author devotes some attention to Maximilla, ampli-
fying her Mary-like acceptance of her lot to the end of
reinforcing Christian dogma as well as certain kinds of
behavior for women.

According to legend, Maximilla is the first person
to die for Christ. Living at the time of Solomon, she
is martyred as a result of visiting Solomon's temple and
sitting on the log that is to become the cross. As her
clothes instantly catch flame, Maximilla calls upon the
yet unborn Jesus to save her, thus revealing to the
astonished and disbelieving world the name of Christ and
the existence of a new god.21 Her outcry does not,
however, simply prophesy Christ's coming; her speeches
also create a bridge between the prefiguring of events
in the Old Testament and their typological working out
in the New Testament. In contrast to Maximilla's spare
presentation in such analogues and possible sources as
The Northern Passion and Cursor Mundi, the Cornish play
uses Maximilla to link the past and future history of
the cross, thus affirming the connection between Adam
and Christ.

By providing Maximilla with more speaking oppor-
tunities than she has in other versions of the story,
the author allows her to display her Mary-like faith and
acquiescence as she endures torture because she pre-
dicted the crucifixion, the harrowing of hell, the
trinity, the nativity, and the fulfillment of the oil of

mercy through David's three rods and the cross. Moreover, by adding and developing the scene wherein the
Torturers beat and stone Maximilla to death with great
exuberance and relish because she will not recant, the
author allows Maximilla as proto-martyr to experience
the same mockery and hateful treatment as Christ in the
buffeting and and scourging. At the same time, the
author again supports the cultural desire for meekness
in women as he also panders to an audience taste for
violence, particularly violence against women. Even
though the Torturers similarly abuse Christ before the
Crucifixion, one cannot ignore the specific misogyny
displayed in the glee with which the Torturers beat
Maximilla directly on the breast, and in the names they
call her during the beating: "jade," "foul wench," and
"vile strumpet" (PPH 297-301: 2717-41).

In the similarly one-dimensional characterization of
the mother of Christ, the author emphasizes Mary's
motherliness and prepares it as a context for the presentation of crucial doctrine. In the play, when Jesus
breaks free of the tomb and appears to Mary on the third
day, she asks in a touching and fully credible motherly
fashion if he still suffers pain from the wounds made by
nails and spear. Reassuring her that he does not suffer
and never will again, Jesus explains that he has overcome sorrow and death and has been made whole and perfect. Profoundly grateful that he suffers no more, Mary
thanks God for allowing her to see her son and to learn
that he suffers no pain. The essential information,
that Christ has risen from the dead, is thus presented
as a response to Mary's motherly concern. The author
uses Mary's complete absorption in her son's well-being
as the occasion and context for the announcement of the
resurrection, thereby constituting another significant

example of the way literary representation can reinforce
and embellish cultural ideals.

In addition to Mary and the predictable Mary-
figures, The Ordinalia surprisingly casts some other
female characters as good women, among them Noah's
wife. In much medieval drama Noah's wife is the stereo-
typic shrew, disobedient, bad-natured, and belligerent;
in this play, however, Noah's wife is a Mary-figure.
Entirely obedient and mild-mannered, she hastens to
enter the ark when bidden and never once engages her
husband in any sort of dispute, either verbal or
physical. Also surprising as a type of Mary is Pilate's
wife; in her one-dimensional characterization she is
like Mary in her concern for her children, and by
accepting Beelzebub's statement that Jesus was the son
of God, she aligns herself with the image of the good
woman. For the most part, however, with the notable
exception of Eve herself, the author of The Ordinalia
employs conventional stereotypes and reflects traditional attitudes toward women, portraying them in
one-dimensional terms as types of Eve or as types of
Mary, and focusing on particular attributes associated
with those types.

A departure from this tradition in the depiction of
Veronica is therefore of special interest. In the
episode concerning the death of Pilate,[22] Veronica's
character shifts between the two polar images. Beginning as a Mary-type, as the gentle Christian solicitous
for her Emperor's health, Veronica is transformed in the
play into a cruel and willful Fury, bent on vengeance.
Having suggested that Pilate be killed, Veronica inter-
venes when the Emperor would stab him with a sword and
insists instead on torture for Pilate and the most
hideous death possible. Yet, in spite of her ruthless-

ness and implacable cruelty, we are certainly intended to view Veronica positively; not only does she become a saint, but she is the most powerful character in the episode, stronger willed even than the Emperor, and only she is able to resist Pilate's charm and magical powers and conceive of ways to overcome him. But, in so doing, and in demanding his torture and death, Veronica is inevitably presented as an utterly heartless being; in fact, she is assigned the same qualities of coldness, cruelty, and brutality that are given to the Smith's Wife. Yet, because she functions in the play as a militant saint, Veronica is not only freed from the confinements of the Eve-Mary ideals--and can, in fact, embody qualities of both--but she is also freed from negative associations attached to Eve-like behavior. Because her willfulness, arrogance, and cruelty are acceptably channeled toward Christian ends, Veronica is neither presented nor recognized as the twin she is to the Smith's Wife, but as a Christian hero.

The author's depiction of Veronica as a strong, independent, and forceful female is thus acceptable only because he advances a saintly female rather than a human female. A human female displaying Veronica's qualities for anything other than Christian ends would of necessity be a negative character, a type of Eve, like the Smith's Wife. Only because this legendary figure of Veronica is more than human and therefore barely female is the _Ordinalia_ author able, in her characterization, to depart so significantly from convention.

The second extant piece of Cornish literature, which dates from roughly the same period as _The Ordinalia_, is a small bit of Middle Cornish dialogue that was written down on the back of a Cornish land charter.23 The charter itself is dated 1340, and Jenner believed the dramatic fragment was written on the charter some time prior to 1400 ("Fragment" 698). Although one cannot be certain, the dialogue appears to be the speeches for one actor in a play. Further, since the speeches seem to be for a match-maker or go-between,[24] the play may have been a popular type of interlude wherein a man and a woman are brought together for marital or extramarital amorous purposes (Axton 21). The first speech is addressed to a man who is riding by; the second is addressed to the man again, with the bride-to-be present; and the last speeches seem to be addressed to the woman in the man's absence.

In the first speech the matchmaker invites the male passerby to stop and be given a wife, a fair maiden who will not refuse him and who will be a good housekeeper. In the second speech, the matchmaker gives the maiden into the man's hand, perhaps in a form of betrothal. Urging the man to be good to the maiden, the matchmaker explains that she is a child, well-behaved, and not at all willful. However, the matchmaker's third speech, obviously addressed to the maiden in the absence of the man, is very different in tone and intent. Counseling the maiden to begin at once to prevent the man from opposing or controlling her, the matchmaker advises how to accomplish this. If, for example, the man should command her to do something, she is to refuse, and to tell him to do it himself. The maiden is also cautioned to begin to do this early, so that the man will fear to set himself against her. Even though the man possesses grace and courtesy, the matchmaker explains that the maiden should render him ineffectual; she can then be mistress and lady as long as she lives, and will have her husband in her power.

The sex of the matchmaker is not stipulated and although Nance posits "a greybeard" ("Charter" 35), my own assumption is the opposite. To begin with, this fragment does seem to be in the tradition of the wooing play, wherein a couple is brought together by what Axton has termed a "female bawd" (21). More persuasive, however, is the unlikelihood that a male speaker, in what is certainly not an aristocratic or courtly piece of literature, would advise a young wife when and how to acquire control over her husband. We might, then, tentatively accept the matchmaker as female.

On the play's surface, it is obvious that the matchmaker and the maiden alike are stereotypically characterized. Revealing herself to be corrupt, dishonest, and conniving, the matchmaker advises the maiden to use the man's very courtesy and gentleness against him to obtain control. Revealing the character of the maiden as well, the matchmaker assumes the young woman to be hiding, beneath her fair face and her ostensibly sweet nature, an innate and Eve-like desire to dominate and deceive. To the audience in medieval Cornwall, the surface level of this dialogue presents a male nightmare of the false and black-hearted bride and the evil hag who teaches young women to manipulate, control, and deceive men.

At the same time, however, this snippet of a play offers another level of meaning which conveys a more realistic if less comic message. In essence, the matchmaker addresses the realities of life for women in the Middle Ages and advises the maiden how to behave in light of those realities. For instance, to secure the marriage necessary to women's existence, the maiden must be a daughter of Mary, quiet, mild, and obedient. However, if that maiden is to survive in her marriage with

any self-determination at all, she must begin immediately to be Eve, vocal, assertive, and independent. In
providing the maiden her assistance, the matchmaker functions as the "wise woman" possessed of special learning,
while the maiden represents a younger version of the
Wife of Bath, a woman who will endure by virtue of her
own wit and strength, augmented by the advice and coun-
sel of her female friends.

Thus, this tiny fragment of a drama, while following
rigidly stereotypical depictions of women, presents a
comic situation that overlies a dramatization of survival strategies for medieval women. To be sure, the
comic level of the dialogue confirms misogynistic
beliefs, but the dialogue's deeper level not only manifests women's realities, but testifies to the real
strength available in the qualities and attributes for
which Eve is usually denounced.

In addition to having its own versions of the cycle
drama and the tantalizing "Charter Fragment," medieval
Cornwall also possessed its own particularized saint's
play, Beunans Meriasek.25 Believed to date from late
in the fifteenth century (Thomas 23), this play concerns
the life and miracles of Meriasek, the patron saint of
Camborne, whose arena included not just Cornwall but
Britanny and Italy, and whose life spanned several centuries. The play was apparently intended to be performed over a period of two days, since diagrams in the
manuscript depict stage plans for the first and second
days.

There are very few female characters in this play,
and they have little dialogue; except for a single
instance, women in the play testify to the author's
reliance on stereotypes for female characterization.
The mother of Meriasek, for instance, is strictly one-

dimensional; like Noah's wife in The Ordinalia, she is
focused on worldly matters, particularly a good marriage
for her son. Similarly limited in role are the mothers
of the innocents, the 1,900 children whose blood will be
used to cure Constantine's leprosy;26 entirely func-
tional, the mothers display anguish at the possibility
of the slaughter and then joy when the children are
saved. Undeveloped figures, they serve only to empha-
size the magnitude of the slaughter and the corresponding greatness of Constantine's conversion when he
decides against it.

An exception in Meriasek to such narrow treatment of
women is the interlude concerning "Mary and the Woman's
Son."27 The source for this interlude could have been
a paragraph in The Golden Legend (Ryan and Ribberger
526-27), although the author of Meriasek considerably
expands upon the Legend's account. Interestingly, he
adds by his expansion a thematic strand concerning the
relationship and the commonality between Mary and a
female worshiper, the catalyst for their interaction
being the kidnapping of the woman's son.

Since she had previously consigned her son to Mary's
special care, this mother prays repeatedly and confi-
dently for Mary to rescue him. When her prayers have
long gone unanswered, the mother in the play goes to the
church, perhaps the Church of St. Mary in Camborne,
where she testily chastises Mary for her tardiness,
charges the Virgin with a lack of sympathy, takes as
hostage the infant Jesus from the statue's arms, and
goes off in a huff, announcing to Mary that she is
cancelling her allegiance:

> Farewell to thee, Mary
> I will not annoy thee
>> Here praying more (Stokes 211: 3536-38).

This provocative action earns Mary's immediate attention and, after consulting with Christ in heaven (in contrast to the Golden Legend, where Mary apparently had authority to act on her own), Mary goes to earth and frees the young man from prison. By way of explanation and in an effort at reconciliation, Mary urges the young man to assure his mother that even though Mary may have appeared neglectful and uncaring, she never intended to forget her loyal worshiper. Of course, to this divine magnanimity and graciousness the mother responds in kind. Amusingly acknowledging the awesome burden of having taken Jesus from his mother's arms, she confides to her son that the statue of the infant is still wrapped as when taken, since she had not dared to open it. Gratefully returning the infant to the statue's arms, the mother admits to Mary that she, too, has been lax in her devotional duties, and promises to do better in the future.

Adding considerably to the characterization of both women, the author of **Meriasek** thereby creates in the interlude further thematic depth. He depicts the mother individualistically, as a mix of good and bad qualities, and as a woman credible in her attitudes and her action--as, most intriguingly, he depicts the Virgin. The author thus demonstrates the commonality the two women have as less-than-perfect, and therefore human, beings. In fact, Mary and the woman are disclosed as parallel figures in their concern for their children and in their respective recognitions and admissions of personal shortcomings. For the mother, this treatment manifests an authorial conception of her as a real woman, rather than as one of two undesirable or impossible types. For Mary, of course, this treatment has the effect of humanizing her to a very unusual degree.

The author of Meriasek thus contrives, at least in this
interlude if not in the rest of the play, to depart from
the usual polarities of female characterization and,
additionally, to place Mary ever so slightly outside her
stereotypical image.

The last piece of extant drama in Middle Cornish is
Gwryans an Bys or The Creacion of the World.28 Since
this work is sub-titled "The First Daie of Playe," and
since at the play's end the character of Noah invites
the audience to attend the next day and see redemption,
it seems likely that The Creacion was but the first
segment of a longer work.29 Although Nance believed
the play to date from between 1530 and 1540 ("Windows"
244), the earliest existing manuscript is much later,
the colophon having been dated by the scribe, William
Jordan, as 12 August 1611.

There are few female characters in the play, and of
those only Eve herself seems to have received much more
than minimal or perfunctory attention; nevertheless, the
snake, whose body the devil assumes for the temptation
and who is female, also represents an interesting perspective. Of the other two female characters, Cain's
wife, Calmana, and Noah's wife are undeveloped types
respectively of Mary and Eve. Because Calmana's primary
quality is her faithfulness to Cain even though fully
recognizing his sin, she is cast as Mary-like in
accepting her lot and devoting herself to husband and
children. Full of grief at Cain's deed, Calmana nevertheless obediently packs up children and belongings so
as to accompany Cain on his wanderings. Similarly one-
dimensional is Noah's wife, who is shown, in her one
speech in The Creacion, to be stereotypical in her
concern for possessions she does not wish to abandon.
This slight materialism may be a hint in her of cross-

fertilization from the English cycles, but more likely
it simply reflects traditional beliefs about women.

Although The Creacion devotes some attention to the
character of Eve, this later play contrasts The Ordinalia considerably in the degree to which the figure is
stereotyped; the Creacion author presents Eve as weak,
unpleasantly cunning, and much less intelligent than she
is in The Ordinalia.[30] Testifying to her frailty, the
serpent voices conventional anti-woman attitudes,
explaining that he chooses to tempt Adam through Eve
because "she is easier to deceive" and "more simple-
minded" (Creacion 39: 473- 75).[31] More damning to
Eve in The Creacion than the devil's remarks, however,
are the misogynistic comments she makes herself. During
the temptation, for instance, she states that "Woman's
wit is weak," and after the expulsion she laments that
she was simply not equipped to deal with the devil
(Creacion 51: 615; and 87: 1015). Even her naivete,
though touching on one level, seriously undercuts her
character, since it betrays so openly the shallowness of
her understanding; she decides, for example, to trust
the serpent simply because he says he came from heaven,
and after eating the apple she uncomprehendingly asserts
that Adam will thank and praise her "for undertaking so
noble a venture" (Creacion 59: 708-12).

In addition to this weakness in intellect and her
lack of self-esteem, an unpleasant deceitfulness is also
revealed in Eve's temptation of Adam. Calling him to
come to her because she has something for him, she urges
Adam not to fear a trick. Although one would think that
this very caution might well arouse Adam's suspicions,
it does not, but it does communicate to the audience an
unattractive disingenuousness in Eve. As becomes
obvious, her intent is to manipulate Adam into eating,

and she first attempts this by telling him of potential
monetary gains, of profit he will earn if he eats; in an
amusing anachronism that nonetheless reveals her very
limited understanding of what it would mean to be a god,
she promises him he will get "thousands of Pounds" if he
eats (Creacion 61: 741). When Adam, resisting, questions her and then, understanding, condemns her for
breaking the commandment, she coldly and bluntly exercises her only power, declaring that she will be angry
with him and their love will therefore fail if he does
not taste the apple. Although in both The Ordinalia and
The Creacion Eve used Adam's love as a means of manipulation, The Creacion focuses much more closely on this
action, thus offering a more severely limited and contracted delineation of character in Eve.

One final, curious bit of nastiness assigned to Eve
is evident in the curse she places upon her son, Cain,
after Abel's murder. In a passage of considerable psychological interest she damns Cain, places her curse
upon him forever, berates him for having done this deed,
and heaps guilt upon him by charging that "God and the
earth too are / crying out on you continually" (Creacion
105: 1267-68). Echoing the very speeches God and Adam
made to her after the temptation, Eve passes to Cain
responsibility for the loss of human happiness:

> Therefore, after this,
> We shall never rejoice,
> but for ever all be mourning,
> without any joy or gladness,
> because of your bad deed here (Creacion
>   107: 1269-73).

Her action is, of course, understandable on doctrinal
grounds, since God's curse on Cain makes him anathema to

all other beings, but the <u>Creacion</u> author makes possible
several additional effects by placing in the mouth of
Eve, the first sinner, the same condemnations that had
been placed upon her. To begin with, the author thus
establishes a connection from Cain back to Eve, a connection which summons up and reminds us again of that first
sin. In creating a link between the sin of Eve and the
sin of Cain, the author displays how the first made
possible the second, thus underscoring the magnitude of
Eve's original deed.[32] Eve's curse also, however,
discloses additional disagreeable qualities in her; not
only does it specify that she, unlike the faithful
Calaman, has no feeling for her son, and that she will
eagerly transfer responsibility for the loss of happiness elsewhere--even to her own flesh--but, more importantly, her curse manifests a total lack of sympathy for
a human being very like herself, a person who has
sinned. The curse, then, proves that her own experience
of condemnation has given her no empathy at all for one
similarly afflicted; instead, we see her giving to Cain
the same harsh and absolute treatment she herself
received. Although her actions can, as indicated, be
defended on religious grounds, the author also by that
action defines the limitations of both her mind and her
heart.

The character of Eve seems clearly to degenerate
between <u>The Ordinalia</u> and <u>The Creacion</u>. Her primary
attributes in <u>The Creacion</u> are weakness and stupidity,
coupled with an innate and easy deceitfulness. Narrowly
conceived by the <u>Creacion</u> author as a flawed individual,
she possesses none of the pride, intelligence, confidence, and curiosity of her energetic and admirable
counterpart in <u>The Ordinalia</u>. Ultimately, Eve is unable
to transcend, in <u>The Creacion</u>, the conventions established for her.

The remaining female character in The Creacion is
the snake; although she has no lines, she is an
important reflection of cultural attitudes, offering
compelling evidence of the widespread belief in women's
inherent evil. The snake's attributes and exterior
form--her subtlety and her beautiful maiden's face--
unmistakably categorize her as female and place her
firmly among the daughters of Eve.

Artistic depictions of the fall often portray the
snake, even before the temptation, with the face of a
woman, thus testifying to the misogyny in our culture.
In "The Garden of Eden" in The Très Riches Heures of
Jean, Duke of Berry, for example, Eve is handed the
fruit by a voluptuous serpent whose hair, upper torso,
and posture are almost mirror reflections of Eve's own
(Longnon and Cazelles, plate 20). Similarly, in Michelangelo's depiction of "Original Sin and the Expulsion
from Earthly Paradise" in the Sistine Chapel, the fruit
is given to Eve by a blonde creature whose female body
extends to the thigh before the body of a snake begins;
moreover, because the snake is the central and pivotal
figure in the scene--Adam and Eve being tempted on the
one side, balanced by Adam and Eve being driven out of
the Garden on the other--both visual and thematic attention is riveted on the snake and on her very considerable femaleness (Mariani, plate IX). Finally, in yet
another example from The Visconti Hours, Eve is tempted
by a creature in a tree who has the body, wings, and
feet of a bat, but who nonetheless has the head of a
woman (Meiss and Kirsch, LF 51).

This same tradition in art that accords femaleness
to the snake,[33] which creature, incidentally, is
referred to as male in the Bible (Genesis 3:1), is
strongly in evidence in The Creacion. One might, in

fact, speculate whether the greater strength and longer
tenure in Cornwall of pagan belief and folklore manifests itself in a connection between the snake and the
ancient goddess. This speculation may even find support
within the play since God, when he creates all the other
animals for Adam to name, fashions the snake with "a
virgyn face, and yolowe heare upon her head" (Creacion
34). In any case, because God did create the snake as a
subtle female with a beautiful face who can easily be
controlled (Creacion 41-43:   500-02), Lucifer is able to
employ her to tempt Eve. In The Creacion's account of
the fall, then, womankind suffers doubly since Eve, who
is going to be blamed for the loss of paradise anyway,
is tempted as well by a being who looks exactly like
herself.

Yet the snake is not unrelievedly evil. When
Lucifer approaches to take over her body, to her credit
the snake resists, and she and Lucifer struggle vigorously. One would give a lot to have witnessed this
scene performed in medieval Cornwall, since the stage
directions command at this point the following intriguing actions:

> Let Lucyfer com to the Serpent and offer
> to goe in to her. The Serpent voydeth
> [attempts to get away]. And stayety [is
> kept], and [Lucifer] ofeeth to go in to
> her (Creacion 42).

While Lucifer struggles mightily to get inside the snake
suit with the snake, he explains that Eve will not fear
him as the snake because he will be so beautiful. This
belief that exterior female beauty disguises dreadful
interior evil is, of course, a basic tenet of misogyny

that was evident in "The Charter Fragment" and that is
by no means peculiar to the Middle Ages. And Lucifer's
plan works; Eve indeed has no fear of Lucifer in the
serpent's form because the serpent's face is that of a
beautiful woman. Of course, Eve's lack of fear testifies further to her shallowness and gullibility, since
she is so easily fooled by exterior appearances.

Thus, even though the snake has no voice in the
play, she is an important indicator of medieval attitudes towards women, the womanliness of her face and
form alone sufficient to predispose her to evil and suit
her for its accomplishment. Her usefulness to Lucifer
in the temptation because of her female appearance thus
casts her, even before the first woman has sinned,
squarely in the tradition of female evil that the play
itself has yet to establish.

The Cornish plays, as a whole, are not rich in the
number of female characters they contain, probably a
result of attitudes toward women and women's marginal
status in the culture. But as my discussion suggests,
even as these plays betray the limitations the two primary models impose on the drama, the female characters
indicate important societal beliefs by pointing collec-
tively to the strength and persistence of Eve and Mary
as models in the culture. The plays do seem to suggest
that these cultural constructs can best receive literary
reinforcement from genres other than the drama. Perhaps
more significant, however, is the commentary the plays
ultimately make about the Eve and Mary models themselves. When the authors become engaged in the literary, as opposed to the purely doctrinal, possibilities
of their texts, their female characters inevitably
challenge and call into question, by their very being,
the validity and possibility of Eve and Mary as ideals
in literature or in culture.

NOTES

[1] For studies of these two figures in western culture see Phillips, Eve: The History of an Idea; and Warner, Alone of All Her Sex: The Myth and the Cult of the Virgin Mary.

[2] McLaughlin discusses theological perspectives on women in the Middle Ages in "Equality of Souls, Inequality of Sexes: Woman in Medieval Theology." See also Ruether's "Misogynism and Virginal Feminism in the Fathers of the Church."

[3] For other discussions of this symbolism see Phillips (44 and passim); Vawter (84-85); and of course Freud, who labels the snake the "most important symbol of the male organ" in The Interpretation of Dreams (V, 357).

[4] Janeway notes the conflicts in women today between the Eve and Mary impulses in "Who is Sylvia? On the Loss of Sexual Paradigms."

[5] Henderson and McManus observe that the three traditional female stereotypes used by misogynistic writers are the seductress, the shrew, and the vain woman; the positive images are women who are chaste, holy, and nurturing (47-50). Bornstein, in The Lady in the Tower, summarizes the ideals put forth in medieval courtesy books for women in such roles as virgin, wife, ruler, and worker.

[6] Only the first part of The Ordinalia exists in the modern scholarly edition; see Phyllis Pier Harris's Origo Mundi. The entire play is available in Norris's earlier edition and translation, The Ancient Cornish Drama. A modern popular translation is Markham Harris's The Cornish Ordinalia. References to the first section of the play will be to Phyllis Pier Harris's edition, cited as "PH" and followed by page and line numbers. For a study of The Ordinalia manuscript, see Hawke's essay on scribal transmission. Fowler discusses possible provenance in "The Date of the Cornish Ordinalia." For a complete bibliography on all the Cornish plays see my Cornish Drama of the Middle Ages: A Bibliography, forthcoming from the Institute of Cornish Studies, Truro.

[7] For studies of this legend, see Halliday, The Legend of the Rood, and Quinn, The Quest of Seth for the Oil of Life.

[8]One very interesting aspect of the medieval Cornish drama is its performance in a plain-an-gwary, a round open-air amphitheater. For discussions of staging see Borlase; Whitley; Holman; Jenner, "Peran Round"; and Nancy, "The Plen an gwary."

[9]This type in later literature is the subject of Allen's The Femme Fatale.

[10]Bakere asserts in The Cornish Ordinalia: A Critical Study, that "the first suggestion for Uriah's murder comes from her [Bathsheba], not from David" (57); however, the scholarly translations by Phyllis Pier Harris and by Norris do not confirm this reading, which is found in Markham Harris's popular translation.

[11]The idea that female sexuality freely exercised is a greater and more grievous sin than male sexuality freely exercised is found in art as well as in literature. In his chapter on "Eve and Mary: Conflicting Images of Medieval Woman," Kraus points out that in twelfth-century church sculpture the "typical 'male' vice" is pride or avarice, while the typical female vice is "unchastity" (42). Haskell writes similarly of later medieval literature that while "male characters might be judged in relation to the entire gamut of morality, a woman's physical virtue superseded all other moral considerations" (6).

[12]For a similar, current-day interpretation of Bathsheba see Frontain and Wojcik's The David Myth in Western Literature, which states that Bathsheba's "unchecked animal appetites had tragic consequences for him [David], his family, and the community he governed" (3).

[13]See the play of Noah and "The Second Shepherds' Play" in England and Pollard's edition of The Towneley Plays; or in Martial Rose's modernized edition, The Wakefield Mystery Plays. Davidson discusses the stereotypical images of Noah's wife and Pilate's wife in "Women and the Medieval Stage" (106-07); as my remarks indicate, however, we differ regarding the effectiveness in effectiveness in drama of the Mary type.

[14]One possible source is The Northern Passion, ed. Foster (I, 172-73), although the story exists elsewhere, including the continental passion plays (Frank 127).

[15]Cross studies the Torturers' role and function in "Torturers as Tricksters in the Cornish Ordinalia."

[16]Longsworth suggests further that "the smith and his woman may in a small way be intended, on the verge of the crucifixion, to recall as well the folly of the first woman" (67).

[17]See, for example, Deferrari's edition of Hugh of Saint Victor on the Sacraments of the Christian Faith (122-23).

[18]Another curious connection between Paradise Lost and the Cornish drama is that the Cornish plays give to Satan as motivation jealousy of Adam and Eve's happiness, as does Paradise Lost; when God in The Ordinalia asks why he deceived Eve, the serpent confesses, "Because they had a joy so great, / And I every hour was burning" (PPH 75, 11. 306-07). The serpent in The Creacion says virtually the same thing. Compare Satan's jealousy of the first couple's happiness in Paradise Lost, IV: 505-09 (Hughes 290).

[19]This suggestion may, of course, echo various myths wherein the ancient goddess, in the form of a snake, is killed and supplanted by the new gods of the patriarchy, as when Apollo slew the python at Delphi and established his temple on the site.

[20]Fudge notes that the absence in The Ordinalia of Lucifer's fall puts even greater emphasis on the fall of Adam and Eve (460).

[21]Kolve discusses the anachronisms in Maximilla's knowledge of Christ in The Play Called Corpus Christi (121).

[22]A possible source for this story is The Golden Legend; see Granger and Ripperger (214-15). See also "The Death of Pilate" in the Gospel of Nicodemus (James 157-59).

[23]Although no definitive edition of this fragment exists, early editions are those of Jenner, Stokes, Nance, and Campanile.

[24]Nance, however, has speculated that "it may deal with the early life of one who afterwards became a Cornish saint" ("Charter" 35).

[25]Stokes's 1872 edition and Markham Harris's popular translation provide the only access to Beunans Meriasek, although Combellack-Harris edited and translated the play as her Ph.D. dissertation in 1985 for the

University of Exeter. References are to Stokes's
edition.

[26]Turk and Combellack study the use of illness in the
play in "Doctoring and Disease in Medieval Cornwall:
Exegetical Notes in Some Passages in 'Beunans
Meriasek.'"

[27]This interlude may have been added to provide
padding in the second day's play (Halliday 17), or it
may have been intended to publicize the "local cult" of
Saint Mary in the parish of Camborne (Harris, _Meriasek_
11).

[28]A modern edition and translation is Neuss's _The
Creacion of the World_. See also Hooper's edition of
Nance and Smith's earlier edition and translation,
Gwryans _an_ _Bys_, in Unified Cornish; and Stokes's early
edition and translation, _Gwreans_ _an_ _bys_. Rawe's translation was used for the 1973 production of the play at
Piran Round in Cornwall. Since close correspondences
exist between _The_ _Creacion_ and the first portion of _The
Ordinalia_, particularly in the speeches of God, Neuss
suggests that _The_ _Creacion_ was reconstructed through the
memory of an actor who played God in _The_ _Ordinalia_ ("Reconstruction" 131).

[29]If _The_ _Creacion_ were a three-day play, perhaps the
second and third days' plays, like _The_ _Ordinalia_, would
have been concerned with Christ's passion and resurrection. On the other hand, since _The_ _Creacion_ covers less
ground than the corresponding first part of _The_ _Ordi-
nalia_, Neuss suggests that a larger, complete play might
have taken more than three days to present (_Creacion_
207, note to title). Historical records documenting
dramatic activity in St. Ives, Cornwall, may also suggest this possibility, since they cite profits received
over the six days of a play; these records also refer to
the purchase of lamb skins (Matthews 147-48). Perhaps
these lamb skins became the "whytt lether" costumes
stipulated in the stage directions for Adam and Eve.

[30]Quotations are from Neuss's edition which will be
cited as "_Creacion_."

[31]Vawter suggests that the serpent approaches Eve
rather than Adam not because she is weaker but because
the writer of Genesis wanted to set up the estrangement
between the woman and the serpent, and that Adam was not
present simply because "Ancient literary conventions

dictated that there be dialogue between two persons only
'on stage' at one time" (79).

[32]The _Ordinalia_ author reinforces this connection in a
different way, by having Eve, after the murder of Abel,
lament that she listened to the devil and made possible
such evils. Significantly, at this point, when Eve is
regretting that she is alive, God directs Adam to end
their 200-year period of abstinence and lie with Eve
once again (PPH 103: 626-37).

[33]Phillips discusses possible beginnings of this
convention in _Eve: The History of an Idea_ (61-62).
Interestingly, only one of the English cycles also
portrays the snake as female. In the York, Towneley,
and N-town cycles the tempter is simply a serpent, sex
undesignated. In the Chester cycle, although the
tempter is an "Adder" with "a maydens face," the devil
does not take over the adder's body as in _The Creacion_,
but merely puts on an "adders coate" (Deimling 28:
193-95, 206).

WORKS CITED

Allen, Virginia M. The Femme Fatale: Erotic Icon.
Troy: Whitston, 1982.

Auerbach, Erich. Mimesis: The Representation of
Reality in Western Literature. Trans. Willard R.
Trask. 1946; rpt. Princeton, NJ: Princeton
University Press, 1971.

Axton, Richard. European Drama of the Early Middle
Ages. London: Hutchison University Library, 1974.

Bakere, Jane. The Cornish Ordinalia: A Critical Study.
Cardiff: University of Wales Press, 1980.

Block, K. S., ed. Ludus Coventriae or the Plaie called
Corpus Christi. E.E.T.S., E.S. 120. 1922; rpt.
London, New York, and Toronto: Oxford University
Press, 1960.

Borlase, William. The Natural History of Cornwall.
Oxford: W. Jackson, 1758.

Bornstein, Diane. The Lady in the Tower: Medieval
Courtesy Literature for Women. Hamden, CT: Archon,
1983.

Campanile, Enrico, ed. and trans. "Un frammento scenico
medio-cornico." Studi e Saggi Linguistici 3
(1963): 60-80.

Combellack-Harris, Myrna May, ed. and trans. A Critical
Edition of Beunans Meriasek. Ph.D. Dissertation,
University of Exeter, 1985.

Cross, Sally Joyce. "Torturers as Tricksters in the
Cornish Ordinalia." Neuphilologische Mitteilungen
84 (1983): 448-55.

Davidson, Clifford. "Women and the Medieval Stage."
Women's Studies 11 (1984): 99-113.

Deimling, Hermann, ed. The Chester Plays. 2 vols.
E.E.T.S., E.S. 62 and 115. 1981; rpt. London, New
York, and Toronto: Oxford University Press, 1968.

England, George, and Alfred W. Pollard, eds. The
Towneley Plays. E.E.T.S., E.S. 71. 1986; rpt.
London: Oxford University Press, 1966.

Foster, Frances A., ed. The Northern Passion. 2 vols.
E.E.T.S., O.S. 145 and 147. 1913; rpt. New York:
Kraus, 1971.

Fowler, David C. "The Date of the Cornish Ordinalia."
Medieval Studies 23 (1961): 91-125.

Frank, Grace. The Medieval French Drama. Oxford and
New York: Oxford University Press, 1954.

Freud, Sigmund. The Interpretation of Dreams. Vol. V.
In The Complete Psychological Works of Sigmund
Freud. Trans. James Strachey. The Standard
Edition. 24 vols. London: Hogarth, 1953-62.

Frontain, Raymond-Jean, and Jan Wojcik. The David Myth
in Western Literature. West Lafayette, IN: Purdue
University Press, 1980.

Fudge, C. "Aspects of Form in the Cornish Ordinalia
with Special Reference to Origo Mundi." Old
Cornwall 8 (1973-79): 457-64.

Gold, Penny Schine. The Lady and the Virgin: Image,
Attitude, and Experience in Twelfth-Century France.
Chicago: University of Chicago Press, 1985.

Halliday, Frank E. The Legend of the Rood. London:
Gerald Duckworth, 1955.

Harris, Markham, trans. The Cornish Ordinalia: A
Medieval Dramatic Trilogy. Washington, DC:
Catholic University of America Press, 1977.

_____, trans. The Life of Meriasek: A Medieval
Cornish Miracle Play. Washington, DC: Catholic
University of America Press, 1977.

Harris, Phyllis Pier, ed. and trans. Origo Mundi, First
Play of the Cornish Mystery Cycle, The Ordinalia: A
New Edition. Ann Arbor: University Microfilms,
1963. Ph.D. Dissertation, University of Washington,
1964.

Haskell, Ann. "The Portrayal of Women by Chaucer and
His Age." In What Manner of Woman: Essays on
English and American Life and Literature. Ed.
Marlene Springer. New York: New York University
Press, 1977.

Hawke, Andrew. "A Lost Manuscript of the Cornish
Ordinalia?" Cornish Studies 7 (1979): 45-60.

Henderson, Katherine Usher, and Barbara F. McManus, eds. Half Humankind. Urbana and Chicago: University of Illinois Press, 1985.

Holman, Treve. "Cornish Plays and Playing Places." Theatre Notebook 4 (1950): 52-54.

Hooper, E.G.R., ed. 2nd. ed. of Gwryans an Bys. Eds. and trans. R. Morton Nance and A.S.D. Smith. Redruth: Dyllansow Truran, 1985.

Horrall, Sarah M., ed. The Southern Version of Cursor Mundi. Vol. I. Ottawa: University of Ottawa Press, 1978.

Hughes, Merritt Y., ed. John Milton: Complete Poems and Major Prose. Indianapolis and New York: Odyssey, 1957.

James, Montague R., trans. The Apocryphal New Testament. 1924; rpt. Oxford: Clarendon, 1983.

Janeway, Elizabeth. "Who is Sylvia? On the Loss of Sexual Paradigms." In Women: Sex and Sexuality. Eds. Catherine R. Stimpson and Ethel Spector Person. Chicago: University of Chicago Press, 1980.

Jenner, Henry, ed. "An Early Cornish Fragment." Athenaeum, 1 Dec. 1988: 698-99.

_____. "Perran Round and the Cornish Drama." 79th Annual Report of the Royal Cornwall Polytechnic Society. Falmouth, 1912.

Kolve, V. A. The Play Called Corpus Christi. Stanford: Stanford University Press, 1966.

Kraus, Henry. The Living Theatre of Medieval Art. Philadelphia: University of Pennsylvania Press, 1967.

Lerner, Gerda. The Creation of Patriarchy. Oxford: Oxford University Press, 1986.

Longnon, Jean, and Raymond Cazelles, eds. The Très Riches Heures of Jean, Duke of Berry. New York: George Braziller, 1969.

Longsworth, Robert. The Cornish Ordinalia: Religion and Dramaturgy. Cambridge: Harvard University Press, 1967.

Mariani, Valerio. *Michelangelo the Painter*. New York: Harry N. Abrams, 1964.

Matthews, John H. *A History of the Parishes of Saint Ives, Lelant, Towednack and Zennor*. London: Elliot Stock, 1892.

McLaughlin, Eleanor Commo. "Equality of Souls, Inequality of Sexes: Woman in Medieval Theology." In *Images of Woman in the Jewish and Christian Tradition*. New York: Simon and Schuster, 1974.

Meiss, Millard, and Edith W. Kirsch. *The Visconti Hours*. London: Thames and Hudson, 1972.

Meyer, Robert T. "The Middle-Cornish Play *Beunans Meriasek*." *Comparative Drama* 3 (1969): 54-64.

Nance, R. Morton, ed. and trans. "The Charter Endorsement in Cornish." *Old Cornwall*, 2.4 (1932), 34-36.

_____. "New Light on Cornish." *Old Cornwall* 4.6 (1947): 214-16.

_____. "Painted Windows and Miracle Plays." *Old Cornwall* 5 (1955): 244-48.

_____. "The Plen an gwary or Cornish Playing Place." *Journal of the Royal Institution of Cornwall* 24.3 (1935): 190-212.

Neuss, Paula, ed. and trans. *The Creacion of the World: A Critical Edition and Translation*. New York: Garland, 1983.

_____. "Memorial Reconstruction in a Cornish Miracle Play." *Comparative Drama* 5.2 (1971): 129-37.

Norris, Edwin, ed. and trans. *The Ancient Cornish Drama*. 2 vols. 1859; rpt. New York and London: Benjamin Blom, 1968.

Phillips, John A. *Eve: The History of an Idea*. New York: Harper and Row, 1984.

Power, Eileen. "The Position of Women." In *The Legacy of the Middle Ages*. Eds. C. G. Crump and E. F. Jacob. Oxford: Clarendon, 1926.

Quinn, Esther Casier. *The Quest of Seth for the Oil of Life*. Chicago and London: University of Chicago Press, 1962.

Rawe, Donald R., trans. The Creation of the World
(Gwryans an Bys). Padstow: Lodenek, 1978.

Rose, Martial, ed. The Wakefield Mystery Plays. New
York: Norton, 1961.

Ruether, Rosemary Radford. "Misogynism and Virginal
Feminism in the Fathers of the Church." In Religion
and Sexism: Images of Woman in the Jewish and
Christian Traditions. Ed. Rosemary Radford
Ruether. New York: Simon and Schuster, 1974.

Ryan, Granger, and Helmut Ripperger, trans. The Golden
Legend of Jacobus de Voragine. New York: Arno,
1969.

Schulenburg, Jane Tibbets. "The Heroics of Virginity:
Brides of Christ and Sacrificial Mutilation." In
Women in the Middle Ages and the Renaissance. Ed.
Mary Beth Rose. Syracuse: Syracuse University
Press, 1986.

Smith, Lucy Toulmin, ed. York Plays. 1885; rpt. New
York: Russell and Russell, 1963.

Stokes, Whitley, ed. and trans. "The Fragments of a
Drama in Add. Ch. 19, 491, Mus. Brit." Revue
celtique 4 (1880): 258-62.

_____, ed. and trans. Gwreans an bys: The Creation
of the World. Berlin, 1863; and London and Edin-
burgh, 1864.

_____, ed. and trans. The Life of Saint Meriasek,
Bishop and Confessor: A Cornish Drama. London:
Trubner, 1872.

Thomas, Charles. Christian Antiquities of Camborne.
St. Austell: H. E. Warne, 1967.

Turk, Frank A., and Myrna M. Combellack. "Doctoring and
Disease in Medieval Cornwall: Exegetical Notes on
Some Passages in 'Beunans Meriasek.'" Cornish
Studies 4-5 (1976-77): 56-76.

Vawter, Bruce. On Genesis: A New Reading. Garden
City, NY: Doubleday, 1977.

Warner, Marina. Alone of All Her Sex: The Myth and the
Cult of the Virgin Mary. 1976; rpt. New York:
Vintage, 1982.

Whitley, H. Michell.   "Cornish Rounds or Playing
    Places." _Devon and Cornwall Notes and Queries_ 7
    (1912-13):   172-74.

Woolf, Rosemary.   _The English Mystery Plays_.   Berkeley
    and Los Angeles: University of California Press,
    1972.

FEMALE NUDITY AND SEXUALITY IN MEDIEVAL ART

by John A. Nichols

Historians who write about women in the Middle Ages
are frustrated by the lack of information either written
by medieval women themselves or material that accurately
represents women. Instead of taking the easy way out
and abandoning the subject, scholars have devised new
and imaginative ways to collect evidence on the lives of
women from that time period. Most of this innovative
research is to look at documents in ways never used
before and glean from these manuscripts bits of data
which must be analyzed and interpreted. Such is the
task of an historian. Seldom, however, does the historian turn to medieval art to look at the images of
these women. To be sure, medieval art historians abound
as is evidenced by the number of articles and books
which are published each year, but these studies for the
most part do not touch on the lives of women as conveyed
by art.

One might challenge the methodology of using these
images because the art which has survived was almost
always the work of male rather than female artists. Yet
it is also true, based on the extant works, that nearly
all manuscripts written in the Middle Ages were also the
product of male authors. Historians do not and should
not ignore information just because it was the work of
men. The images we must deal with are images of women

as given to us by men; and Margaret Miles warns in her
new book that "we must not assume, however, that the
meaning received from the image or group of images was
the same for men and for women."[1] Nor must we assume
that the meaning must be a negative one for women just
because it was the work of men. One might also question
the use of visual images rather than the traditional
verbal texts in an attempt to discover information about
the lives of women. Yet medieval art can give us an
insight to the roles and activities of women that are
not mentioned in manuscripts. Perhaps the reason
medieval art has not been employed by historians to
discover more accurate information about the past is the
belief that the art which was produced was subject to
ecclesiastical supervision and censorship. It is
assumed that because the art was commissioned by the
church that it would have to be highly stylized and
seldom representative of what real men and women of the
Middle Ages looked like. Fortunately not all medieval
art was so regulated.

There exists a large collection of wooden sculpture
in medieval churches and cathedrals which, for the most
part, was free of the normal limitations imposed by
pious clerics. As evidence of this see Figure 1 which
shows a carving of a young girl standing in a leafy pod
that conceals the lower part of her body.[2] She holds
in her hands an object which is unmistakable: the
artist has carved testicles and a penis which is clearly
grasped by the woman. There can be no other interpretation of this piece than to describe it as oral stimula-
tion of the male sex organ by a female. In other words,
we are witnessing an act of fellation. Such an act was
forbidden by canon law and considered a sin by the medieval church. To show such an act in a church would be

unacceptable by the clergy but nevertheless here it is
as proof that such subjects can be found in the churches
of the Middle Ages.

This sculpture and many others are found on the
underside of choir seats, and the artist was given considerable license in the carving of subjects which range
from ancient fable traditions and early church liturgy
to popular romances and everyday life scenes.3 In the
medieval church, the divine offices were said daily and
it was expected that the celebrant do so standing. Even
when it became customary to kneel, sitting during the
offices was forbidden. As a concession to the old,
infirm, or weak, an act of mercy (misericordia) was
extended by allowing seats to be so constructed that
persons could rest by leaning against the seat when it
was in an upright position. The support on the underside of the seat was carved, and such a seat has come to
be known as a misericord, thousands of which were carved
throughout Europe in the Middle Ages.4

In Great Britain nearly every extant misericord has
a central figure carved under the ledge with wing supporters left and right, which many times, but not
always, relate to the subject in the center.5 Some of
the chapels, churches, and cathedrals in England which
have an impressive collection of misericords in which
women are depicted are: Ely; Winchester; Bristol; St.
George's Chapel, Windsor; Chichester; Worcester; All
Souls College Chapel, Oxford; Holy Trinity Church,
Stratford-upon-Avon; and Henry VII's Chapel, Westminster
Abbey. Using the images of nude women found on the
misericords of these buildings, I propose to take one
aspect of women as revealed in medieval art, compare it
when possible with written sources and other art media,

and draw some tentative conclusions based on this information.

As expected, the female nude most frequently found
on the misericords and undoubtedly in all medieval art
is Eve. After God created Adam, he was warned by the
Lord not to eat from the Tree of Life which contained
the knowledge of good and evil. The Lord then caused a
nude Adam to fall asleep (Figure 2) and Eve was created
from Adam's rib. God's prohibition not to eat the
forbidden fruit was extended to Eve as well. Eve is
then seen alone with the serpent who convinces her to
eat the apple, and she in turn is shown seducing (Figure
3) her husband to eat of the Tree of Life. The serpent
normally has the head (Figure 4) and torso of a woman
with the tail of a snake that is coiled around the Tree
of Conscience. The serpent is now always shown as a
woman but sometimes as a monster (Figure 5) and at other
times a neuter being.

After the couple ate the fruit, the Lord walked in
the Garden and found Adam and Eve hiding among the
trees. The embarrassment of Adam and Eve is conveyed by
their trying to hide their genitals either with their
hands or with fig leaves. Because of their disobedience, God orders that they be expelled from the Garden
of Eden, and the humiliation the first man and woman
experience is evident in their faces and by their gestures (Figure 6). The Lord cursed Eve to bear children
in intense pain and forced Adam to work for his food in
order to survive. As a consequence, Adam is normally
shown digging the earth with a spade while Eve spins by
distaff (Figure 7). And so banished from the Garden of
Eden forever, the first couple became the parents of all
humankind.[6]

The account of this story is important for our
purposes because the actions of Eve establish a link

between nudity and sexuality. In The City of God, St.
Augustine argued that before the original sin Adam and
Eve, though naked, were not ashamed of their nakedness.
Nor did the first couple experience any lust for one
another because they were created innocent. By their
disobedience, not only did Adam and Eve recognize that
they were naked, but they lost their ability to control
the feelings of lust for one another since their eyes
were now open to the differences between good and evil.
As a consequence, there was no connection between
nudity, sexuality, and evil. Since Eve was the first to
eat the forbidden fruit, she became the means by which
sexual desires and evil were introduced in the world.[7]

In a recent work titled Eve, The History of an Idea,
John Phillips found that early Christian writers using
intertestamental sources, mostly misogynistic in outlook, held that Eve was demonically tainted from the
moment of her creation. She was tempted because she was
weaker than Adam, and she in turn teamed with the serpent and tempted Adam. Phillips said that "in this
interpretation, the eating of the forbidden fruit
becomes a euphemism for sexual congress between Eve and
the snake, or between Eve and her husband; or the eating
of the forbidden fruit imparts to Eve a sexual consciousness that leads her to seduce her husband . . . ,
because she is filled with the power of the Devil."[8]
Since she and the serpent are in league by the time Adam
eats the fruit, the cunning that the snake represents is
really within Eve herself. This is the reason that the
serpent is portrayed in most Christian art as a female
head rather than something else.[9]

The image of the nude Eve and what she came to
represent is also important for our purposes because
nearly all females who are found in medieval art in a

state of full or partial undress are associated with
evil and seduction. This, however, does not always
apply to a woman exposing her breasts, since the nursing
of a baby was a natural act. There are many scenes
where the Virgin Mary offers her breast to the infant
Jesus as well as occasions where ordinary women nurse
their children. The exposure of a breast does not evoke
the feelings of sex in a medieval person as it does in a
person today.10 In the same vein, scenes of naked
women giving birth, although a more private event today
than it was in the Middle Ages, are, nevertheless, free
of the sexual overtones that have been identified with
nudity.

With these exceptions, the female nude in the art of
the Middle Ages must be considered, for those who see
her as a lustful creature, capable of tempting another
to commit base deeds. This lust can be seen most graphi-
cally in a misericord in Worcester Cathedral (Figure 8)
where a woman wearing a see-through net mesh covering is
riding a goat. Under the woman's arm is a rabbit which
is the symbol of fecundity and lust. The goat is a sign
of the damned with reference to the biblical notion of
how Christ, as the shepherd, will separate the sheep
from the goats. As shown, the woman represents Luxuria
or lechery.11

One must be careful, however, and not assume that
all nude riding women represent this vice. In a seat
(Figure 9) at Holy Trinity Church in Stratford-upon-Avon
there is also a naked woman, but this time riding a
stag. The woman holds a branch in her right hand while
her left is outstretched towards a scroll. The figures
are flanked by two trees, and single leaves of foliage
make up the supporters. The stag or hart is normally
symbolic of Christ or regeneration. If this is true in

this scene, then the woman could very well be Eve who
holds a branch from the Tree of Knowledge in her right
hand. The scroll would mean the biblical promise of
salvation by a saviour or the need of Christ's sacrifice
because of the original sin of Eve.12

In St. George's Chapel, Windsor (Figure 10) is a
misericord of a wodehouse or wild woman riding a cloven-
footed, bull-like animal, while a wodehouse horse-riding
man charges towards her. Neither of the couple wear
clothes but their bodies are concealed because of the
hair which covers them from head to foot--assuming they
had feet, of course. The image of the wild person is a
common one found in medieval art recalling the more
primitive, pre-civilized period in European history.13

There are any number of meanings the sculptor might
have had in mind when this work was carved, but the
notion of the wodehouse riding an animal may be related
to the myth of Solinus. According to the legend there
were creatures called Troglodytes who lived in caves and
fed on snakes. They were also known to capture wild
animals by jumping on their backs and riding them.14

Naked persons in the wild can also be seen in a
misericord in Henry VII's Chapel in Westminster Abbey
(Figure 11). There is a seated nude adult woman and man
who are separated by a naked child. On the left side
behind the woman is a child whose back is seen by the
viewer, and on the right are two more naked youths at
play. The background, filled with vines and foliage,
depicts the out-of-doors. One must assume that such a
naturalistic scene of a nude family frolicking in the
woods would have been no more acceptable in medieval
times than it would be today. It is a well-known fact
that most persons in the Middle Ages slept in the nude,
and while it is believed that private nudity was

commonplace, public nudity seems to be unacceptable
given the lack of references made to it in medieval
literature. Even in the celebrated Lady Godiva story,
the understanding people of Coventry hid behind closed
doors to avoid looking at her.[15] Yet as another
misericord (Figure 12) in Henry VII's Chapel in Westminster shows, it would be possible for a couple to be
naked in the comfort of their home. The man on the
right plays a fiddle while his Rubenesque companion
probably played a flute which can no longer be seen
because of the unfortunate mutilation.

An interesting contrast is seen in two well-pre-
served misericords in St. George's Chapel, Windsor. The
first (Figure 13), shows a naked woman sitting on a
sofa, who is reaching across her body with her left hand
and is helping a bald-headed man take off his cloak. By
the expression on his face, it appears that he is
looking forward to getting undressed. Two birds are in
the background: an eagle which in this case means a
bird of prey or the symbol of sinful pride and worldly
concerns rather than its usual meaning of St. John the
Evangelist, and a falcon perched above the left arm of
the man which should be read as a sign of evil thought
or action.[16] The other (Figure 14) is almost a copy
of Figure 13 but this time the naked woman reaches out
with her right hand to grasp the coat of an equally
anxious, but still clothed, man. A modern-looking
wooden fence curves around the back of the couple while
a three-branched tree stands between them. The coiled
plaits of hair on either side of her face which were in
fashion in the last half of the fourteenth century[17]
and the head band worn by the woman are most becoming
and obviously used by the artist to suggest attractiveness. It seems certain that both women are shown as

the aggressors in these sexually charged scenes and that they may well represent prostitutes in medieval society.18

Sexual foreplay, as everyone knows, can lead to sexual intercourse, but such loving scenes between the sexes are not always the case. Women committed violence towards men (Figure 15) and men in turn abused women physically (Figure 16). As a misericord in Holy Trinity Church in Stratford-upon-Avon demonstrates (Figure 17), a naked woman in the right supporter has her leg grasped firmly in the jaws of a dog while a hooded man straddles her head and beats her with a birch. If one looks closely at the hind quarters of the female figure one can see that she is anatomically incorrect. The artist may well have wanted to carve her as a grotesque, however, since it is common to find such a treatment in medieval art.19 The heads of women (Figure 18) with the bodies of beasts are frequently found as subjects for misericord seats. But the most numerous of female nudes, second only to Eve in the art of the Middle Ages, happens to be just such a creature in the form of a mermaid or siren.20

Mermaids come in all shapes and sizes; some have legs and tails and some even have their breasts covered. Some are found with other beasts (Figure 19), and some are shown alone (Figure 20). Some are seen in the company of mermen (Figure 21), and others are under attack by creatures. The attributes most frequently associated with mermaids are their comb and mirror (Figure 22) which are symbols of vanity and the allurement of the flesh.21 Their breasts are usually exposed and a seductive smile graces their faces. From a medieval bestiary, the source from which the carvers of misericords took many of their designs,22 comes the following warning:

There are many marvels in the sea.
The mermaid, for example, is like a girl
In breast and torso, but it is limited to
    that.
From the navel downward she is like no
    human
But wholly a fish, with fins growing from
    her.
This wondrous creature lives in troubled
    regions,
Where the water gurgles,
And ships go down, and thus she works her
    ruin:
This mermaid sings sweetly and has many
    voices,
Varied and charmed.
But they are all evil.
Sailors steering nearby forget their
    course,
Become drowsy and fall asleep,
And awaken only too late.
The ship sinks with a sucking sound,
Nor does it ever come up again.[23]

Is it any wonder then that when a bishop (Figure 23)
exorcises an evil spirit, the demon would come forth
from the genital area of a nude woman? Or when persons
(Figure 24) are driven by long-necked dragons into the
jaws of hell, one of the damned is always seen as a nude
woman? In sum then, what do these images of the female
nude as found in medieval art tell us?

For one thing, women were stereotyped as good and
necessary because they gave birth and were charged with
the nurturement of children. On the other hand, women

were evil because they were believed to be lustful and
seductive by nature. Medieval artists and their patrons
chose to depict this evil side as a nude woman because
of the original sin of the first female nude, Eve.
Rather than accepting a woman as an individual and
judging her on her own merits, women were defined in
terms that regretfully set the norms for future members
of her sex. In the same vein, nudity and sexuality
rather than being seen as natural and wholesome were
regarded as abnormal and wicked. The nude woman then,
as seen in a seat in Holy Trinity Church in Stratford-
upon-Avon (Figure 25), is not allowed to be shown as a
person relaxed and content with her sexuality but as one
who exhibits herself to seduce the viewer. The erect
and protruding nipples, as seen in this misericord, are
a clue that she is a sexually aroused woman. The
enticing manner of her smile says that she knows the
effect of her appearance. It is unfortunate that this
effect was considered unnatural in medieval times
because it set the standard for the way in which nude
women are still viewed in the world in which we live.

Women and men in modern Western society have had to
struggle with the medieval notion that nude women are
corrupters. The female's sexual nature, depicted graphi-
cally in a state of full or partial undress, was seen as
a destructive force. Women who used their bodies, or
were forced to use their bodies, to seduce men were condemned for doing so. The sexual revolution of this century changed many modern persons' ideas about sex, but
the female nude is still seen as unacceptable by both
conservatives and liberals alike. The former attack the
nude body because they believe it is associated with
evil, while the latter censure the display of flesh
because they feel it demeans the female sex. While the

reasons for their contempt differ, both ideologies oppose the exhibition of the female nude. It is ironic that two philosophies so contrasting on many issues are united on this one. The reason that they are in agreement, however, is that both views are a product of the same medieval concept that the female nude is an unnatural and immoral state for a woman.

NOTES

[1] Margaret R. Miles, _Image as Insight, Visual Understanding in Western Christianity and Secular Culture_ (Boston: Beacon Press, 1985), p. 64.

[2] This illustration, and those that follow, were photographed or purchased by the author from the chapels, churches, cathedrals, and museums in England where the misericords can be found. Permission to publish the photographs for instructional purposes was given to the author by the governing bodies concerned. The list of illustrations which follows gives first a short description of the picture, next, in parentheses, the date of the work, followed by its current location, and finally, the place in the choir where the piece can be found. The dating and locations are taken from G. L. Remnant, _A Catalogue of Misericords in Great Britain_ (Oxford: Clarendon Press, 1969).

[3] Dorothy and Henry Kraus, _The Hidden World of Misericords_ (New York: George Braziller, 1975), pp. ix-x.

[4] Remnant, _Catalogue_, p. xvii.

[5] A good treatment of the style and subject matter can be found in J.C.D. Smith, _A Guide to Church Woodcarvings: Misericords and Bench-Ends_ (Newton Abbot, Eng.: David and Charles, 1974).

[6] _Holy Bible_, Genesis 2 and 3.

[7] St. Augustine, "Sexual Lust and Original Sin," as taken from _The City of God_, as printed in _Sexual Love and Western Morality_, ed. by D. V. Verene (New York: Harper Torchbooks, 1972), pp. 100-102.

[8] John A. Phillips, _Eve, The History of an Idea_ (San Francisco: Harper and Row, 1984), pp. 62-64.

[9] Ibid., pp. 57-69.

[10] Vern Bullough and Bonnie Bullough, _Sin, Sickness, and Sanity: A History of Sexual Attitudes_ (New York: New America Library, 1977), p. 177.

[11] George Ferguson, _Signs and Symbols in Christian Art_ (Oxford: Oxford University Press, 1954), pp. 19-20.

[12]Ibid., pp. 25, 180 and Jaun E. Cirlot, A Dictionary of Symbols (New York: Philosophical Library, 1962), p. 294.

[13]Ibid., p. 353; M. D. Anderson, "The Iconography of British Misericords," p. xxxvii; and Ronald Sheridan and Anne Ross, Gargoyles and Grotesques (Boston: New York Graphic Society, 1975), pp. 13-16.

[14]Mary F. White, Fifteenth Century Misericords in the Collegiate Church of Holy Trinity, Stratford-upon-Avon (Stratford-upon-Avon: Bennett, 1974), p. 7.

[15]Bullough, Sin, pp. 181-82.

[16]Ferguson, Signs, pp. 17-18.

[17]Iris Brooke, English Costume of the Later Middle Ages (London: Adam and Charles Black, 1935), pp. 28-29.

[18]See: Vern Bullough and James Brundage, Sexual Practices and the Medieval Church (Buffalo: Prometheus, 1982), for chapters on prostitution.

[19]White, Fifteenth Century, p. 21.

[20]Ernst and Johanna Lehner, A Fantastic Bestiary; Beasts and Monsters in Myth and Folklore (New York: Tudor Pub., 1969), pp. 90-98 and Cirlot, Dictionary, pp. 283-84.

[21]White, Fifteenth Century, p. 6.

[22]Anderson, Iconography, p. xxvi.

[23]Anonymous, A Medieval Bestiary, trans. by T. J. Elliott (Boston: Godine, 1971), n.p.

ILLUSTRATIONS

Figure 1: Fellation by Woman (dated 1520)
           Bristol Cathedral, Gloucestershire
           North side from west, #9, left supporter

Figure 2: Sleeping Adam (14th Century)
           Victoria and Albert Museum, London
           From East Anglian collection

Figure 3: Temptation of Adam and Eve (1340-41)
           Ely Cathedral, Cambridgeshire
           North side from west, #20, upper

Figure 4: Woman as Serpent (1520)
           Bristol Cathedral, Gloucestershire
           North side from west, #12

Figure 5: Monster as Serpent (late 14th century)
           Worcester Cathedral, Worcestershire
           North side from east, #1

Figure 6: Expulsion of Adam and Eve (1340-41)
           Ely Cathedral, Cambridgeshire
           North side from west, #5, lower

Figure 7: Eve Spins while Adam Spades (15th century)
           Victoria and Albert Museum, London
           From English collection

Figure 8: Nude Woman Rides Goat (late 14th century)
           Worcester Cathedral, Worcestershire
           North side from east, #15

Figure 9: Nude Woman Rides Stag (late 15th century)
           Holy Trinity Church, Stratford-upon-Avon
           North side, #4

Figure 10: Wodehouse Couple Tilting (1477 to 1483)
           St. George's Chapel, Windsor
           South side, #16, upper

Figure 11: Nude Family (16th century)
           Henry VII's Chapel, Westminster Abbey
           South upper range, Return stall

Figure 12: Nude Couple (16th century)
           Henry VII's Chapel, Westminster Abbey
           North side from east, #5, upper third bay

180

Figure 13: Nude Woman on Sofa (1477 to 1483)
St. George's Chapel, Windsor
South side, #14, upper

Figure 14: Nude Female Prostitute (1477 to 1483)
St. George's Chapel, Windsor
North side, #3, upper

Figure 15: Woman Throwing Bowl at Man (1520)
Bristol Cathedral, Gloucestershire
South side from west, #11

Figure 16: Man Seizes Woman's Hair (late 15th century)
Holy Trinity Church, Stratford-upon-Avon
South side, #12, left supporter

Figure 17: Nude Woman under Attack (late 15th century)
Holy Trinity Church, Stratford-upon-Avon
South side, #12, right supporter

Figure 18: Winged Monster with Head of Nun (late 15th century)
Holy Trinity Church, Stratford-upon-Avon
South side, #1, right supporter

Figure 19: Mermaid with Beasts (1520)
Bristol Cathedral, Gloucestershire
North side from west, #11

Figure 20: Single Mermaid (1442)
All Souls College Chapel, Oxford
North side from west, #20,

Figure 21: Mermaid with Comb and Merman (late 15th century)
Holy Trinity Church, Stratford-upon-Avon
North side, #3

Figure 22: Mermaid with Mirror (1477 to 1483)
St. George's Chapel, Windsor
North side, #2, upper

Figure 23: Bishop Exorcises Female Nude (1340-41)
Ely Cathedral, Cambridgeshire
South side from west, #1, lower, right supporter

Figure 24: Nudes Driven by Dragon (1520)
Bristol Cathedral, Gloucestershire
South side from west, #7

Figure 25: Demi-Figure of Nude Woman (late 15th
century)
Holy Trinity Church, Stratford-upon-Avon
South side, #7

Figure 1: Fellation by Woman (dated 1520)
Bristol Cathedral, Gloucestershire
North side from west, #9, left supporter

Figure 2: Sleeping Adam (Fourteenth Century)
Victoria and Albert Museum, London
From East Anglian collection

Figure 3: Temptation of Adam and Eve (1340-41)
Ely Cathedral, Cambridgeshire
North side from west, #20, upper

Figure 4: Woman as Serpent (1520)
Bristol Cathedral, Gloucestershire
North side from west, #12

Figure 5: Monster as Serpent
(late Fourteenth Century)
Worcester Cathedral, Worcestershire
North side from east, #1

Figure 6: Expulsion of Adam and Eve (1340-41)
Ely Cathedral, Cambridgeshire
North side from west, #5, lower

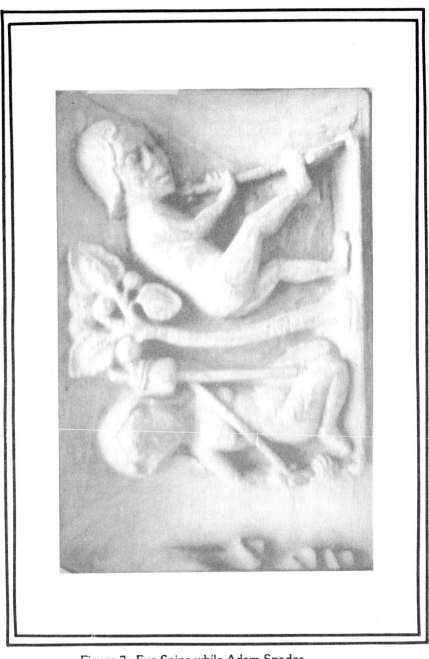

Figure 7: Eve Spins while Adam Spades
(Fifteenth Century)
Victoria and Albert Museum, London
From English collection

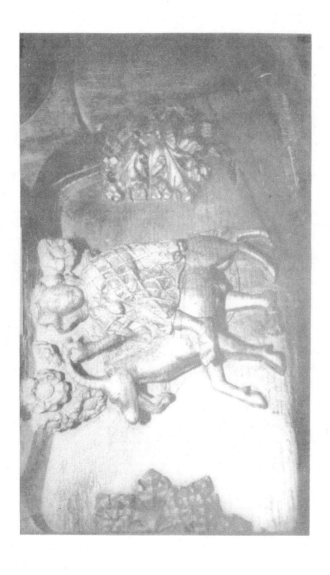

Figure 8: Nude Woman rides Goat
            (late Fourteenth Century)
            Worcester Cathedral, Worcestershire
            North side from east, #15

Figure 9: Nude Woman rides Stag
(late Fifteenth Century)
Holy Trinity Church, Stratford-upon-Avon
North side, #4

Figure 10: Wodehouse Couple Tilting (1477 to1483)
St. George's Chapel, Windsor
South side, # 16, upper

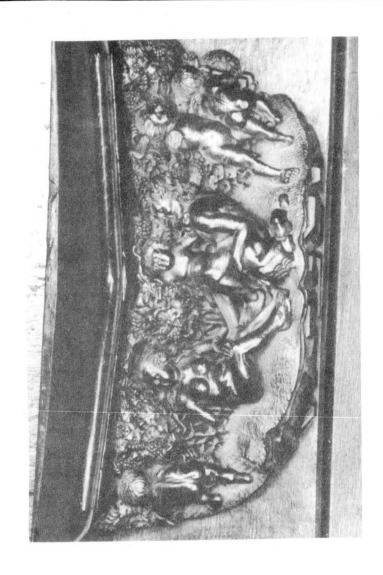

Figure 11: Nude Family (Sixteenth Century)
Henry VII's Chapel, Westminster Abbey
South upper range, Return stall

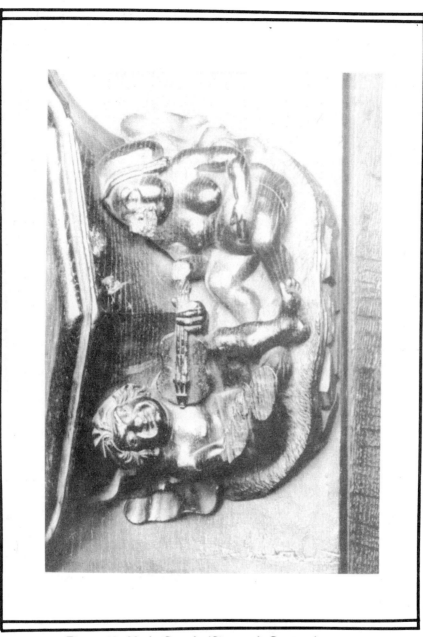

Figure 12: Nude Couple (Sixteenth Century)
Henry VII's Chapel, Westminster Abbey
North side from east, #5, upper 3rd bay

Figure 13: Nude Woman on Sofa (1477 to 1483)
St. George's Chapel, Windsor
South side, #14, upper

Figure 14: Nude Female Prostitute (1477 to 1483)
St. George's Chapel, Windsor
North side, #3, upper

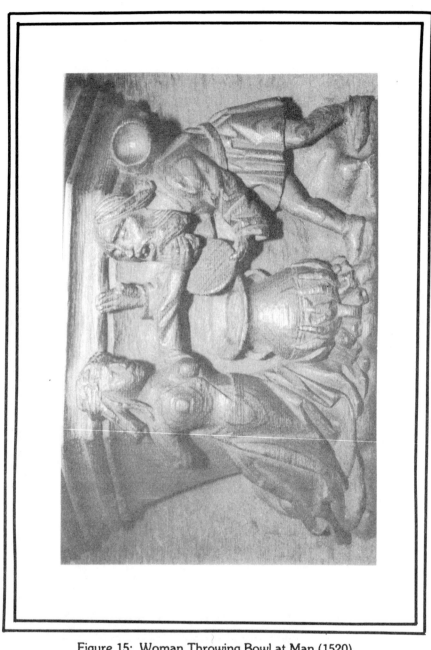

Figure 15: Woman Throwing Bowl at Man (1520)
Bristol Cathedral, Gloucestershire
South side from west, #11

Figure 16: Man Seizes Woman's Hair (late Fifteenth Century)
Holy Trinity Church, Stratford-upon-Avon
South side, #12, left supporter

Figure 17: Nude Woman Under Attack (late Fifteenth Century)
Holy Trinity Church, Stratford-upon-Avon
South side, #12, right supporter

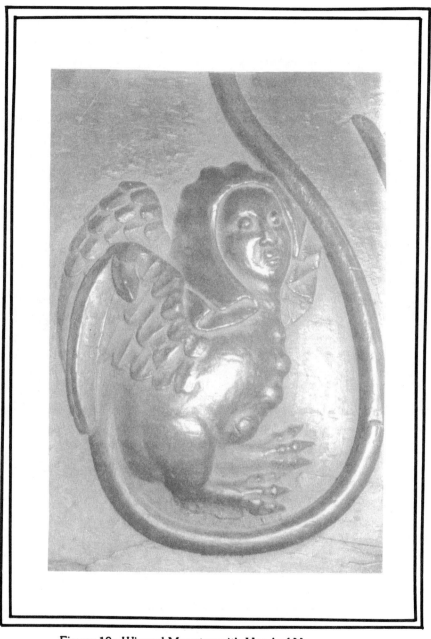

Figure 18: Winged Monster with Head of Nun
(late Fifteenth Century)
Holy Trinity Church, Stratford-upon-Avon
South side, #1, right supporter

Figure 19: Mermaid with Beasts (1520)
Bristol Cathedral, Gloucestershire
North side from west, #11

Figure 20: Single Mermaid (1442)
All Souls College Chapel, Oxford
North side from west, #20

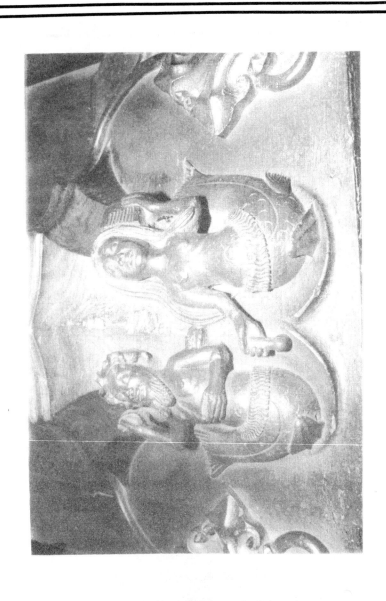

Figure 21: Mermaid with Comb and Merman (late Fifteenth Century)
Holy Trinity Church, Stratford-upon-Avon
North side, #3

Figure 22: Mermaid with Mirror (1477 to 1483)
St. George's Chapel, Windsor
North side, #2, upper

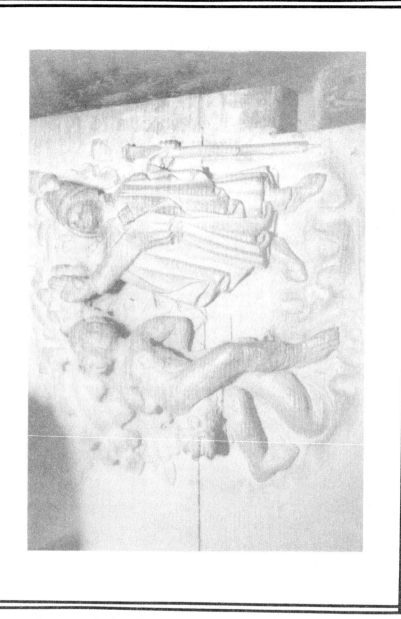

Figure 23: Bishop Exorcises Female Nude (1340-41)
Ely Cathedral, Cambridgeshire
South side from west, #1, lower, right supporter

Figure 24: Nudes Driven by Dragon (1520)
Bristol Cathedral, Gloucestershire
South side from west, #7

Figrue 25: Demi-Figure of Nude Woman (late Fifteenth Century)
Holy Trinity Church, Stratford-upon-Avon
South side, #7

ISRAHEL VAN MECKENEM'S
MARRIAGE A LA MODE: THE ALLTAGSLEBEN

by Diane G. Scillia

Around 1495, Israhel van Meckenem executed the so-
called _Alltagsleben_ or scenes of everyday life (Figures
1-12).1 This series of twelve engravings shows six
couples standing before simple landscapes and six
couples sitting in comfortable interiors. Close study
reveals that they are not just pictures of daily life.
For one thing, the absence of children is striking.
Moreover, the figures are posed--some formally, others
informally--and several can be traced back to earlier
representations. Clearly the _Alltagsleben_ deal with
love and marriage.

Love and marriage were important themes in art and
literature of the fifteenth century. Marriage was one
of the Church's Seven Sacraments and it was the way most
people chose to live. What is unique about the _Alltags-
leben_ engravings is their secular outlook; there is no
overt christological content in these images. Marriage
is not treated as a sacrament of the Church, but as a
virtuous way of life, and licentiousness is treated as
folly. Notice, however, that virtuousness does not mean
solemnity and that folly is not equated with death.
Meckenem used the comic mode to underscore both virtue
and lechery.2

Israhel van Meckenem was primarily a goldsmith, active in the Lower Rhineland.[3] His earliest prints were made ca. 1465, and he continued to augment his income from goblets and jewelry by producing several new engravings each year until his death in 1503.[4] He was the most prolific engraver of the fifteenth century. Many of his secular scenes copy works by other artists, but the Alltagsleben are among his most original inventions (compositionally and thematically), together with the famous Double Portrait of the Artist and His Wife, Ida (Figure 13) and The Dance at Herod's Court.[5] In these works, he examined the sexual relationships between man and woman, although in The Dance at Herod's Court, he used this theme in a hagiographical context emphasizing more traditional misogynous interpretations of female sexuality. The Alltagsleben prints and the Double Portrait of the Artist and His Wife, Ida—which is both the earliest self-portrait as well as the earliest engraved double portrait of real people—differ in focus and intention. As we shall see, Meckenem's Alltagsleben engravings give us insight into the changing ideas on marriage and its role in society around 1500.

The Alltagsleben series are humorous. Many of the couples depicted in these engravings are also found in the vernacular literature and drama of the period.[6] Meckenem addressed his message to the urban middle classes, who would have known these types and could afford his prints. He did more than just document the popularity of these late medieval comic types. Meckenem also, consciously or not, built upon a classical tradition linking comedy with the institution of marriage.[7]

Then, as now, humor depended upon the juxtaposition of incongruous elements set within a common experi-

ence.[8] In the Alltagsleben prints, Meckenem's primary
incongruity is that of the sexes: male and female,
while his second incongruity is that of social class and
position. He included clues to the social standings of
his lovers, even when he used otherwise stock figures,
and he placed his couples squarely in his own world.
His third incongruity comes from the opposition of
specific types of lovers. In the first six couples, he
contrasted two sets of mismatched lovers (Figures 1-2),
The Monk and Nun and The Lord and His Fiancee—who are
also opposite pairs (Figures 3-4)—and The Knight and
His Lady and The Henpecked Husband—again, direct opposites (Figures 5-6). In the second (Figures 7-12), he
opposed decorous married lovers with couples of far less
respectability. The older happy and unhappy lovers of
medieval literature, found among the first six, in turn,
oppose the more modern licit and illicit lovers of the
second.

The six happy and unhappy lovers (Figures 1-6) are
emblematic, and even the simple landscapes and flut-
tering scrolls stress their conventionality. Because of
this, we need not spend too much time examining all the
literary references; nevertheless, seeing how the members of this subset function is primary to understanding
all twelve of the engravings.

The two pairs of mismatched lovers are direct com-
plements: The Older Man and His Young Bride (Figure 1)
and The Older Woman and Her Foolish Young Man (Figure
2).[9] In the first, the older man is a prosperous
burgher, and his young bride is well fed (with still a
hint of late adolescent plumpness about her figure) and
well dressed and pleased with herself.[10] In the
second, the older woman has just wed a young scallywag
whose youth contrasts with her maturity.[11] His

unlaced shoes and insouciant pose tell us that he is a
very callow youth.[12] If things run their hoped-for
course, the young bride will inherit her husband's shops
at his death and remarry, perhaps another older man.[13]
The young husband will reap the rewards of his marriage,
the prospering shops his old wife inherited from her
former husbands, if he does not squander them first (and
just look where his purse is!).[14] After her death, he
would inherit these shops outright and be free to marry
a sweet young thing.

Both kinds of mismatched couples were common in the
fifteenth century.[15] Their venal nature is indicated
by their outward appearance. We cannot miss the self-
satisfied smile of the young bride or her slightly out-
of-date gown and the moonstruck gaze of her old husband
as well as the visual metaphor of his sword handle.[16]
The silly posture of the youth and his old wife's look
of suffering tell us that they are to be pitied: his
greed and her lust (older women were considered lust
personified) have led them to their present state.[17]
The old man is happy with his young bride, as she is
with his money, but the older wife finds little comfort
and no satisfaction with her young man.[18]

The lovelorn **Monk and Nun** (Figure 3), who can resist
the longings of the flesh no better than the little dog
can resist scratching a flea bite, are also unhappy
lovers. Their soulful and lustful glances as well as
the way he holds his book bag are designed to make us
laugh out loud. Couples like this one, members of the
clergy or religious orders who have failed to live up to
their vows of chastity and celibacy, appear throughout
fabliaux and farces popular in France, Italy, and
Germany in Boccaccio's and in Chaucer's tales.[19]
Celibacy is hardly held up as an ideal!

The Lord and His Fiancée (Figure 4) is the
countering image to The Monk and Nun. This pair is
newly engaged or have just pledged their troth, as they
stand before us in their youth and handsomeness. Even
their poses and headdresses echo the engagement portraits of the fifteenth century.[20] Their courtly
elegance contrasts with the bourgeois practicality of
the three others already considered. They are the
reciprocal image to The Monk and Nun, for this young
couple is free to pledge their love. The hooded falcon,
still tied to his owner's wrist by jesses, illustrates
their sexual restraint and is yet another contrast to
The Monk and Nun.[21] This couple and The Knight and
His Lady (Figure 5) follow chivalric traditions missing
in the other couples. Curiously, Meckenem legitimizes
his two sets of courtly lovers.[22]

In The Knight and His Lady we see a pair of newly-
weds. She wears a chatelain hanging from her girdle and
shyly points to it.[23] It symbolizes her new role as
mistress of the house. Her proud husband turns as if to
introduce her, his beautiful bashful bride. Their
poses, more informal than that of the engaged pair, also
recall the Arnolfini couple in Jan van Eyck's double
portrait of 1434, even though the knight and his lady
have nothing sacramental in their stances and surroundings.[24] Meckenem's fashionably dressed knight
and his lady belong to the wealthy upper-middle class,
and their main purpose in this subset is to balance the
henpecked husband and his shrewish wife (Figure 6),
their exact opposites, socially, physically, and psychologically.

Where The Knight and His Lady represent the ideal,
the man as head of the family with his wife, an equal,
if submissive partner, The Henpecked Husband is a

burlesque of that ideal.[25] A harridan abusing her
spouse still figures in our own popular entertainments.[26] The humor in this scene is in the reversal
of roles; it was a husband's prerogative to beat an
unruly wife.[27] Here, however, is a clear case of
"husband abuse," and his spouse has usurped the male
role. Even the little pooch reacts to her anger: the
dog, together with the monster, signal to the fifteenth-
century viewer that things are not as they should
be.[28] Here the monster completely replaces the blank
winding scroll seen behind the other lovers of the first
six scenes and probably also symbolizes anger.[29]
These people are workers. She beats him with her
distaff (the symbol of Eve, the first woman) and she
treads upon his foot, adding injuries to her
insults.[30] The garment in the foreground is a
breechcloth.[31] In the late fifteenth century many
women wore no closed undergarments.[32] Thus, this is a
battle over who will wear the pants in the family.

In the second set of six scenes (Figures 7-12),
Meckenem omitted the archaic scrolls and presented his
prosperous townspeople in contemporary interiors. Where
he pictured his fellow citizens in the guises of the
traditional courting and married or unmarried lovers in
the first set, now they are the new lovers of his own
day: the wise licit and foolish illicit lovers, that
is, married or engaged couples as opposed to couples of
convenience, prostitutes and their clients.[33] Each
pair comfortably sits singing or playing musical instruments or conversing or playing a game of cards. There
are few pictorial prototypes for these scenes.[34]
Meckenem's second set are not only among the earliest
pictures of married couples, they are also among the
earliest scenes of amorous folly associated with

brothels and taverns very popular later in the sixteenth century.

If we find few examples for Meckenem's second set, we can trace several of his sources, paramount among these The Lovers by the Master of the Housebook (Figure 14).[35] The young man losing at cards in The Card Players (Figure 7) wears the same hat as the youth in The Lovers. Meckenem also included the cooling basic complete with carafe of wine and tumbler that the Housebook Master had set out for his lovers.[36] The Card Players has a different meaning than the Housebook Master's image. Where in the earlier print, a young couple shares a quiet interlude, in The Card Players, a female of questionable virtue gets the better of her companion.[37] This is the reversal of the norm! In spite of the hanging basin and towel, the interior looks like a tavern.[38] There is a sense of exploitation here: the man raises his right arm as if to protect himself from her aggressiveness, just as the henpecked husband did (Figure 6).[39] This image, like that of The Henpecked Husband, echoes the "power of women" theme so popular in the fifteenth and sixteenth centuries.[40]

In The Couple Sitting on a Bed (Figure 8), Meckenem again based his own figures upon those in the Housebook Master's The Lovers. The resemblance becomes clearer when we look at Meckenem's own version, in reverse, of the Housebook Master's print (Figure 15).[41] The man's profile, the tilt of the woman's head, the position of his left arm and the placement of the fingers of his left hand are copied directly from the Housebook Master. This scene is also close in spirit to that of the original, although the couple depicted is a married pair.

Nothing could be farther in mood from The Card
Players. Domestic tranquility reigns in The Couple
Sitting on a Bed. We read the essentials of their relationship, not only in their choice of seat and attitude
towards one another, but also in the details of their
home and dress. This is a married pair. The tender
concern of each for the other seen in the Housebook
Master's lovers has been transferred to the husband and
his wife. He has taken off his sword and has laid it
aside, momentarily, and she seems to be with child.42
Who else, but a married pair would leave their slippers
and chamber pot beneath the bed where we can see them?
The Card Players and The Couple Sitting on a Bed, therefore, reflect the same play of opposites as in the first
set of six lovers.

In The Organ Player and His Wife (Figure 9), the man
strokes the keyboard while his spouse pumps the bel-
lows.43 He cannot produce a note without her help and
her work is futile without his playing. They work
together and they make music together, and obviously,
their music-making is a metaphor for other activi-
ties.44 Around them are the trappings of domestic
bliss, including their well-upholstered marriage
bed.45 The loyal Fido signifies fidelity and, as in
the Arnolfini double portrait, Fido is unleashed. He
may symbolize the freedom from lechery enjoyed by well-
married couples.46 Thus, these faithful help mates
work together and achieve physical harmony.47 In all,
this is a picture of the benefits of marriage, and the
pair is often called Israhel van Meckenem and his wife,
Ida.48

Countering The Organ Player and His Wife is The
Harpist and the Lute Player (Figure 10), in which two
attractive young people each play their own instru-

ment.[49] This setting is devoid of personal possessions. It looks like an inn or tavern, compared with
the cozy domesticity of The Couple Sitting on a Bed and
The Organ Player and His Wife. The box in the foreground, in front of the harpist, may be a case for her
instrument or a foot warmer.[50] The open lute case in
front of the young man is a visual pun based upon one of
the erotic meanings traditionally given that instrument.[51] There is a note of detachment in the postures
and attitudes of the two figures. Each seems preoccu-
pied with his own activity.

This pair comes from popular imagery. A similar
couple playing a harp and a lute represent the phlegmatic lovers in the Strasbourg Calendar of ca. 1500.
They belong to a set illustrating the four humors.[52]
The phlegmatic temperament is dull, slow to respond to
stimuli. It can be aroused, however, by music.[53] In
Meckenem's engraving the two figures are strumming up
their own passions—the support for his lute tells us
his physical state—but without touching upon the true
meaning of cooperation, companionship, or partnership.

In The Singer and the Lute Player (Figure 11), the
same young man as in The Harpist and the Lute Player has
stopped playing his instrument to lean forward and
listen to his partner's song. She, not the same young
woman as that playing the harp, sings the notes cau-
tiously, carefully following the music book. Yet, it is
a duet, as it is sometimes called, for both individuals
work together towards one goal.[54] The interior shown
has those touches, cushions and other decorative
details, that were lacking in The Harpist and the Lute
Player. The mirror, for example, resembles that in The
Organ Player and His Wife, as does the dog.[55] Here,
the animal is leashed, signifying that this man and this
woman are in control of their passions.[56]

The Gentleman and the Spinner (Figure 12), yet
another couple of questionable virtue, is the contrasting image. This scene is also called The Visit to
the Spinner.[57] The man has just arrived and still
wears his hat, cloak, and boots. He sits rather
stiffly, fondling the handle of his sword--again, this
is a visual pun.[58] She, more lightly dressed, sits
spinning. The differences in dress are significant and
illustrate the estrangement of the two and the business-
like nature of their relationship. In each of the other
scenes, the man and woman were dressed for the same
conditions, whether indoors or out.[59] This is also
the only scene in which he is of a different social
class than she. They are not a married pair.

Meckenem evidently drew his inspiration for this
scene from the meanings associated with the distaff. It
can be an attribute of the virtuous wife and mother, but
it may also mean any number of less favorable
things.[60] Meckenem had already referred to some of
these negative meanings in his The Henpecked Husband
(Figure 6). Here, there is an additional pejorative
implication touching upon both witchcraft and the "power
of women." Witches were the ultimate femmes fatales,
known for their sexual license as well as for their
abilities to cast spells over men.[61] Through a triple
association (distaff=woman=Eve-witch) the distaff came
to symbolize female sexuality in general.[62] Moreover,
the spinner herself is likened to another female who
ensnares, the female spider.[63]

Our spinner, like the card player and the harpist,
has enticed her companion through his own weakness,
leading him to lechery and lust. These young women and
their clients form the illicit lovers of the six
scenes. Our spinner entertains her visitor at home,

with or without the knowledge of her own mate. The
ostentatious display of tankards and tumblers atop the
fancy chest has no counterparts in the other interiors
shown and refers to her pecuniary zeal.[64] She even
lets him cool his heals while she finishes spinning.[65] The cat's presence may illustrate one of the
proverbs based upon the animal's sensual nature. Two
from the _Proverbia Communis_ of 1495 will suffice. The
first may explain his presence: "Where the cat is
stroked, it likes to be."[66] The second, "All cats are
grey in the dark," may comment upon her.[67]

The scenes making up the _Alltagsleben_ were chosen
carefully. The various "common leisure activities"
depicted are not as innocent as they may appear at
first. Limited to visual imagery, Meckenem had to rely
upon well-known literary types, proverbs, and popular
erotic symbols to carry his meaning. It is remarkable
that all of the scrolls in the first set are blank. The
inscriptions around the mirror frames in two scenes are
simply variations on the letters in Meckenem's monogram,
which may indicate a more personal identification with
these couples, since he also signed each of the twelve
plates.

Nowhere in these twelve engravings is there any
indication that marriage came under control of the
Church. This aspect departs from most of the handbooks
on marriage written and printed in the late fifteenth
century. With one exception, these books were the work
of jurists, clerics, and theologians.[68] Meckenem was
a layman and he was married. The canonical impediments
to marriage, the debate whether a scholar should marry,
and the theological investives on the fickleness of
women, did not interest him. Marriage was a fact of his
life. Ida was his wife and probably also his business
partner, as was usual with artisan families.

In the Alltagsleben, Meckenem depicts marriage as an
institution with its roots in the world at large.
Hence, folly is a human failing, but not a sin in the
theological definition of sin.[69] The punishments for
Meckenem's lecherous couples are their extreme discom-
forts here on earth: their present physical pain or
emotional distance from each other, or their mutual
material and physical exploitation.[70] In contrast,
the married lovers and the wise and happy couples quite
literally find their heaven on earth in their marriage
bonds and vows.[71] Virtue (i.e., self-denial, moderation, and self-control) is its own reward, spiritually,
physically, and materially.

In part, this message stems from Church teachings
and, as such, is stated in an ironical way in Chaucer's
Merchant's Tale, but Meckenem departed from both Church
tradition and from Chaucer's irony.[72] Wise men and
women marry and marry well; fools do not. There is
nothing ironical about Meckenem's scenes (except, perhaps, for The Monk and Nun); his criticism is leveled
at the foolish unhappy and illicit lovers. Sexual intercourse outside of marriage is folly because it wastes
time, money, and threatens one's security, both now and
eternally. A good marriage is both virtuous and cost-
effective: two generous, loyal, and loving spouses
living together and working together are indeed companions and help mates. This is a very middle-class,
nay burgherlijk, point of view, for marriage insures the
continuity of a family line (and a family's wealth) as
well as a livelihood. It brings both children and prosperity. Although Meckenem only implied the eventuality
of children in two of the scenes (Figures 8 and 9), he
emphasized the material comforts and benefits of a good
marriage in his well-mated couples.[73]

The later German reformers, townsmen themselves and
allies with other burghers in their reconstruction of
German society after the religious, social, and political upheavals of the 1520's and 1530's, took a similar
position around 1550.74 These reformers, basing their
theological arguments on careful study of texts from the
Old and New Testaments, held that marriage was the best
estate for man. They supported marriage as a cure for
lechery or concupiscense and as a "holy estate in which
God's service could best be done," thus exalting marriage over celibacy.75 Steven Ozment holds that the
new marriage laws worked out by these reformers "became
the most emphatic statement on the ideal of sharing,
companionable marriage."76 Self-control, sharing, and
companionship are precisely what Meckenem stressed in
his wise married and engaged couples of the Alltagsleben.

What is missing in Meckenem's engravings is the note
of paternalism, especially the misogyny, implicit in the
later reformers' Biblical interpretations of mar-
riage.77 A misogynous interpretation can be made of
some of the Alltagsleben scenes--The Older Woman and Her
Foolish Young Man, The Card Player, and The Gentleman
and the Spinner--but in these cases it is coupled with
male lechery and greed, and both members deserve whatever they get. The sole exception is The Henpecked
Husband, in which we see no redeeming moral lesson. In
his wise and happy married pairs (as in his foolish
unhappy couples) Meckenem showed both the man and woman
jointly sharing the responsibility for living virtuously
and avoiding lust. This is a balanced outlook for the
fifteenth century and is yet another unprecedented facet
of the Alltagsleben.

I cannot help but believe that Meckenem's careful
tone in these engravings was influenced by his own
experience. His _Double Portrait with His Wife, Ida_
(Figure 13), shows them as equals, precisely as he had
pictured the well-mated, virtuous pairs in the _Alltags-
leben_.[78] These couples, by living together, working
together, and loving together, found their paradise at
their own hearths.

NOTES

[1] Walter Strauss (editor), The Illustrated Bartsch, 9,
Early German Artists (New York: Abaris Books, Inc.,
1981), no. 171 (267) - 179 (270), 182 (272) - 183 (272),
and Appendix 114 (302). Fitzroy Carrington, "'After a
Lost Original,' Twelve Scenes from Daily Life Engraved
by Israhel van Meckenem," The Print Collector's
Quarterly, 27 (1940), 320-36, discusses the entire
series. Alan Shestack, Fifteenth Century Engravings of
Northern Europe from the National Gallery of Art
(Washington, DC: The National Gallery of Art, 1967),
nos. 233-43, omits only The Card Players. This is the
first study since Carrington's to deal with all twelve
thematically.

[2] Compare, Derek Brewer, "Afterword: Notes Towards a
Theory of Medieval Comedy," in Medieval Comic Tales,
Translated by Peter Rickard, Alan Deyermond, Derek
Brewer, David Blamaires, Peter King and Michael Lapridge
(Totowa, NJ: Rowman and Littlefield, 1973), 141-45,
especially 142-43 and 144-45.

[3] Shestack, Engravings of Northern Europe, nos. 152-54,
cites relevant bibliography. Also, see James E. Snyder,
Northern Renaissance Art (New York and Englewood Cliffs,
NJ: Prentice-Hall, Inc., 1985), 289-92.

[4] Kleves Städtisches Museum Hauskoekoek, Klevisches
Silber, 15. - 19. Jahrhundert, 10 Dezember, 1978 - 28
Januar, 1979, 7-9, and catalogue numbers 3, 4, 7, 15,
and 18.

[5] For these, see Strauss, The Illustrated Bartsch, 1
(202) and 9 (206); and Shestack, Engravings of Northern
Europe, nos. 232 and 255.

[6] See Medieval Comic Tales, passim, but especially
7-10, 16-17, 79-89,. and 128.

[7] Ernst Robert Curtius, European Literature and the
Latin Middle Ages (New York: Harper and Row, Publishers, Inc., 1963), 386n, 435n, and 437. Also see
Henry Ansgar Kelly, Love and Marriage in the Age of
Chaucer (Ithaca: Cornell University Press, 1975),
71-100. Meckenem is not a humanist. His inspiration for
these engravings stem from the literary traditions of
the late Middle Ages, for which, see Brewer, "Afterword," 146-49, and those derived, however indirectly,
from Ovid.

[8]Brewer, "Afterword," 141-43.

[9]Alison G. Stewart, Unequal Lovers: A Study of Unequal Couples in Northern Art (New York: Abaris Books, Inc., 1977), passim.

[10]Stewart, 82-9, especially 86.

[11]Stewart, 59, 77, 93, and 104. Also, see Emerson Brown, Jr., "Biblical Women in the Merchant's Tale: Feminism, Anti-feminism, and Beyond," Viator: Medieval and Renaissance Studies, 5 (1974), 387-412; and William Matthews, "The Wife of Bath and All Her Sect," Viator: Medieval and Renaissance Studies, 5 (1974), 413-43, who cite earlier bibliography on important questions such as "when did old age begin in the middle ages?"

[12]Richard Jente, Proverbia Communis: A Fifteenth Century Collection of Dutch Proverbs Together with the Low German Version. Edited with Commentary by Richard Jente (Bloomington, IN: Indiana University Publications, Folklore Series, no. 4, 1947), no. 444: Hi danset als op enen foet ("he is dancing on one foot," i.e., he is a fool). Both editions edited by Jente were published in 1495. Also, see Hoffman von Fallersleben, Die Aelteste Niederdeutsche Sprichwörtersammlung von Antonius Tunnicius (Berlin: Robert Oppenheim, 1870),no. 589: He danset al up einem beine. Tunnicius was schooled at Deventer, around 1480, and returned to his native Münster, ca. 1500. His collection was first printed ca. 1515.

[13]There are parallels with another well-known much younger bride, Alison of Bath. Also, see Clair C. Olson, "The Interludes of the Marriage Group in the Canterbury Tales," in Chaucer and Middle English Studies in Honor of Rossell Hope Robbins (Kent, OH: The Kent State University Press, 164-72).

[14]See Friedrich Zarncke, Sebastian Brants Narrenschiff (Hildesheim: Georg Olms, 1961), no. 52, 54:

> Wer schlüfft jnn esel, umb das schmår
> Der ist vernunfft, und wifzheyt Iår
> Das er eyn alt wib nymbt zůr ee
> Eyn gůtten tag, und keynen me
> Er hatt ouch weing freůd dar von
> keyn frücht mag im dar ufz entston
> Und hatt ouch nyemer gůtten tagk
> Dann so er sicht den pfening sagk.
> Der gatt jm ouch dick umb die oren

Durch den er worden ist zům doren
Dar viz entspringt ouch offt und dick
Das dar zů schlecht gar wenig glůck.

(Compare, Sebastian Brant, The Ship of Fools, Translated
into Rhyming Couplets with Introduction and Commentary
by Edwin H. Zeydel [New York: Dover Publications, Inc.,
1961], no. 52, 182-83:

Who flays a donkey for its fat
He has no brains beneath his hat
Who weds an old wife just for gain
Makes one grand splurge, then ne'er again,
And he has very little joy,
No children, either girl or boy,
And happy, carefree days he lacks
Save when he sees the money sacks.
The money bag is often stressed
That's made of him a fool at best,
And by this truth I'm often struck
That such a marriage brings ill luck.

[15]By the later middle ages, it was common practice for
a young journeyman to marry his master's daughter or
widow simply so he could work at his trade. The regu-
lations of the local guilds were then so restrictive,
due to the number of artisans already working, that no
new workshops could be opened. The widow inherited her
husband's shop and guild membership and could bestow
these upon her new husband. See Frances and Joseph
Gies, Women in the Middle Ages (New York: Barnes and
Noble Books, Inc., 1978), 178-80; and David Herlihy,
Medieval Households (Cambridge, MA: Harvard University
Press, 1985), 135-38.

[16]Stewart, 82-89; and Lucy Freeman Sandler, "A Bawdy
Betrothal in the Ormesby Psalter," Tribute to Lotte
Brand Philip: Detective and Art Historian (New York:
Abaris Books, Inc., 1985), 154-59.

[17]Brants Narrenschiff, no. 52. Also, see above, n.
11; and Stewart, 67 and 128, n. 106.

[18]Kelly, 247 and 265-66, on the "double standard"
applied to these May/December marriages. Also, see
Stewart, 34. Compare the example of Chaucer's Merchant's Tale and similar tales based upon the same theme
in Medieval Comic Tales, x-xi. Here (Figure 1), even
the plant growing behind the young bride may refer to

her husband's age. The plantain "is good also against evil customs of man's stones (i.e., cures impotence)," see The book of Secrets of Albertus Magnus of the Virtues of Herbs, Stones and Certain Beasts also a Book of the Marvels of the World. Edited by Michael R. Best and Frank H. Brightman (Oxford: Oxford University Press, 1975), 20.

[19]Lecherous monks and nuns figure prominently in Boccaccio's Decameron. Dirk Bax (Hieronymus Bosch: His Picture-Writing Deciphered, translated by M. A. Bax-Botha, Rotterdam: A. A. Balkema, 1979, 252) cites a fifteenth-century proverb: erm broerkens soeken erm susterluytkens which relies upon the image of such licentious members of the clergy. In Meckenem's engraving (Figure 3), the little dog, unrestrained in his enjoyment as he satisfies his itch, sums up the "natural" means by which this pair relieves their itch. The Proverbia Communis, no. 625: Ten sijn niet alle papen die cruyne draghen ("all are not priests who wear the tonsure"), and no. 792: Zy en sign niet alle hey-lich die gheerne ter kerken gaen ("all are not saints that go to church"), seem to illustrate that such couples were not uncommon, ca. 1495. Tunnicius gives a variant of no. 792 in Se sint nicht al hillich de hillich schyner (see von Fallersleben, no. 1144). Also, see Curtius, 434, who cites passages from works dating from the eleventh and twelfth centuries suggesting the origins of this theme.

[20]Compare the costumes and poses of this couple with those in the panel by an Anonymous Southern German Master, see The Cleveland Museum of Art: Paintings before 1500 (Cleveland: The Cleveland Museum of Art, 1974), 35, no. 12; with the couples painted and engraved by the Master of the Housebook, see Jan P. Filedt-Kok (Compilor), Livelier than Life: The Master of the Amsterdam Cabinet or the Housebook Master, ca. 1475-1500 (Amsterdam: Rijksprentenkabinet/Rijksmuseum in Amsterdam, in Association with Gary Schwartz in Maarssen, 1985), 150, no. 55; 236, no. 133; by the Master b x g (Livelier than Life, 204, no. 105); and by Israhel van Meckenem in reverse (Livelier than Life, no. 55b).

[21]For the meanings given to both the falcon and the blossom, see Een Abel Spel van Lanseloet van Denemerken, Klassiek Galerij, nummer 123 (uitgegeven door Dr. Rob Roemans en Dra. Hilda van Assche, Antwerp: Uitgeverij de Nederlandsche Boekhandels, 1982, 121-22):

O Sanderijn, ghi waert die gheerde,
Die scone met haren bloemen stoet,
Ende ic die valke, dies benic vroet,
Die ene bloeme daer af nam,
Want mi nie sint vroude en bequam,
Dat ic die edele gheerde verloes,
Soe hebbic ghequolen altoes,
Uut vercoren vrouwe mijn.
Alle vroude es mi nu een pijn
Die ic op der eerden mach bescouwen . . .

("Oh, Sanerlijn, you were the bough, so lovely in all
its blossoms, and I was the falcon, I know well, who
plucked one flower from it, for I have never known peace
since I lost that noble bough and have been in endless
torment . . . ," in Reynard the Fox and Other Medieval
Secular Literature, Translated by Professor Adriaan J.
Barnouw and R. Colledge [Leyden: Sithoff and London:
Heinemann, 1967, 182].) An almost identical text
appears in Nederlandse Letterkunde, III, Middeleeuws
Toneel--Esmoreit, Glorient, Lanseloet van Denemerken, Nu
Noch, Elckerlijc, Marijken van Nieumeghen, Utrecht/
Antwerp: Uitgeverij Het Spectrum, 1984, 117. The play
was first printed at Gouda in 1486. Professor Therese
Decker of Lehigh University is preparing a critical
edition of this late fourteenth-century play. Also, see
Bax, 106. In this engraving (Figure 4), the falcon is
both hooded (i.e., blinded) and tied to his owner's
wrist. He cannot fly. Beside the young lady is a
flowering plant (a marguerite or daisy) with one blossom
in place. The restraint and temperance of this couple
is exemplary.

[22]See Kelly, 20, 31-33, for a discussion of the adulterous nature of courtly love and how it changed in the
mid-fourteenth century. Also, see Andreas Capellanus,
The Art of Courtly Love, Translated with Introduction
and Notes by John Jay Parry (New York: W. W. Norton and
Co., Inc., 1969), 171, and the "rules of love" listed on
184-86.

[23]Proverbia Communis, no. 286: Die Slotele en hangh
en niet al aen eens wijfs eers ("all keys hang not on
one wife's girdle") demonstrates that the chatelain as
an attribute of a wife had become proverbial by 1495.
Compare, von Fallersleben, no. 379: De slottelen en
hangen nicht (al) an eines ewynes aerse.

[24]See Lucy Freeman Sandler, "The Handclasp in the Arnolfini Wedding: A Manuscript Precedent," _The Art Bulletin_, 68 (1984), 488-91; _idem_, "Bawdy Betrothal," 155-56; and Robert W. Baldwin, "Marriage as a Sacramental Reflection of the Passion: The Mirror in Jan van Eyck's 'Arnolfini Wedding,'" _Oud Holland_, 98 (1984), 57-75, for the sacramental nature of this painting. For a countering interpretation, see Peter E. Schabacker, "De Matrimonio ad Morganaticiam Contracto: Jan van Eyck's 'Arnolfini Portrait' Reconsidered," _The Art Bulletin_, 35 (1972), 375-98, who includes an extensive bibliography. Compare Kelly, 173-74.

[25]Kelly, 40-1, cites Gratian and Thomas Aquinas. In his _Summa, Supplemental Question 64, Article 5_, Aquinas comments upon Paul's Epistle to the Ephesians, 23 (see Thomas Aquinas, _Summa Theologica, First Complete American Edition, Literally Translated by the Fathers of the English Dominican Province_, New York: Benziger Brothers, Inc., 1947-48, III, 2803): ". . . Husband and wife are not equal in marriage; neither as regards the marriage act, wherein the noble part is due to the husband, nor as regards the household management, wherein the wife is ruled and the husband rules. But with reference to the second kind of equality, they are equal in both matters, because just as both in the marriage act and in the management of the household the husband is bound to the wife in all things pertaining to the husband, so is the wife bound to the husband in all things pertaining to the wife."

[26]For this image, see Walter S. Gibson, "Some Flemish Popular Prints from Hieronymus Cock and His Contemporaries," _The Art Bulletin_, 60 (1978), 577-79, who gives other Netherlandic and German texts; and _idem_, "Bruegel, _Dulle Griet_, and Sexist Politics in the Sixteenth Century," _Bruegel und Seine Welt_ (Berlin: Gebr. Mann Verlag, 1979), 9-15, especially 1-2. Also, see Christiane Andersson and Charles Talbot, _From a Mighty Fortress: Prints, Drawings and Books in the Age of Luther, 1483-1546_ (Detroit: The Detroit Institute of Arts, 1983), 320; Keith P. F. Moxey, "Chivalry and the Housebook Master," in _Livelier than Life_, 78, n. 33; and Sandler, "Bawdy Betrothal," 138. Moxey is currently working on this theme.

[27]Gies, 46-8, give an objective account of this husbandly right. Also, see Angela M. Lucas, _Women of the Middle Ages, Religion, Marriage and Letters_ (New York: St. Martin's Press, 1983), 127-28, who cites feminist literature on this subject.

[28]The same pooch holds exactly the same pose in Meckenem's The Dance at Herod's Court (Bartsch, n. 9 [206]):
he points out humans who shock even the animals with
their wild behavior.

[29]Andersson and Talbot, Mighty Fortress, 320.

[30]For the bibliography on the distaff as a feminine
symbol, see Christiane Andersson, "Symbolik und Gebärdesprache bei Niklaus Manuel und Urs Graf," Zeitschrift
für Schweizerische Archäologie und Kunstgeschichte, 37
(1980), 276-88, especially 278-79. Spinning itself was
frequently equated with underhanded deeds, see Thomas
Murner, Die Schelmenzunft (1512) (Berlin: Königliche
Hof-Steindruckerei, Gebr. Burckard, 1881), Chapter 16,
entitled "Gut Garn Spynnen," which is introduced by a
woodcut showing a rogue spinning. For the insult
incurred by the wife's stepping on her husband's foot,
see Christiane Andersson, Dirnen-Krieger-Narren: Ausge-
wählte Zeichnungen von Urs Graf (Basel: GS-Verlag,
1978), 61-62.

[31]See above, n. 26 (especially Gibson, "Bruegel, Dulle
Griet and Sexist Politics," 10-2), and, add Keith P. F.
Moxey, "Pieter Bruegel and the Feast of Fools," The Art
Bulletin, 64 (1982), 644 and Figure 4, where the fools
dance around a pole decorated with both a breechcloth
and a cod-piece. A breechcloth also appears on the
banner carried by the guards of Maximilian I's baggage
train in The Triumph of Maximilian I, executed between
1514-18 (see The Triumph of Maximilian I. 137 Woodcuts
by Hans Burgkmair and Others, with a Translation of
Descriptive Text, Introduction and Notes by S. Appelbaum
[New York: Dover Publications, Inc., n.d.], pl. 135).

[32]Andersson and Talbot, Mighty Fortress, 320, states
that many women, ca. 1500, wore no undergarments. In
the eleventh and twelfth centuries a comic tradition
existed which made fun of certain religious orders who
wore no undergarments (see Curtius, 434).

[33]Meckenem's opposing couples reflect the distinction
outlined by Aquinas in Summa, Suppl. Q. 49, Art. 1
(Summa, III, 1736: ". . . the intercourse of fornication and that of marriage are of the same species as
regards the species of nature. But the intercourse of
fornication is wrong in itself. Therefore, in order
that the marriage intercourse be not wrong, something
must be added to it to make it right, and draw it to
another species." It is precisely that "something" (the
marriage goods) which distinguish our licit and illicit

couples. The goods are a) proles (or the procreation of children), b) fides (or the promise and acceptance of that promise), and c) sacramenta (or the indivisibility of the contract). Also, see Cynthia Hahn, "Joseph Will Perfect, Mary Enlighten, and Jesus Save Thee: The Holy Family as Marriage Model in the Merode Triptych," The Art Bulletin, 68 (1986), 54-66, especially 61-63, where additional texts on marriage are cited; and Kelly, 245-58, and 255, and 265-66, who discusses the motives for marriage and cites many pre-Aquinian authorities. The motives are among those somethings, like the goods, that draw the intercourse of marriage to "another species."

[34]Van Eyck's Arnolfini double portrait of 1434 is again the closest comparison. Also, see Quentin Massys's Money Lender and His Wife (Max J. Friedländer, Early Netherlandish Painting, Vol. VII, Quentin Massys, Leiden: A. W. Sijthoff and Brussels; La Connaissance, 1971, pl. 51; and Stewart, 68). Many later engravings, brothel scenes, exist of couples playing cards or games of chance or musical instruments in richly appointed rooms (Gibson, "Flemish Popular Prints," 679-81; Andersson and Talbot, Mighty Fortress, 320; and Stewart, passim). Double portraits of husbands and wives also occur in which the partners each work at some symbolic task (Friedländer, vol. XII, pl. 201, for Jan van Scorel's Portraits of Pieter Bicker and His Wife, Anna Codde, Amsterdam, Rijksmuseum; and Maerten van Heemskerck's Portrait of a Lady with Spindle and Distaff, Lugano, The Thyssen-Bornemisza Collection). Also, see E. de Jongh, "Pearls of Virtue and Perils of Vice," Simiolus, 8 (1974/75), 69-97; and Simon Schama, "Wives and Wantons: Versions of Womanhood in Seventeenth-Century Dutch Art," The Oxford Art Journal, 14 (1980), 5-13, for some of the emblems associated with wives as well as a discussion of how these emblems work.

[35]Livelier than Life, no. 75, 173-75.

[36]This motif reappears in engravings by the Master b x g (Livelier than Life, no. 99, 199), and in Peter Flotner's Complaint of Two Lovers Against Death, dated 1536 (see Keith P. F. Moxey, "Master E. S. and the Folly of Love," Simiolus, 11, 1980, Figure 15). The presence of wine shades any reading of lovers, see Stewart, 51 and 81; Brants Narrenschiff, no. 16, 18:

> Eyn schadlich ding ist umb den wyn
> By dem mag nyeman witzie zyn
> Wer freüd und lust dar jnn jm sücht

Eyn drunckner mensch gar nyemas rûht
Und weiss keyn molz moch underscheit,
Vil unkusch kumbt ufz trunckenheyt,
Vil vhels ouch dar ufz entsprinct,
Eyn wiser its, wer syttlich drinckt . . .
(For wine is a very harmful thing,
A man shows no sound reasoning
Who only drinks for sordid ends,
A drunken man neglects his friends
And knows no prudent moderation,
And drinking leads to fornication:
It oft indices grave offense,
A wise man drinks with common sense . . . ,

Brant's The Ship of Fools, no. 16, 97), and Chaucer's
well-known comment, "For wyn and youthe toon Venus
encrece."

[37]Jane C. Hutchinson, The Master of the Housebook (New
York: The Collector's Edition, 1972), cat. no. 1, I.
75; and, compare Moxey, "Chivalry and the Housebook
Master," 67-69.

[38]In earlier fifteenth-century panels these motifs
symbolize Mary's cleanliness and virginity (see Charles
I. Minott, "The Theme of the Merode Altarpiece," The Art
Bulletin, 51 (196[], 267-71; William S. Heckscher, "The
Annunciation of the Merode Altarpiece, An Iconographical
Study," Miscellanea Josef Duverger, Gent: Uitg.
Vereniging voor de geschiedenis der textielkunsters,
1968, 37-65; and Erwin Panofsky, Early Netherlandish
Painting, New York: Icon Editions, 1971, I, 131-48, for
earlier citations). For more recent studies, see Hahn,
63; and Barbara G. Lane, The Altar and the Altarpiece:
Sacramental Themes in Early Netherlandish Art (New
York: Harper and Row Publishers, 1984), 42-43. In this
scene (Figure 7), the laver and towel must be read in a
different way. Already in the fifteenth century, card
playing and gambling were considered dubious activities
at best; see Brants Narrenschiff, no. 77, 75:

Sunst fynd ich nårrscher narren vil
Dieall jr freůd hant inn dem spyl
Meynend, sie môchten leben nit
Soltten sie nit umbgon do mit
Und tag, und nacht spyelen, und rassen
Mitt karten, würfflen, und mit brassen
Die gantz nacht, . . .
(Some foolish idiots I could name,
They love the cards, the dice, the game,

Preferring never to exist
Before from gambling they'd desist,
And day and night they game and rattle
With cards and dice, and drink and prattle . . .,

Brant's The Ship of Fools, no. 77, 255). Also, see P.
J. Harrebonne, Spreekwoorden der Nederlandsche Taal
(Utrecht: Keminck en zoon, 1853-70), I, 371: De hoeren
hebben de kaart ("the whores have the cards") and Kaart,
keurs en kan Bederven mening men ("cards, women, and
wine ruin many men"). Stewart, 68, 70, 98, and 138;
Moxey, "Chivalry and the Housebook Master," 71-73; and
Livelier than Life, nos. 73 and 99, illustrate card
playing by fifteenth-century lovers.

[39]This scene also calls to mind the tavern scene in
"Marijken van Nijmeghen," where through the workings of
the devil Moenen Emma outwits several young men, leading
them to their doom (in Medieval Netherlands Religious
Literature, Translated and Introduced by E. Colledge,
Leyden: Sythoff and London: Heinemann, 1965, espe-
cially 103-106. The Netherlandic text appears in
Middeleeuwse Toneel, cited above, n. 21).

[40]Stewart, 34, 39, 47, 75, 101-102, 106, 144, and 128,
no. 106, touches upon this motif. See also Moxey,
"Master E. S. and the Folly of Love," 141-44; and
Andersson, "Symbolik und Gebärdesprache," 278-79.

[41]See Livelier than Life, no. 75c.

[42]The sword or knife as a phallic symbol goes back to
Roman times, or even earlier. The Latin term for the
female genitalia (vagina) literally means "a sheath for
a sword." In this engraving (Figure 8), in removing his
sword and laying it aside, the young man conquers lust.
For medieval puns using a knife or sword as a penis symbol, see Sandler, "Bawdy Betrothal," 158-59. Pregnancy
is difficult to diagnose in works of art. The young
woman's swelling belly, her hands carefully folded over
her stomach, and the neatly, but suggestively arranged
pillows and bed curtain, all hint at a pregnancy. Likewise, her husband's sword, which lies on the floor,
suggests that this couple conquered lust by frequent
marital intercourse, for which, see Kelly, 241-48 and
254-61, who cites the theological texts defending this
form of continence. Moreover, with his left foot, he
"steps on" his wife's right foot, thereby completing the
secular ritual determining spousal dominance (see also,
above, n. 30).

[43]The verbal metaphors and puns are clear: "he strokes, while she pumps" uses several derived meanings (to stroke = slagen (Dutch); slagen (German); to pump = pompslagen (Dutch); pumpen (German). In Dutch, the "proper" term for sexual intercourse is geslachtelijke omgang, while in German it is geschlechtlicher Verkehr. One need not look to a classical text for this image. Plutarch's Coniugalia Praecepta was not available in Latin until 1497. This engraved series was executed and circulated before 1495, for our organ player (Figure 9) reappears among the musicians performing in a synagogue in the Lobkovice Breviary (Prague, The University Library), dated 1494 (for which, see Alexander Buchner, Musical Instruments through the Ages, London: Artia for Spring Books, 1961, no. 139). Compare Robert Baldwin, "Plutarch's Wife as Mirror in a German Renaissance Marriage Portrait," Source: Notes in the History of Art, 4 (1985), 68-71, especially 70. Baldwin also errs in counting Shestack, Engravings of Northern Europe, Figures, 233-43.

[44]The bibliography on music-making as a sexual metaphor is not extensive. Usually, the texts concern a particular instrument, especially the strings of woodwinds, see Bax, 88, 252-53. Also, see Bert Meijer, "Harmony and Satire in the Work of Niccolo Frangipani: Problems in the Depiction of Music," Simiolus, 6 (1972/73), 94-99. B. A. Bowles, "The Symbolism of the Organ in the Middle Ages: A Study in the History of Ideas," Aspects of Medieval and Renaissance Music: A Birthday Offering to Gustave Reese, Jan La Rue, editor (New York: W. W. Norton, Co., 1966), 27-39, focuses on the liturgical function and associations of the instrument. Following Bowles, the organ in Figure 9 supports my reading of this couple as a married pair and tempers any meaning implied by the vulgar terms for their actions.

[45]Even today, in French-speaking countries, a double bed is called un lit matrimonial. One function of such a bed may be suggested by the "curtain sack" hanging from the canopy. This idea was presented by Susan Koslow in "The Curtain Sack: A Newly Discovered Incarnation Motif in Roger van der Weyden's Columbia Altarpiece," at the Seventy-Third Annual Meeting of the College Art Association of America, Los Angeles, February 16, 1985. Also, see Hahn, 63.

[46]Traditionally, the dog is a symbol of fidelity, as in van Eyck's Arnolfini portrait. But a dog running free ("a running dog") can symbolize lust or any unrestrained passion. Meckenem opposed two such animals in

his Hunting for Fidelity (see Max Lehrs, Late Gothic Engravings of Germany and The Netherlands: 682 Copperplates from the "Kritischer Katalog" by Max Lehrs, New York: Dover Publications, Inc., 1969, no. 650). This sitting animal (Figure 9) conveys the meaning of fidelity as well as freedom from lust.

[47]This is also the object of Chaucer's Merchant's Tale.

[48]Carrington, 336.

[49]Stringed instruments have a special erotic symbolism, see Ellen Jacobowicz and Stephanie Loeb Stepanek, The Prints of Lucas van Leyden and His Contemporaries (Washington, DC: The National Gallery of Art, 1983), 220 (who cite Plutarchian sources); and Bax, 88 and 252-53. Bax (88) notes that de snaren bespelen ("to play on the strings") is a vulgar expression, while (253) spelen met der luten ("to play with the lute") means to indulge in love making. Also, see Keith P. F. Moxey, "The Social Function of Secular Woodcuts in Sixteenth Century Nuremberg," New Perspectives on the Art of Renaissance Nuremberg: Five Essays Edited by Jeffery Chipps Smith (Austin, Texas: The Archer M. Huntington Art Gallery, 1985), 66, who discusses the engraving by Frans Huys with women, lutes, and a lutemaker. Bosch's linking of the lute and the harp in his Hell panel from The Garden of Earthly Delights (Madrid, the Prado) further underscores the erotic associations of these two stringed instruments.

[50]For the erotic meanings of the foot warmer, see Peter C. Sutton, et al., Masters of Seventeenth Century Dutch Genre Painting. An Exhibition Organized by the Philadelphia Museum of Art in Cooperation with the Gemäldegalerie, Staatliche Museen Preussischer Kulturbesitz, Berlin (West), and the Royal Academy of Arts, London (Philadelphia: The University of Philadelphia Press, 1984), especially, 244 and 261.

[51]See above, n. 49. Also, see Sutton, et al., 261 and 304. Here, the erotic meaning is enhanced by the anthropomorphic forms of the open lute case.

[52]This woodcut copies an engraving by Master E. S., who may have been Meckenem's teacher. Meckenem made his own versions of E. S.'s original early in his career (Bartsch, no. 208 [283]). For the Strasbourg Calendar of ca. 1500, see Erwin Panofsky, Raymond Klibansky, and Fritz Saxl, Saturn and Melancholy: Studies in the

History of _Natural_ _Philosophy_, _Religion_, and _Art_ (New York: New York University Press, 1964), pl. 90b; and compare pl. 89a from the Augsburg Calendar (ca. 1480).

[53]Panofsky, Klibansky, and Saxl, _Saturn_ and _Melancholy_, _passim_, but especially 296, n. 56; 298, and 299-300, on the phlegmatic temperament as opposed to the melancholic, choleric, and sanguine.

[54]Shestack, _Engravings_ of _Northern_ _Europe_, 154 and 240. This young man and woman are refraining from sexual intercourse (compare above, n. 49). The couple may not yet be married (compare Meijer, 99). The leashed dog who sits before them is a symbol of restraint and temperance (compare P.J.J. van Thiel, "Marriage Symbolism in a Musical Party by Jan Mieris Molenaar," _Simiolus_, 2 [1967/68], 91-99, in which he plays the lute and she sings). Compare also, Baldwin, "Plutarch's Wife," 70.

[55]Both hark back to the Arnolfini double portrait. Neither of Meckenem's mirrors (Figures 9 and 11) reflects anything and the inscriptions are without Christian or classical allusions, the letters being those of the artist's name. Compare Baldwin, "Plutarch's Wife," 70.

[56]See above, n. 46. Also, see H. W. Janson, _Apes_ and _Apelore_ in _Western_ _Art_ (London: Warburg Institute of the University of London, 1952), _passim_, for chained monkeys representing the control of passions; and van Thiel, 91-99, for a dog (fidelity) responding to a chained monkey (temperance) and a cat (lasciviousness). For Meckenem's monkeys, see Strauss, _The_ _Illustrated_ _Bartsch_, no. 190 (276).

[57]Shestack, _Engravings_ of _Northern_ _Europe_, 154, and 243; and Snyder, 291-92. Snyder follows Brant's _Narrenschiff_, no. 77, 75:

> . . . Und geschlechts sich nit schême
> Und spyelen, rasslen, spat, und frü
> Das doch den frowen nit stat zů
> Sie soltten an der kunckel lucken
> Und nit in spyel byn mannen ståcken . . .
> (For all good women great the same.
> The distaff they should tend and wet
> and gamble not with men and bet . . . ,

Brant's _The_ _Ship_ of _Fools_, no. 77, 256). Shestack describes Meckenem's twelve scenes (Figures 1-12) as

depicting "common leisure activities," which undoubtedly
influenced Snyder. Compare Andersson and Talbot, **Mighty
Fortress**, 320; and the examples cited above, n. 30.

[58]See above, n. 42; Sandler, "Bawdy Betrothal,"
158-59; and Snyder, 291-92.

[59]Stewart, 87 and 89; and David R. Smith, **Masks of
Wedlock: Seventeenth-Century Dutch Marriage Portraiture**
(Ann Arbor, MI: University of Michigan Research Press,
1982), **passim**.

[60]Chapter 31 of **The Book of Proverbs** is the source of
many symbols for the virtuous wife and mother. See Hahn,
64, especially n. 71 and n. 74, for examples of Mary
spinning. Also, see above, n. 34. This tradition
supports Brant's verses in the **Narrenschiff** (see above,
n. 57). Moreover, David Kunzle, **The Early Comic Strip:
Narrative Strips and Pictures in European Broadsheets
from ca. 1450 to 1825, The History of the Comic Strips**
(Berkeley and Los Angeles: The University of California
Press, 1975), I, Figure 1-17 reproduces a woodcut dating
ca. 1470 showing a couple enframed by the goods necessary to the well run household, including the distaff
and spindle. The pejorative associations of the distaff
are discussed in Andersson, "Symbolik und Gebärdesprache," 278-79; also, see **Proverbia Communis**, no. 11:
Als horen spinnen is die neeringhe cranck ("when whores
spin there is small gain"). The same proverb appears in
von Fallersleben, no. 20: **Als sik de horen schelden, so
is de neringe klein**.

[61]Heinrich Kramer and James Sprenger, **Malleus Malefi-
carum, Translated with Introduction, Bibliography and
Notes by Rev. Montague Summers** (New York: Dover Publi-
cations, Inc., 1971), 7, 41-43, and 47. For witches as
young, beautiful, sexual beings, see Charles Talbot,
"Baldung and the Female Nude," in James H. Marrow and
Alan Shestack, **Hans Baldung Grien: Prints and Drawings**
(New Haven and Washington, DC: The National Gallery of
Art, 1981), 31-36, especially, Figure 31.

[62]Andersson, "Symbolik und Gebärdesprache," 278-79.
The popularity of the witch in European art exactly
parallels the paternalistic interpretations of female
sexuality (see Stewart, 28-34; Talbot, "Baldung and the
Female Nude," 31-36; and Gibson, "Bruegel, **Dulle Griet**
and Sexist Politics," 9-15).

[63]T. H. White, The Bestiary: A Book of Beasts (New
York: G. P. Putnam's Sons, 1960), 213. Spider = spinne
in both Dutch and German. Harrebonne, II, 290, cites
several proverbs about the spider; and Bax, 106-107,
includes references to the spider and her web as love
omens.

[64]Strauss, The Illustrated Bartsch, German Book Illustration Before 1500, Vol. 87, Part VIII, Anonymous
Artists, 1489-91 (New York: Abaris Books, Inc., 1985),
8789/1488-92, which depicts the Ninth Commandment. A
similar association of a spinner and ostentatious possessions is seen in the Sin of Greed in The Last Judgment
with Scenes of the Seven Works of Mercy and the Seven
Deadly Sins, dating ca. 1490-1500, by an Unknown Antwerp
Master (see Geert Groet en de Moderne Devotie, Utrecht:
Rijksmuseum het Catharijneconvent, 1984, 34). In
Figures 7-11 the furnishings seem to complement the
couples. Here, too, the gaudy cups and pitchers and
elaborate chest must reflect the character of the
couple, especially of the lady of the house.

[65]The spindles in the box may refer to her other con-
quests (see Andersson, "Symbolik und Gebardesprache,"
278-79). They are not fully wound (see above, n. 60).
Compare those in the "Allegorical Engraving," reproduced
in Andersson, Figure 3, where the theme of erotic folly
is clear and the visual metaphors are explicit.

[66]Proverbia Communis, no. 314: Die catte es gheerne
daer meanse cloet.

[67]Proverbia Communis, no. 126: By nachte sinn alle
catten graen. For a more benign reading of Puss, see
Snyder, 291-92; and compare Sandler, "Bawdy Betrothal,"
157-59.

[68]Archer Taylor, Problems in German Literary History
of the Fifteenth and Sixteenth Centuries (1939: rpt.
New York: Kraus Reprint Corporation, 1966), 124-43 and
the appendices, 167-72.

[69]Compare Moxey, "Master E. S. and the Folly of Love,"
11125-48.

[70]Compare the sentiments voiced by the badly married
men and women in Chaucer's The Canterbury Tales, or in
various other medieval comic tales, or in the satiric
lament, Les Quinze Joyes de Mariage.

[71] Proverbia Communis, no. 336: Eyghen heert es gout
weert ("one's own hearth is worth gold"). Compare this
passage from Albrecht von Eyb's Ehebuchlein: "What
could be happier and sweeter than the name of father,
mother, and children (that is, family), where the children hang on their parent's arms and exchange many sweet
kisses with them, and where husband and wife are so
drawn to one another by love and choice, and experience
such friendship between themselves that what one wants
the other also chooses, and what one says, the other
maintains in silence as if he had said it himself; where
all good and evil is held in common, the good all the
happier, the adversity all the lighter because shared by
two" (in Steven Ozment, When Fathers Ruled: Family Life
in Reformation Europe, Cambridge, MA: Harvard University Press, 1983, 55 and 59). Ozment cites Albrecht
von Eyb, Ehebuchlein, Faksimile der Originalausgabe von
Anton Koberger, Nuremberg, 1472 (Wiesbaden, 1966), 81.
Von Eyb's Ehebuchlein is the one fifteenth-century tract
not written by a jurist, theologian, or cleric.

[72] Chaucer's "Merchant's Tale" is replete with ironic
statements, which undermine the words praising the
institution. Also, compare Hahn, 64-65; and von Eyb,
Ehebuchlein, for contemporary statements on marriage.

[73] In these two scenes the curtain sack and the plumped
pillows may be signs of a pregnancy. Both echo the
shape of the female body carrying a child. Also, see
above, n. 42 and n. 45.

[74] George Hayward Joyce, Christian Marriage: An
Historical and Doctrinal Study (London: Sheed and Ward,
1948), 390-99, and 409-29, follows the legalistic tradition of Catholic scholars. Recent studies by sympathetic writers have focused on the positive changes worked
by these reformers. Ozment and Thomas Max Safley, Let
No Man Put Asunder: The Control of Marriage in the
German Southwest, 1550-1600, Sixteenth-Century Studies
and Texts, II (Kirkville, MO: The Sixteenth Century
Journal Publications, Inc., 1984), are excellent over-
views of this period. Significantly, it was the members
of the city councils and the leading artisan families
who were in the forefront of these marriage reforms.
Meckenem, a goldsmith who had been elected to the town
council at Bocholt, belonged to both groups.

[75] This argument (with its Apostolic injunction)
continued after the Reformation. Compare Aquinas's

commentary on Paul's Epistle to the Ephesians, cited above, n. 25; and Ozment, 3-9.

[76]Ozment, 50-72, especially 59-63.

[77]For which see Ozment, 23, and 63-78. The reformers, in effect, sought to control women in order to contain their own lechery. Also, see Susan C. Karant-Nunn, "Continuity and Change: Some Effects of the Reformation on the Women of Zwickau," The Sixteenth-Century Journal, 13, no. 2 (1982), 17-42, especially 21-26 and 35-42.

[78]See Livelier than Life, 214-15, for an examination of this engraving as the portraits of specific people in comparison with two sets of "unequal lovers" (Cat. nos. 113-16).

ILLUSTRATIONS

Note: While researching this essay and obtaining permissions for the accompanying illustrations, Dianne Scillia could not reach agreement with The National Gallery of Art on the correct captions for the van Meckenem engravings. Thus they appear with the caption requested by the National Gallery, though Scillia refers to several of them by a different name in her text. Her alternatives appear below.

Figure 1:   Israhel van Meckenem, The Old Man and His Young Bride (Washington, DC: The National Gallery of Art)

Figure 2:   Israhel van Meckenem, The Older Woman and Her Foolish Young Man (Washington, DC: The National Gallery of Art)

Figure 3:   Israhel van Meckenem, The Monk and Nun (Washington, DC: The National Gallery of Art)

Figure 4:   Israhel van Meckenem, The Lord and His Fiancée (Washington, DC: The National Gallery of Art)

Figure 5:   Israhel van Meckenem, The Knight and His Lady (Washington, DC: The National Gallery of Art)

Figure 6:   Israhel van Meckenem, The Henpecked Husband (Washington, DC: The National Gallery of Art)

Figure 7:   Israhel van Meckenem, The Card Players (after Carrington, 335)

Figure 8:   Israhel van Meckenem, The Couple Sitting on a Bed (Washington, DC: The National Gallery of Art)

Figure 9:   Israhel van Meckenem, The Organ Player and His Wife (Washington, DC: The National Gallery of Art)

Figure 10: Israhel van Meckenem, _The Harpist and the Lute Player_ (Washington, DC: The National Gallery of Art)

Figure 11: Israhel van Meckenem, _The Lute Player and the Singer_ (Washington, DC: The National Gallery of Art)

Figure 12: Israhel van Meckenem, _The Gentleman and the Spinner_ (Washington, DC: The National Gallery of Art)

Figure 13: Israhel van Meckenem, _Double Portrait of Israhel van Meckenem and His Wife, Ida_ (Washington, DC: The National Gallery of Art)

Figure 14: The Master of the Housebook/Master of the Amsterdam Cabinet, _The Lovers_ (after _Livelier than Life_, cat. no. 75. 2)

Figure 15: Israhel van Meckenem, _The Lovers_ (after the Housebook Master) (Lawrence, KS: The Spencer Museum of the University of Kansas).

Figure 1:

Unglieches Paar, c. 1495/1503
(Israhel van Meckenem, c. 1445-1503; National Gallery of Art, Washington, DC; Rosenwald Collection)

Figure 2:

The Juggler and The Woman, c. 1495/1503
(Israhel van Meckenem, c. 1445-1503; National Gallery of Art, Washington, DC; Rosenwald Collection)

Figure 3:

The Church Goers, c. 1495/1503
(Israhel van Meckenem, c. 1445-1503; National Gallery of Art, Washington, DC; Rosenwald Collection)

Figure 4

Falconer and Lady of Nobility, c.1495/1503
*(Israhel van Meckenem, c. 1445-1503; National
Gallery of Art, Washington, DC; Rosenwald
Collection)*

Figure 5:

Knight and Lady, c. 1495/1503
(Israhel van Meckenem, c. 1445-1503; National
Gallery of Art, Washington, DC; Rosenwald
Collection)

Figure 6:

Jealous Wife, c. 1495/1503
(Israhel van Meckenem, c. 1445-1503; National
Gallery of Art, Washington, DC; Rosenwald
Collection)

Figure 7:

The Card Players
(Israhel van Meckenem, after Carrington, 335)

Figure 8:

Man and Woman Seated on Bed, c. 1495/1503
(Israhel van Meckenem, c. 1445-1503; National Gallery of Art, Washington, DC; Rosenwald Collection)

Figure 9:

The Organ Player and His Wife, c. 1495-1503
(Israhel van Meckenem, c. 1445-1503; National Gallery of Art, Washington, DC; Rosenwald Collection)

Figure 10:

Lute Player and Harpist, c. 1495/1503
(Israhel van Meckenem, c. 1445-1503; National Gallery of Art, Washington, DC; Rosenwald Collection)

Figure 11:

The Lute Player and the Singer, c. 1495/1503
(Israhel van Meckenem, c. 1445-1503; National Gallery of Art, Washington, DC; Rosenwald Collection)

Figure 12:

Visit With The Spinner, c. 1495/1503
(Israhel van Meckenem, c. 1445-1503; National Gallery of Art, Washington, DC; Rosenwald Collection)

Figure 13:

**Double Portrait of Israhel Van Meckenem and His
Wife Ada, c. 1490**
*(Israhel Van Meckenem, c. 1445-1503; National
Gallery of Art, Washington, DC; Rosenwald
Collection)*

Figure 14:

The Lovers
*(The Master of the Housebook/Master of the
Amsterdam Cabinet, after 'Livelier than Life',
catalog no. 75. 2)*

Figure 15:

The Lovers (after the Housebook Master, see previous page)
(Israhel van Meckenem; from the collections of The Spencer Museum of the University of Kansas, Lawrence, KS)

ELAINE AND GUINEVERE:
GENDER AND HISTORICAL CONSCIOUSNESS IN THE MIDDLE AGES

by Martin B. Shichtman

Scholars have long viewed the women of medieval
literature simply as being imitators of paradigms,
daughters of Eve or Mary for instance. In fact, judgment of female characters has all too often been based
on how well they fill their paradigmatic roles. But
this perception of female characters neglects to take
into consideration the many striking changes in con-
sciousness--particularly those changes relating to
historical reckoning--which developed from the twelfth
century onwards. The understanding of the progress of
time and history which began during the twelfth century
and flourished throughout the Middle Ages was not only
partially responsible for the rise of the concept of the
individual--and individuality--but affected the manner
in which the individual was recognized as a component of
medieval clerical and secular institutions. Scholars
have, perhaps, overemphasized the importance of the
medieval belief in a cyclical pattern of time, and their
overemphasis has led them to lend excessive attention to
the continuous regeneration of paradigms that would
necessarily result from such an appreciation of time's
progress. Certainly during the Middle Ages there was a
tendency to "mythologize," and, as Jessie Gelrich notes,
the "similarity between medieval and 'totemic' classifi-
cation is hardly coincidental; both are expressions of a

common perspective that 'reads' existing phenomena as
connected by a preexistent design and then catalogs and
indexes from a seemingly unquestioned sense of the unity
and continuity of the universe."[1] This tendency to
"mythologize," this outgrowth of what Claude Levi-
Strauss refers to as "the savage mind," conceives of the
past not as a stage in the historical process but rather
as a timeless model and "expresses a consciously or
unconsciously adopted attitude, the systematic nature of
which is attested all over the world by that endlessly
repeated justification of every technique, rule, and
custom in the single argument: the ancestors taught it
to us."[2] Mircea Eliade in The Myth of the Eternal
Return similarly notes that when "an act (or an object)
acquires a certain reality through the repetition of
certain paradigmatic gestures, and acquires it through
that alone, there is an implicit abolition of profane
time, of duration, of 'history'; and he who reproduces
the exemplary gesture thus finds himself transported
into the mythical epoch in which its revelation took
place."[3] If during the Middle Ages history was in
fact perceived as a series of eternal returns, then
female characters would necessarily be reflections of
the paradigms on which they were based, and their easy
categorization by recent scholars would be completely
justified.

There is, however, considerable evidence arguing for
a medieval understanding--albeit a sometimes limited
one--of the progress of time and history. Along with
the "mythologizing" he recognizes to be so much a part
of medieval culture, Gellrich also maintains that many
"medieval theories of the sign emerge from the effort to
depart from the myths of precedent societies."[4]
According to Lee Patterson:

As often has been noted (but rarely
explored) . . . deference [to the past]
. . . renders a genuinely historical consciousness elusive. Indeed, the most
common of medieval historical writings,
those that moralize the historical record
into illustrative instances of success and
failure, vice and virtue, are manifestly
ahistorical: the past is rendered not as
a process that has its own temporality,
but as a storehouse of disconnected and
timeless _exempla_ that assume authority
precisely because they are no longer time
bound. Nevertheless, we should remember
that medieval writers also used the past
historiographically--sometimes to deline-
ate an instructive chronology of secular
empire, more commonly to apprehend a plan
of providential dispensation--and it would
be a mistake to assent too quickly to the
common proposition that the Middle Ages
lacked historical sense.[5]

M. D. Chenu similarly writes that within the twelfth
century there arose a "new awareness of history" and "at
just the very time when the influence and attraction of
a philosophy of the world was being exerted, especially
the various platonizing philosophies which tended to
eliminate time and history, we have a prime example of
the ineradicable view of Christianity as an itinerary of
man's journey toward the divine, a view which could not
be reduced to a cyclical conception of the cosmos with
neither commencement nor consummation."[6] Indeed,
throughout the Middle Ages both churchmen as well as

secular writers were attempting to come to terms with a
conception of time and history still undergoing revi-
sion. Morton Bloomfield has demonstrated that even by
Chaucer's time acceptance was by no means completely
certain. Chaucer, in fact, differs from many of his
contemporaries in that his "art unrolls in time aware of
itself through the author, the commentator on his work.
It has duration, and it conveys an awareness of this
duration even as events come and go."7

Recent scholarship suggests that for the male protagonists of Arthurian romance--a genre whose evolution
may parallel the development of the sense of chronology
during the Middle Ages--paradigms are not always repeat-
able and attempts at repetition do not always end satis-
factorily; these protagonists often learn during their
adventures that they are not so much copiers of paradigmatic acts but rather individuals who must take responsibility for their own deeds. As Robert W. Hanning notes:

> In the romance genre generally, man is
> defined in terms of becoming, not being;
> that is, what he is is a function of what
> time brings him. The sequence of events
> whereby protagonists are separated from and
> then returned to their "normal" world, or
> grow from helpless children to capable
> adults, shows them (and us) what they can
> do and presents them as the sum total of
> their experiences, as more than they were
> when they started, even though in a physi-
> cal sense they remain the same person . . .
> The passage of time brings discovery,
> recovery, truth. But if time shapes man,
> man shapes time: it is the individual

life at the center of the romance which
gives to time the meaning it has.[8]

Arthurian romance allows for male protagonists a clear
contrast between the old form of historical reckoning
and the new, between a history which demands acts of
repetition, romantic and religious rituals, eternal
returns, and one which emphasizes the individuality and
accountability of its participants. The choice as to
the more preferable of the two forms is never in doubt;
the Arthurian hero, at least in part, realizes his identity from his situation, his narrative, his adventure in
sequential time.

For the women of Arthurian romance, the choice is
not so clear. They are caught between the conflicting
perceptions of time; archetype never fully enters
history. In the characters of Elaine of Astolat and
Guinevere, Thomas Malory presents the tensions which
arise when two positions are given equal recognition.
Elaine of Astolat exists in a timeless world where she
can remain forever young. She is woman as idealized by
man: attractive, obedient, adoring. But once Elaine
falls in love with Lancelot, she is drawn into the power
of continuous time. This love shatters Elaine's world
of ever constant potential. Once rejected, her potential is ended, and there is little left for her other
than the despair of having to grow old alone. Elaine
takes her own life because she desires to function in
time but is forbidden to do so by the institutions that
define her. Elaine's suicide represents her most strident attempt to break from the paradigms imposed upon
her. But even this gesture amounts to little more than
Elaine's final repetition, her final submission, and
society recognizes it as such. Following her suicide,

Elaine is restored to the position she held prior to
falling in love with Lancelot; she is immortalized,
remembered always as being young, beautiful, loving, and
filled with potential. Guinevere, on the other hand,
like the Arthurian story itself, evolves in time; it is
her narrative situation to mature and eventually grow
old as the story progresses. As a character functioning
in chronological history, Guinevere develops a distinct
identity; she becomes assertive, perhaps even aggressive, in proclaiming her individuality. Nor is Guinevere unable to endure the responsibilities which come
with her historical position; she accepts the consequences of her actions. Unfortunately, Guinevere is
never granted the freedom which time and history provide
for her male Arthurian counterparts. The spirit of
Elaine haunts Guinevere. While Elaine lives in mythic
moments, Guinevere functions in profane time. The ideals
Guinevere strives for, the ideals which her society
demands women attain, are forever out of reach. She is
fated, as a character living in historical time, to
recognize perfection and stoically suffer its inaccessi-
bility. Thus both Elaine and Guinevere are placed in
situations which allow for no satisfactory choices and
offer no satisfactory rewards. They are both ultimately
damned because they cannot find a place in time.

Malory's introduction of Elaine of Astolat capsu-
lizes her entire history in two sentences: "This old
baron had a doghter that was called that tyme the Faire
Mayden of Astolat, and euer she beheld Sir Launcelot
wonderfully. And as the book sayth, she cast suche a
loue vnto Sir Launcelot that she could neuer withdrawe
her loue, wherefore she dyed, and her name was Elayne le
Blank."9 Prior to Lancelot's arrival at her father's
court, Elaine's life has been shaped by the series of

rituals she has been taught to perform. In this
respect, her name is very appropriate (neither of
Malory's sources for the episode concerning the Fair
Maid of Astolat--the French prose La Mort le Roi Artu
and the English stanzaic Le Morte Arthur--provide a
given name for this character): her life has been a
blank, a whiteness to be written on, to be inscribed.
Malory speaks little about Elaine's past, leaving the
reader to conclude simply that her character has been
shaped by the various medieval institutions governing
the behavior of women. Had Lancelot not interrupted
Elaine's existence of eternal returns, she likely would
have gone on similarly, flawlessly, unremarkably. There
can be no doubt that Elaine is a peripheral figure in
Malory's Le Morte Darthur, and this is because she has
no real story beyond that which can be summed up in two
sentences. Her entrance into the realm of historical
time is brief, incomplete, and fatal.

Elaine is drawn into history, into the narrative,
into her "adventure," by what amounts to a misunderstanding. Lancelot, needing a disguise, and realizing
that he has never borne the token of any woman, takes a
red sleeve from Elaine to wear at a tournament. Lancelot understands the confusion that his disguise might
create--indeed he appreciates that the function of disguise is to encourage confusion. But he neglects to
consider what his gesture of wearing the sleeve signifies for Elaine. Elaine hears Lancelot proclaim, "Faire
damoysel . . and yf I graunte yow that, ye may saye I
doo more for youre loue than euer I dyd for lady or
damoysel . . . neuer dyd I erst soo moche for no damoysel" (p. 516), sees him take her sleeve, and draws the
only conclusion possible for one who has perfect faith
in tokens. Felicity Riddy suggests that Lancelot is

being more than ambiguous here, that "what might have
served as a perfectly civil excuse for refusing . . .
now becomes a compliment which is positively misleading
in its implications."10 But it is difficult to fault
Lancelot completely. Elaine is not aware of the rules
of the game Lancelot is playing; she does not even know
that a game is being played. For Elaine, for those who
take comfort in eternal returns,

> No god, no culture hero ever revealed a
> profane act. Everything that the gods or
> ancestors did, hence everything that the
> myths have to tell about their creative
> activity, belongs to the sphere of the
> sacred and therefore participates in
> being. In contrast, what men do on their
> own initiative, what they do without a
> mythical model, belongs to the sphere of
> the profane; hence it is a vain and illu-
> sory activity, and, in the last analysis,
> unreal.11

Elaine, for whom the repetitions of ritual are filled
with significance and truth, reads no duplicity in
Lancelot's gestures. The knight seems to be following a
mythical model, and, given her upbringing, given what
she must necessarily expect from others in relation to
what has been expected from her, Elaine has no hope of
perceiving that Lancelot is, at least within Malory's
work, a master illusionist. Her response, though filled
with emotion, is, naturally, completely decorous: "euer
the Damoysel Elayne was aboute Sire Launcelot alle the
whyle she myghte be suffred" (p. 517). Despite an out-
pouring of feeling, Elaine keeps to her well-defined
place.

Lancelot is injured in the tournament and taken to a
hermitage to be healed. There he is found by Elaine.
Seeing how Elaine cares for Lancelot, Bors presses her
case to the knight: "Why shold ye putte her from you
. . . she is a passynge fayre damoysel, and a wel bisene
and wel taughte. And God wold . . . that ye coude loue
her" (p. 525). The reader is later told: "Thenne were
they there nygh a moneth togyders, and euer this mayden
Elayn dyd euer her dylygent labour nyghte and daye vnto
Syr Launcelot, that ther was neuer child nor wyf more
meker to her fader and husband than was that Fayre Mayden of Astolat; wherfore Sir Bors was gretely pleasyd
with her" (p. 526). Bors admires Elaine's ability to
fill the roles society designates for her. She is what
a woman should be; she does what a woman should do; and
Bors believes she should be appropriately rewarded.
Bors appreciates that which is ahistorical in Elaine,
her complete subservience to ritualistic patterns of
behavior.   _ disagree

Elaine also expects compensation for her performance; she asks that Lancelot marry her, fully expecting
that he will comply with the request. Lancelot's
refusal forces Elaine out of the world of archetype and
into the world of history. The repetition of paradigmatic gestures has brought her nothing but frustration.
The promises made by the institutions she trusted have
proven lies. When Lancelot apologizes that he can never
be a wedded man, Elaine offers to be his lover. This
assertion on her part is both out of character and
shocking, as Lancelot's response suggests. Lancelot
explains: "Ihesu defende me . . . for thenne I rewarded
your fader and your broder ful euylle for their grete
goodeness" (p. 528). Lancelot naturally sees Elaine as
an extension of the principles set forth by the men in

her life; her actions up until this moment have given him no reason to believe otherwise. The issue here is not whether Elaine will be hurt by a brief fling into historical time but whether the people and institutions which have prescribed her activity will be damaged by such a fling. Lancelot has business to attend to, he has his own narrative to get on with, and he expects, upon his departure, that Elaine will fade back into her life of repetitions, eternal returns, that she will again be a good daughter, a good sister, and ultimately some appropriate man will come along so she can become a good wife. Her assertiveness is recognized as an aberration which can be repressed with promises of future prospects, an aberration which can be gotten over.

Elaine does not, however, retreat into ritual in the manner Lancelot expects. Instead of again finding comfort in her household duties, Elaine kills herself, refusing sleep and sustenance. In her final spoken words, Elaine addresses her predicament as well as her unwillingness to return to business as usual:

> why shold I leue suche thoughtes? Am I
> not an erthely woman? And all the whyle
> the brethe is in my body I may compleyne
> me, for my byleue is, I doo none offence
> though I loue an erthely man. And I take
> God to my recorde, I loued neuer none but
> Syr Launcelot du Lake or neuer shal, and a
> clene mayden I am for hym and for al
> other. And sythen hit is the suffraunce
> of God that I shall deye for the loue of
> soo noble a knyght, I beeseche The, Hyghe
> Fader of heuen, to haue mercy vpon my
> soule; and vpon my innumerable paynes that

I suffred may be allygeaunce of parte of
my synnes. For swete Lord Ihesu . . . I
take The to recorde, on The I was neuer
grete offencer ageynste Thy laws, but that
I loued thys noble knyght Syr Launcelot
oute of mesure; and of myself, good Lord,
I myght not wythstande the feruent loue,
wherfore I haue my deth (p. 529).

In this speech--original to Malory's Le Morte Darthur--
Elaine attempts to reject the paradigms that she has
spent her life emulating and to do so with as much conviction as she can muster. Both in her statements and
in her actions--insomnia and fasting--Elaine exhibits
symptoms of an anorexic. That she justifies this sort
of suicide to her confessor suggests that Elaine may
even suffer from what Rudolph M. Bell calls "holy
anorexia." Bell provides a case history of a typical
anorexia patient:

> the girl always lived for others, judged
> herself by their standards, and let them
> define her identity. Raised to strive for
> perfection and to seek approval from nar-
> cissistic parents, she is now able to set
> for herself a daily, relentless, physi-
> cally torturing challenge, one over which
> she alone has control. The immediate
> cause of her desperate choice may be a ·
> lower than expected grade at school or it
> may be the onset of bodily maturation, the
> uncontrollable fattiness of developing
> breasts and rounding hips, or it may be a
> disgusting sexual encounter, but it is the

>underlying psychological need to gain a
>sense of self that is the essence.12

The anorexic, at least in part, torments herself to
achieve the autonomy that has been denied her by
society. For Elaine, however, that autonomy is never
really achieved. Her method of self-destruction turns
out to be just another emulation of institutionally
sanctioned ritual. As Bell notes, holy anorexia during
the Middle Ages "came to be seen as part of a wider
pattern of heroic, ascetic masochism amply justified in
the literature of radical Christian religiosity."13
Elaine's final gestures clearly take on ritualistic
proportions, right down to the selection of the appropriate death bed, clothes for the corpse, and words for
the suicide note. The demands of living in historical
time are too exacting for Elaine, the responsibilities
too great. She has not been prepared for them and is
unable to respond in a healthy manner. Unlike her male
counterparts in Arthurian romance, Elaine suffers too
much agony to appreciate the illumination her situation
might provide. And while her death causes a small stir
in Camelot, Elaine is soon and easily forgotten. Her
life has not been significant enough to cause great
impact. Her demise was that of a follower of arche-
types--and there will be many more followers to come--
not of a woman.

Guinevere's various responses to information
received about Elaine show her to be a character functioning almost always in chronological time. From the
beginnings of Malory's Le Morte Darthur, Guinevere is
introduced as something other than a model woman, and
because she is not an archetype, or an imitator of arche-
types, her introduction barely suffices to describe her

or the career she will follow. Merlin warns Arthur:
"as of her beaute and fayrenes she is one of the fayfest
on lyue; but and ye loued her not so wel as ye doo, I
shold fynde yow a damoysel of beaute and goodenesse that
shold lyke yow and plese yow" (p. 80). He goes on to
call Guinevere "not holsome" (p. 80). Rather than
allowing the institutions and rituals of her society to
define her, Guinevere struggles to define them. Hers is
not a life of doing what is right, what is pleasing to
those in authority, those who formulate the ritualistic
patterns for women to follow, but rather one of attempted self-realization. When Guinevere hears that
Lancelot displayed Elaine's sleeve at a tournament, she
becomes maddeningly jealous. She has grown old in her
affair with Lancelot--it is more than twenty-four years
since the affair began--and she fears the presence of a
young rival. Calling Lancelot a "fals traytour knyghte"
(p. 523), Guinevere suggests to Bors that a fitting
punishment might be execution.

Guinevere is manipulating rather than manipulated.
She exerts authority to her own ends. Instead of minis-
tering to men, they minister to her. And she especially
exerts authority over that greatest man of all, Lancelot. But like all who function in historical time,
Guinevere pays a price. She is not comforted by eternal
returns; there is constant uncertainty in her life. As
Eliade maintains, historical knowledge brings with it
the "tragic discovery that man is a being destined to
death, issuing from Nothingness and on his way to
Nothingness."14 Although her character becomes more
finely delineated because of her willingness to take
part in time reckoned chronologically, such matters
weigh heavily on Guinevere. As a woman of the Middle
Ages, she has, in most senses, failed completely, and

she knows it. After hearing of Elaine's death, Guinevere chides Lancelot: "Ye myght haue shewed her . . .
some bounte and gentilness that myghte haue preserued
her lyf" (p. 531). There are a multiplicity of agendas
in Guinevere's discourse. Her words demonstrate a
modicum of relief that a perceived rival is out of the
way, no longer dangerous. It is, after all, easier to
be charitable to an enemy once that enemy is gone. They
also allow for the continued domination of Lancelot,
putting him on the defensive, making him explain himself, forcing him to go through a series of rituals.
But there is also a kind of melancholy in Guinevere's
statement, for she recognizes, perhaps, that Elaine was
never a serious threat, that she was only a perfect
young woman who could not cope with the imperfections
history is prone to present.

Guinevere ultimately submits/commits herself to a
timeless world, and it is difficult to determine if
Malory actually endorses her actions. Eliade writes
that "justification of a historical event by the simple
fact that it is a historical event, in other words by
the simple fact that 'it happened that way,' will not go
far toward freeing humanity from the terror that the
event inspires."15 Guinevere takes upon herself partial blame for "the deth of the moost noblest knyghtes
of the world" as well as for the death of the "moost
noble lord" (p. 594). But the "terror of history"
proves too much for her. In entering a convent, Guinevere rejects the interpersonal conflicts that categorize
historical time in favor of a comforting world of
rituals. Hers has been a troubled life, and the insti-
tutionalized structure of the convent presents a long
awaited peace in God. Guinevere tells Lancelot: "I am
sette in suche a plyte to gete my soule hele. And yet I

truste thorugh Goddes grace that after my deth to haue a
syght of the blessyd face of Cryst, and at Domesday to
sytte on his ryght syde, for as synful as euer I was are
sayntes in heuen" (pp. 594-95). Guinevere's embrace of
religion nevertheless must be seen as an abdication, not
only of authority but of responsibility as well. Guinevere refuses Lancelot's challenge to struggle to create
new lives, refuses to work to restore what has been lost
of the Arthurian dream. She even refuses her long time
lover one last, consoling kiss. Having left the realm
of chronological time, having left history, Guinevere is
determined not to reenter. For Malory's women, historical time presents great attractions, but not enough to
make the pain worthwhile. In the end there is a regres-
sion into ritual and the solace it offers. Perhaps
Malory presents this as the best way--it is difficult to
imagine that Malory would have rejected altogether the
institutional demands his society placed on women,
especially as those demands related to the spiritual
life--but this way does not provide the kind of material
on which interesting narratives are based. We leave
Guinevere in the convent to die; there is nothing more
we want or need to hear of her.

NOTES

[1] Jessie M. Gellrich, *The Idea of the Book in the Middle Ages* (Ithaca, NY: Cornell University Press, 1985), p. 43.

[2] Claude Levi-Strauss, *The Savage Mind* (Chicago: University of Chicago Press, 1966), p. 236.

[3] Mircea Eliade, *The Myth of the Eternal Return*, trans. Willard R. Trask, Bollingen Series 46 (Princeton: Princeton University Press, 1954), p. 35.

[4] Gellrich, p. 93.

[5] Lee Patterson, "The Historiography of Romance and the Alliterative *Morte Arthure*," *Journal of Medieval and Renaissance Studies*, 13 (1983), 2.

[6] M. D. Chenu, *Nature, Man, and Society in the Twelfth Century*, ed. and trans. Jerome Taylor and Lester K. Little (Chicago: University of Chicago Press, 1968), p. 199.

[7] Morton W. Bloomfield, "Chaucer's Sense of History," in *Essays and Explorations*, ed. Morton W. Bloomfield (Cambridge, MA: Harvard University Press, 1970), p. 25.

[8] Robert W. Hanning, *The Individual in Twelfth-Century Romance* (New Haven: Yale University Press, 1977), p. 139.

[9] *Caxton's Malory, A New Edition of Sir Thomas Malory's Le Morte Darthur*, ed. James W. Spisak and William Matthews (Berkeley: University of California Press, 1983), p. 516. All further references to Malory's *Le Morte Darthur* will be cited hereafter within the text of this paper.

[10] Felicity Riddy, "Structure and Meaning in Malory's 'The Fair Maid of Astolat,'" *Forum for Modern Language Studies* 12 (1976), 362.

[11] Mircea Eliade, *The Sacred and the Profane*, trans. Willard R. Trask (New York: Harcourt Brace Jovanovich, 1959), 96.

[12] Rudolph M. Bell, *Holy Anorexia* (Chicago: University of Chicago Pres, 1985), pp. 18-19.

[13]Bell, p. 21.

[14]Mircea Eliade, _Myths, Dreams, and Mysteries_, trans. Phillip Mairet (New York: Harper and Row, 1960), p. 239.

[15]Eliade, _The Myth of the Eternal Return_, p. 150.

ARMS AND THE LOVER IN THE
FIFTEENTH-CENTURY SPANISH NOVEL

by James R. Stamm

Love and warfare are very closely interwoven in the
early peninsular novels of chivalry and sentiment.
Being a **caballero**, in these fictions, implied not only
possessing a horse, but being a lover as well, or at
least professing devotion to a mistress, as Don Quijote
makes clear in his invention of Dulcinea. The **Caballero
de la Triste Figura** was well aware, from his reading in
the sources, that one cannot be a champion of truth and
justice without the inspiration of a relatively chaste
and--usually--absent or unobtainable love.[1] A necessary corollary is that the lover improves his status in
the eyes of the lady by his "service" to her in the
lists of honor or through prowess in warfare. Spanish
fiction in the fifteenth century shows a clear predilec-
tion for this tension. While Boccaccio worked his sentimental romance, **Elegia di Madonna Fiammetta**, around
political and commercial interests, essentially bourgeois rather than courtly milieu, and while Piccolomini
was content, in **Historia de Duobus Amantibus**, with
amorous intrigue for its own sake, Castilian and Catalan
writers felt it desirable to prove their heroes' devotion in the trial by arms. And not alone in fiction:
one curious example of the mating of martial valor with
masochistic surrender to the feminine will is the **Libro**

del Passo Honroso defendido por el excelente caballero
Suero de Quiñones, the true account of a prolonged
journey reported in precise detail in a Leonese chronicle of 1434. This tension or dichotomy is also a factor
in two little-studied novels, the recently published
Triste deleytación and the Catalan Curial y Güelfa, both
anonymous works, in which combat and the obstacles to
love interact in a more or less complementary fashion.

Triste deleytación comes to us in a single manuscript from the Biblioteca de Catalunya of Barce-
lona.2 Internal evidence dates the novel between 1458
and 1467, and it is the work of a Catalan author writing
in Castilian; in fact, it includes a quantity of verse
in Catalan. The title itself, which might be prosai-
cally translated as "Sad Delight," identifies the genre
of the work, if we still care to think in those terms,
as being that of the sentimental novel. In fact, the
title indulges in one of those oxymora so dear to the
poets of the fifteenth-century cancioneros and parodied
by Celestina in her definition of love for Melibea: "Es
un fuego escondido, una agradable llaga, un sabroso
veneno, una dulce amargura, una delectable dolencia, un
alegre tormento, una dulce y fiera herida, una blanda
muerte."3

The central figure of the work, identified only as
the Lover (Enamorado), is initially rejected by his lady
and he resolves to go off to the wars. This decision
comes as a result of analytical thinking; he realizes
that this rejection may not be entirely arbitrary on the
part of the Lady, and that it may be the result of some
lack of virtue in himself: "Vino a ymaginar que no de
[ella] mas dél algunas faltas fuesen causa. . . .
delibró d'alí partir para la g[u]erra, por que fuese de
sus trabajos y infinito querer brevemente de quien tanto

quería por muerte a remuneración satisfecho."[4] He
feels certain that his going to war equates with death
and that his sacrifice will serve to convince the Lady
of his sincere devotion. His act represents to the
Lover neither bravado nor desperation, but rather the
opportunity for "virtuosa inmienda." To signal this new
course which his life will follow, he changes his colors
from black and tan to blue and white, and we find in
this action an element of symbolism which will be
developed at considerable length in the later sentimental novel. Black represents mourning and despair,
while tan signifies worry and anguish; blue indicates a
range of positive feelings and white, of course, the
purity of his intentions.

The Lover is not entirely bent on self-destruction;
he reflects that "muchas vezes una pequenya absençia es
causa de crecentar más amor . . . aun por más mostrar
quánto es el querer suyo por algunos peligros[os]
serviçios."[5] He is so lost in introspection that he
rather comically falls off his horse as he waves farewell to the Lady. She is impressed by his devotion,
since "siguiendo el exerçiçio militar morir y no naçer
se acostumbra,"[6] so impressed that she sends a message
and some money to love's exile. The message is one of
encouragement rather than a call to the Lover to return;
he determines to face combat and either put an end to
his suffering through death or prove to the Lady that he
is worthy of her consideration. We soon learn that the
most intrepid soldiers in this war are expelled and
suffering practitioners of courtly love: "todos
aquél[l]os que quemados d'amor se sintían."[7] What a
way to run a war! But this circumstance illustrates the
extent to which love and warfare are linked in the
author's literary canon.

The Lady's letter raises doubts in the Lover's mind: does his true allegiance lie with his commander in a national cause, or with the sovereign demands of love? This is a serious dilemma, a dilemma of duty, but without immediate solution. The Lover goes to the front with the intention of winning the favor of the Lady or dying in the attempt, "no considerando los danyos ni stimando peligros, en son de onbre que ama seguir el fin suyo."8

The hour of combat arrives and the Lover is inspired to valor "en testimonio de la fe que a su Señora tenýa."9 Unlike other heroes of the novels of chivalry, this caballero is not cut out for glory in battle. At the first engagement, "por ser los golpes sin número, forçado, amorteçido, quedar [sic] en el suelo. Y así, sin movimiento, stubo por spaçio de una hora."10 There is no description of the battle or of personal encounters; the names of enemy knights do not appear, nor is there a list of accoutrements. It is a totally anonymous war; one in which neither attackers nor defenders have a name, a country, or a flag. It seems apparent that the author, most probably a cleric, was unfamiliar with the military enterprise and uses the war only as a device to separate the lovers temporarily, thus increasing the psychological tension of the tale. War is completely depersonalized and becomes little more than an abbreviated distraction in the narration. The adventure does serve a topical purpose: word arrives to the Lady that the Lover is dead, killed in battle, and this news provokes a long lament in better-than-average verse. Psychological penetration, so much a part of the sentimental novel, is highly developed in this work: we share the anxiety of the Lady and hear her confession to herself of love and concern for the Lover.

The military exercise ends at this point and the plot takes other and complex turns. As is the case throughout the Castilian sentimental novel, warfare and/or personal combat constitute a recurrent, though minor, ingredient. We recall that the global exploits of Ardanlier, in Siervo libre de amor, were presented simply as a list of wide-ranging travels and faultless victories.11 In the last decade of the fifteenth century, at the apogee of the sentimental novel, Diego de San Pedro will cut short the account of armed combat between Leriano and the false courtier Persio, "por no detenerme en esto que parece cuento de historias viejas."12 We note a new novelistic sensibility, one in which combat and martial activity are still an indispensable means of proving the lover's noble devotion, but which, at this stage in the evolution of the novel, lack pictorial attractiveness and do not warrant extensive development.

Curial y Güelfa is a Catalan romance roughly contemporary with Triste deleytación, but very different in its orientation.13 While it antedates both Tirant lo Blanc and the sixteenth-century text of Amadís de Gaula that we know, its general tone is much closer to those chivalric works than to the sentimental novel, whose atmosphere of anxiety, erotic symbolism, and psychological analysis provide so notable a contrast with the novels of chivalry. It is a broad-canvas novel which traces the career of Curial, son of a poor but virtuous man, who enters the service of the Marquis of Monferrat as a boy. The lad excels all others in beauty and intelligence and, as he grows to manhood, in the exercise of arms. He wins the favor of all but the envious, and particularly that of the Marquis' sister, Güelfa, Lady of Milan. She arranges anonymously to place her wealth

at Curial's disposal, so that he will want for nothing
and may have every opportunity to grow in virtue and
prowess. Undying love is soon generated between the
two, but the young knight has far to go in acquiring
patents of virtue. Güelfa maintains the upper hand in
this relationship; she, though quite young, is the widow
of the Lord of Milan, and thus of the highest nobility.
Her role in the novel is a complex one of tutrix, benefactress, and promised wife, although that promise is
highly contingent on the progress of Curial's exploits,
especially at arms. There is no other female figure
quite like Güelfa in the fifteenth-century peninsular
novel. She guides the young knight into his first
personal combat with the words, "The greater the danger
and the fear, the greater the honor that will accrue to
you from it.14

The project is thus more clearly delineated than in
other novels of chivalry: while fortune has given
Curial a place in the courts of nobility, and innate
qualities have given him preference among knightly
contenders, the dominant spirit of Milady Güelfa takes
his career in hand and directs it toward excellence.
And excellence is here defined in martial terms; it is
well recognized that only through his acquisition of
fame and honor in the lists can Curial hope to become
acceptable as the lady's consort. Again, virtue depends
upon valor. It is not enough that Curial has excelled
in the trivium and the quadrivium, that he is remarkably
handsome and a very pleasant chap at table. Güelfa's
patrimony is spent to accounter him as a champion, and
he must prove himself in foreign combat. Curial's
career becomes a long series of tourneys in which he is,
of course, invincible. One of the more bizarre of
these, and particularly interesting to the theme of this

paper, is proclaimed by the King of France. The participants will be divided into four parties: the knights
who are in love with widows shall wear ornaments of grey
and black; those who love married ladies shall sport
purple; those devoted to damsels shall wear green and
white, and those who love nuns, green and grey. Those
who have never loved may also participate, wearing
white, while those who no longer love shall wear black.

We may be tempted to find parallels between this
novel and some primitive versions of **Amadís** **de** **Gaula**,
and it is quite probable that the author knew the work
in some form, but the structure of the Catalan romance
differs greatly. There is no mystery about Curial's
name or origins, no presence of the supernatural in
enchantments, monsters, or giants, no mysterious mentor
comparable to Urganda la Desconocida, no magical tests
of love. There is, instead, considerable play of allegory. In Book III, the goddess Fortune turns against
Curial and does everything in her power to bring about
his ruin. She tries to enlist the aid of Juno and
Neptune against the hero, but these figures find no
justice in Fortune's demand. Nevertheless, she is able
to make life quite miserable for Curial, causing Güelfa
to reject him and turning all his friends against him.
Worse yet awaits the young knight: seven years of captivity and slavery under the Moors. The fickle goddess
finally relents, Curial regains his freedom and returns
to Monferrat. He is named Grand Constable of the Christian forces in a great battle against the Turks, a battle which is conducted according to the most rigorous
rules of chivalry. The Christians triumph over the
Infidel and Güelfa joyfully accepts Curial, now at the
peak of his glory, as her husband.

While personal combat is the (literally) royal road
to acquiring honor and a good name, Curial is equally
honored for his learning. At a particularly low point
in his misfortune, the god Bacchus, here representing,
oddly enough, reason, learning, and justice, appears to
Curial in a dream and upbraids him for having lapsed
into soft and lascivious ways of life, "as though he had
been an archbishop or a great prelate, forgetting that
he was a knight and a learned man" (254). Says Bacchus,
"You who shone in the world both for your chivalry and
your learning have now won ill-repute in those places
where you are but newly known, and if you do not return
to your former ways this will become even more the
case. I beg, require and warn you to return to your
studies . . . Do not exchange the divine and eternal
gift of learning for earthly and temporal brutishness
and filth" (256). This seems a most curious reversal of
priorities in a genre which we think of as representing
virtue only in the clash of steel and fidelity in love.
The author thus adds an unexpected component, foreign to
both the sentimental novel and the books of chivalry,
which perhaps anticipates the formulae for perfection in
courtly life elaborated later by Machiavelli and Castig-
lione.

Life seems to be imitating art to an astonishing
degree in the famous _Passo honroso defendido por el_
excelente caballero Suero de Quiñones.14 The young
nobleman has been in "prisión de una señora gran tiempo
acá," and as a sign of his servitude, every Thursday he
wears a massive iron ring around his neck. We are not
told whether the lady imposed this penance of love, or
Suero adopted it voluntarily as the outward sign of his
devotion. He seeks to liberate himself from this undoubtedly uncomfortable encumbrance with a grand ges-

ture. He and nine companions, all **hidalgos de limpia
sangre**, will undertake to defend the bridge of Orbigo,
in northwestern Spain, against all knights who attempt
to cross it, for a period of thirty days. All ladies
who wish to pass must surrender their right glove, and
all the knights must give up their right spur until
these tokens are redeemed in armed encounter, where each
challenger shall fight until three lances are broken.
Combat shall not go beyond this limit and no grudges are
allowed to be carried beyond the lists. The tourney is
sponsored by King John II and his constable, Don Alvaro
de Luna, who are gallantly excused from taking up the
challenge. Suero de Quiñones, second son of Don Diego
Hernández de Quiñones, Merino Mayor, or chief civil
judge of the province of Asturias, undertook the enor-
mous expense of the tourney, utilizing three hundred
oxcarts to transport building materials for the stands
and other necessary construction, supplying arms and
horses to the challengers, along with temporary housing
and nightly banquets. Supporting personnel is not
detailed beyond a mention of "carpinteros y cirujanos,"
but there is implied a vast company of backstage workers
in the description of the festivities, the special
livery of pages, and the constant presence of musicians. The trumpeters, incidentally, have their own
competitive blow-out to determine which can play longest
and loudest.

Interesting details and sidelights appear. It has
been forbidden to communicate with the combatants during
the jousts by voice or sign, and when a page of the poet
Lope de Stuniga cries out to his master in encouragement, he is sentenced to have his tongue cut out. This
punishment is swiftly commuted to thirty blows with a
stick and off to jail. Various young nobles are

knighted for the occasion, some by Suero himself, and
they participate as challengers, "to liberate Suero from
his captivity," and thus help him to fulfill his vow.
The challengers are in no sense enemies; it is a point
of honor to receive and treat them as guests. Tempers
do of course flare up, and some of the knights seek to
extend the combat beyond the established terms, but this
is never allowed by the judges or the "king of arms."

One challenger is killed when a lance pierces the
visor of his helmet and penetrates his eye. The Church
refuses him burial in sacred ground, since "la sancta
Iglesia non tiene por fijos á los que mueren en tales
exercicios; porque non se pueden fascer sin pecado
mortal: nin ruega por ellos á Dios, como dexandolos por
condenados: de lo qual dispone el Derecho Canónico en
el título de los Tornéos" (LXIV, 55).15 Suero appeals
this decision to the bishop of Astorga and promises, if
permission is granted, to have the young knight buried
in the family chapel of the Quiñones in León. Again,
permission is denied, and so the unfortunate Esberte de
Claramonte is buried in unsanctified ground near the
bridge, with much honor but without the blessing of the
Church.

The tourney continues for its allotted time; the
Passo honroso ends, as agreed, on August 9, 1434, when
Suero and his companions have fulfilled their vow to
defend the bridge against all challengers until 300
lances have been broken or thirty days have passed. In
fact, the chronicler records, only 166 lances have been
broken and on more than one occasion the defenders--who
could not be substituted--were forced to postpone
encounters owing to wounds, sprains, and other ortho-
pedic disasters. The judges decree that the conditions
of the tourney have been fulfilled and Suero de Quiñones

is relieved of his amorous penance as the iron collar is
ceremoniously removed from his neck.

The chronicle is presented quite factually and there
is no indication that it is in any way exaggerated or
fictionalized. An abbreviated version was included in
the **Historia** del **Rey** **Don** **Juan** **II**, and the full account
was licensed for publication in 1538, "para que los
Caballeros de nuestro tiempo hallassen una buena muestra
de los de aquél, y quietassen de aventura tan peligrosa
como la de los libros de caballerías fingidas, y
escripta con gran rigor de verdad."[16] These words are
at once a condemnation of the novels of chivalry, long
fallen from popular favor when Don Quijote rode forth to
take up knight-errantry, and a celebration of remarkable
deeds of the past.

Love, and the suffering it may cause, will continue
to be celebrated in the Spanish novel, and the resort to
arms either as a proof of virtue and constancy or as a
last resort in winning the lady and upholding her honor
will be an important factor in the novels of San Pedro
and in the novels of chivalry which dominate Spanish
prose fiction in the first half of the sixteenth century.[17] As the practice itself becomes more and more
remote from experience, new fantasies will arise, the
most notable of them being the pastoral novel. We find
then the expression of a new and more poetized sensibility, and love will no longer go hand-in-gauntlet with
warfare and its surrogates.[18]

NOTES

[1]Cervantes' satirical bent makes a strong point of
this sine qua non of chivalric novels very early in Part
I of Don Quijote: "Toda aquella noche no durmió don
Quijote, pensando en su señora Dulcinea, por acomodarse
a lo que había leído en sus libros, cuando los caballeros pasaban sin dormir muchas noches en las florestas
y despoblados, entretenidos con las memorias de sus
señoras." Miguel de Cervantes Saavedra, El ingenioso
hidalgo Don Quijote de la Mancha, I, 8.

[2]Triste deleytación. An Anonymous Fifteenth-Century
Castilian Romance, ed. E. Michael Gerli (Washington,
DC: Georgetown University Press, 1982).

[3]Fernando de Rojas, La Celestina, ed. Dorothy S.
Severin (Madrid: Alianza Editorial, 1969), X, 158-59.
"It's a secret fire, a gentle wound, a delicious poison,
a sweet bitterness, a delectable grief, a welcome torment, a kind yet cruel hurt, an easy death." Fernando
de Rojas, La Celestina, translated with an introduction
by J. M. Cohen (New York: New York University Press,
1966), 157.

[4]"He came to imagine that the fault might lie not with
her, but in his own shortcomings . . . He resolved to go
off to the wars so that she whom he so loved might soon
be satisfied by his deeds and his death." Triste deleytación, 26. All translations from Triste deleytación
are mine. The specific source will be indicated by
reference to page numbers in the Gerli edition.

[5]"Often times a brief absence may serve to increase
love . . . and even to show how great is his love by
death-defying service" (27).

[6]"following the military life, death and not birth is
the customary outcome" (28).

[7]"all those who felt themselves inflamed by love"
(29).

[8]"not considering wounds nor counting dangers, as a
man who seeks his own destiny" (29).

[9]"in testimony of the faith in which he held his lady"
(31).

[10] "as the blows were beyond number, overpowered, he lay on the field like one dead" (31).

[11] Juan Rodriguez del Padron, *Siervo libre de amor*, ed. Antonio Prieto (Madrid: Castalia, 1976). "E después del común passaje en las quatro partes del mundo, y grandes passados peligros, que en loor de aquella que amaua más que a sý, con grand afan andaua a la ventura, fue llegado a las partes de Yria, rryberas del mar Oçéano . . . , p. 87.

[12] "not to bother the reader with stories which appear to be ancient history." Diego de San Pedro, *Cárcel de amor*, ed. Keith Whinnom (Madrid: Castalia, 1971), 117. Whinnom's note (119) to this passage comments: "es de suponer que San Pedro está aludiendo a las novelas de caballerías; pero también parecería una historia vieja porque tales lides formales delante del rey ya no tenían lugar en España." The original date of publication of *Cárcel* is 1491.

[13] *Curial and Güelfa*, trans. Pamela Waley (London: George Allen & Unwin, 1982). Quotations will be identified by page numbers in the text. My use of the form *Curial y Güelfa* in the text corresponds to the usage in early Spanish manuals of literary history, by which the novel is still known to many.

[14] *Libro del passo honroso, defendido por el excelente caballero Suero de Quiñones, copilado de un libro antiguo de mano por Fr. Juan de Pineda Religioso de la Orden de San Francisco* (Madrid: Imprenta de D. Antonio Sancha, 1783. Reimpresión facsímil, Valencia: Anubar, 1970).

[15] "the Holy Church does not consider as her children those who die in such exercises, for they may not be undertaken without incurring mortal sin. Nor does She pray to God for them, but abandons them as condemned, as canon law disposes under the title devoted to tourneys."

[16] *Passo honroso, Licencia*, unpaged, preceding the text. "so that the knights of our present time may find a good example of those of that earlier age and forego their taste for adventures as dangerous as those we find in made-up books of chivalry, and here reported with great respect for the truth." My translation.

[17] The immense popularity of Garci Ordóñez de Montalvo's reworking of *Amadís de Gaula* led to a great many imitations and sequels, bringing to a round dozen the

series related to the original hero, including _Amadís de Grecia_, 1530 (?), _Don Florisel de Niquea_ (1532), _Don Rogel de Grecia_ (1535), and _Don Silves de la Selva_ (1546), written by various authors. Another series, clearly derived from the original novel, includes _Palmerín de Olivia_ (1511), _Primaleón_ (1512), and _Palmerín de Inglaterra_ (1548). We note that the inspiration for composing these (largely imitative) works had died out by mid-century, but there were new editions of some of the works being printed as late as 1599. See Daniel Eisenberg, _Romances of Chivalry in the Spanish Golden Age_ (Newark, DE: Juan de la Cuesta, 1982), especially 97-104.

[18]This is not to say that violence is totally absent from Spanish pastoral fiction. It represents, rather, an intrusive, unexpected variation from the norms of experience and behavior in the tranquil glades of Arcadia. Nowhere does violence take on the formal and organized guise of warfare or personal combat that we have seen in the sentimental novel and the novels of chivalry. For a discussion of this aspect of two of the pastoral works, see James R. Stamm, "_La Galatea_ y el concepto de género," in _Cervantes: Su obra y su mundo: Actas del I Congreso internacional sobre Cervantes_, ed. Manuel Criado de Val (Madrid: EDI-6, 1981), 337-43.

WIFELY WILES: COMIC UNMASKING IN
LES QUINZE JOYES DE MARIAGE

by Steven M. Taylor

As a major work of the fifteenth century in France,
Les Quinze joyes de mariage has elicited considerable
critical comment. For example, some scholars have
indulged in a fruitless search for the identity of its
author.[1] Others have convincingly demonstrated the
anonymous satirist's debt to earlier misogynists, particularly to Jean de Meung and to the French version of
the Lamentations of Matheolus.[2] Lastly, a numerous
group including Söderhjelm, Rychner, and Nykrog, has
sought to come to grips with the work's form, producing
descriptive hypotheses ranging from a series of proto-
typic novellas to, as Nykrog would have it, an elaborate
paradigmatic joke.[3] These prior examinations of the
Quinze joyes, despite their earnestness or perhaps
because of it, have not given sufficient attention to
the timeless comic content of this masterful caricature
of connubiality. Using the theories of Henry Bergson as
a critical grid, the present study will concentrate on
the comic elements of Les Quinze joyes de mariage,
specifically the depiction of marriage itself and the
two individuals it links.[4]

Bergson's basic definition of the comic is "something mechanical encrusted on the living" (Comedy, p.
84). In practical terms, this axiom means that individuals or institutions which fail to adapt themselves

to circumstances become ridiculous by their rigidity.
The French philosopher further states: "Any arrangement
of acts and events is comic which gives us, in a single
combination, the illusion of life and the distinct impression of a mechanical arrangement" (Comedy, p. 105).
The anonymous author of Les Quinze joyes finds such a
comic situation in the institution of marriage, as preva-
lent in fifteenth-century France. As he explains in the
prologue to his work, marriage is inherently incompati-
ble with human happiness, since it perforce limits the
liberty of those involved. His premise seems to be that
all men are born free, but some get married. Despite
his apparent clerical status (QJ, lines 110-13, p. 4),
which he calls "another servitude," he adopts a clini-
cal, cynical and hence comic parti pris: husbands and
wives in Les Quinze joyes are a secular species; there
is not a single Scriptural reference to the duties and
spiritual benefits of marriage partners in the work.
This omission is telling. Prefiguring Balzac by four
centuries, the author of Les Quinze joyes proposes a
physiology of marriage, a description of its banal
biological realities rather than its spiritual dimensions. In so doing, he maximizes the comic potential of
such a bestiary for, as Bergson states, "Any incident is
comic that calls our attention to the physical in a
person, when it is the moral side that is concerned"
(Comedy, p. 93). The fifteenth-century author pursues
his comic purpose of desacralizing and demeaning marriage, then, by a series of metaphors stressing the
constraints of the institution and the animality of
those it binds.

This process of comic mechanization by means of
metaphors begins in the prologue with the comparison of
marriage to a pit designed to trap wild beasts (QJ,

lines 59-66, pp. 2-3). However, the author rapidly
shifts to another metaphor borrowed from the Old Woman
(la Vieille) in Jean de Meung's continuation of Le Roman
de la Rose.5 The Old Woman, like the author of Les
Quinze joyes, finds folly in any restriction of freedom. Hence, she compares men who join monastic orders
to foolish fish, which, lured by the bait, have flocked
into a net (la nasse) only to rue their haste until
captivity shortens and ends their days. The author of
Les Quinze joyes alters the object of the metaphor from
monasticism to marriage, an inspired adaptation which
lends itself to absurd embellishment, for, as we will
see, the "bait" in the later work is sexual gratifica-
tion rather than creature comforts, a wife who in turn
becomes the "baiter." In any event, the image of the
net becomes an obsessive one. The objective correlative
of marital frustration, it recurs as a pervasive refrain
in each of the fifteen episodes, framing the absurd
examples of the folly which marriage, the net, en-
genders.6 The cumulative effect of this rhetorical
strategy produces the comic result which Bergson attributes to repetition (Comedy, p. 119). The reader laughs
at the author's insight that marriage is a "mechanical
arrangement" which is equally inhibiting to any individual who enters into it, whether by free choice or by
coercion.

Before continuing with the enumeration of the comic
metaphors which the author employs to convey his impression of the absurdity of marriage, it is important to
explain his basic intention, which is to unmask in an
amusing way what he feels is the hypocrisy of the conventional view of this institution traditionally considered
as a source of happiness. As Sigmund Freud, another
theorist of the comic, states, unmasking is directed

against people and objects which lay claim to authority
and respect.[7] Our subversive author seeks to elicit
our complicity in this task by pitting us reasonable
human beings of either sex against the "fish," those who
have abdicated their rights and reason to such an extent
that they find contentment in cuckoldry, happiness in
harassment, and pleasure in pain. He therefore concludes his prologue as follows: "Thus, observing these
torments which [married men] take as joys, considering
the incompatibility which exists between their mentality
and mine and that of many others, I have taken great
pleasure in watching them swim in the net in which they
are so enmeshed . . ." (QJ, lines 135-40, p. 5). His
ironic conclusion is that this unmasking will be wasted
on those fated to marry, because their comic idée fixe--
that marriage brings beatitude--blinds them to what he
feels is an obvious truth: that it is a confinement, a
prison which corrupts all its inmates, particularly the
henpecked husbands, primary specimens of the "stir-
crazy" spouse.

To conclude our discussion of the author's metaphors
for marriage, we find in the Fourteenth Joy an image
which continues the idea of confinement while adding the
further complication of conflict. As we will see
shortly in the discussion of the comic of character in
Les Quinze joyes, the author considers men and women as
antithetical, like certain animal species. He explains: "Now consider whether it is well done to put
two contrary things together! It is to be compared to
putting a cat and a dog in a sack: they will war inside
it until the end" (QJ, lines 99-103, p. 102). Like
Jean-Paul Sartre in No Exit, our author makes the Other,
whether wife or husband, a source of continual anguish.
Indeed, throughout the work, the two sexes torment one

another in a burlesque battle for hegemony, like
cellmates struggling for the best bunk. Unlike the
fabliaux, in which husbands normally reassert their
authority after a challenge, however, most male spouses
in Les Quinze joyes relinquish the symbolical trousers
without a fight (QJ, line 77, p. 80).[8] Thus, by using
the concrete metaphors of the pit, the sack and the net,
the author of Les Quinze joyes succeeds in creating a
comic transposition that heightens our appreciation of
the incongruity inherent in marriage as he views it
while it prepares us to accept the spouses themselves as
animal and trainer.

The author of Les Quinze joyes is careful in his
composite caricatures of husbands and wives to avoid any
individualization whatsoever, even to the extent of
refusing to give a stock name to the different avatars
he presents. Rather, his approach corresponds to Bergson's prescription for the creation of comic types:
"Consequently, the effect must appear to us as an
average effect, as expressing an average of mankind"
(Comedy, p. 169). It is marriage which brings about
this leveling metamorphosis in every husband. Unlike
the caterpillar and the butterfly, the carefree young
bachelor ineluctably loses his individuality and becomes
a drab drudge. Moreover, the uxorious husband increases
his absurdity by his masochism. Married men's endurance
and even enjoyment of suffering inspires the wry
satirist to formulate the first of a series of animal
metaphors and comparisons in the conclusion to his
prologue: "But there is one thing, for they take these
torments for joys and pleasures and are as inured to
them as a pack mule and seem to be very content, and for
this reason, there is some doubt as to whether they will
derive any merit from them: (QJ, lines 131-35, pp.

4-5). Evidently, our author is engaging in comic hyper-
bole by reducing men to the level of donkeys. However,
as an acute observer of husbands, he has detected their
comic flaw: in general, they prefer to trade tracta-
bility for relief from tension. Like dogs or donkeys,
men are "broken in" by their wives who, by a comic inversion, become the trainers in a situation where, de jure,
they should be subservient to their husbands. It is
clear that the author of Les Quinze joyes feels that the
routine of marriage, combined with the wife's manipu-
lative techniques, will break the spirit of any man. He
exaggerates this latent pliability in men in each of the
ensuing metaphors, realizing that, as Bergson will later
state, "Caricature is a means which the artist is using
to manifest to our eyes the distortions which he sees in
embryo" (Comedy, p. 77). It is reality raised expo-
nentially to the level of ridicule. By judicious repetition of the animal analogy in varying contexts, the
cynical cleric invites our laughter at the alterity of
such husbands. For example, in the Third Joy, lying-in
provides women the opportunity for further conditioning
of their spouses. After being badgered by his wife and
her cronies because of his inadequacies, the hapless
husband is reduced to the state of a beaten dog so that
"one could lead him off by a leash to guard the sheep"
(QJ, lines 257-58, p. 25).

In the Fourth Joy, the author returns to the image
of the ass as an epithet for a paradigmatic older husband who has become "hardened like an old donkey, which,
by habit, endures the spurs, so that he does not quicken
his pace which he normally uses on their account" (QJ,
lines 11-14, p. 27). In the Seventh Joy, an animal
analogy explains why women thrive and men waste away in
the marriage environment: "So you will see a hen which

lays an egg every day get fatter than a rooster does,
for the rooster is so stupid that he does nothing all
day except to look for food for her and puts it in her
beak, and the hen does no more than eat and cackle and
enjoy herself" (QJ, lines 34-39, p. 58). In the Eighth
Joy, a henpecked husband, seeking to satisfy his wife's
whims during a pilgrimage, runs around more than a dog
(QJ, line 110, p. 69). In the Twelfth Joy, the husband
has been truly broken to the yoke: "If anybody has
business with him he says: 'I will talk about it with
my wife or with the lady of the household,' and if she
wants it to happen, it will, and if she does not,
nothing will, for the good man is so well trained that
he is as docile as the ox at the plow" (QJ, lines 14-19,
p. 90). Even if the urge to rebel does cross a husband's mind, he remains impotent in the topsy-turvy
world view of Les Quinze joyes. The author's most
inspired animal metaphor which evokes the comic calamity
of a henpecked husband is found in the Fourteenth Joy:
"He who has fallen to this point has no recourse, except
to pray God that He give him enough patience to endure
and suffer everything, like an old muzzled bear, which
has no teeth, tied with a thick iron chain and poked and
prodded with a big wooden stick, all he can do is yell;
but when he yells, he gets two or three more pokes" (QJ,
lines 50-57, p. 100). As these examples indicate, the
rhetorical strategy of animal metaphors does succeed in
conveying the cowed status of the married man. The husbands in Les Quinze joyes constitute a meek and mirth-
inspiring menagerie.

Unlike animals, however, married men, whether compared to fish, dogs, bears or donkeys, do not have the
consolation of blaming their capture or captivity on
other agents. They, like Molière's George Dandin, have

made their own bed and must lie in it (even if conditions are somewhat crowded at times). George Dandin is
less comically unaware than his fifteenth-century
counterparts, however, as would indicate his outburst
concerning his disastrous decision to marry at the end
of Act I of Molière's farce: "You got your way, you got
your way, George Dandin, you got your way, it serves you
very right, and here you are treated as you should be,
you have just what you deserve."9 Most of the medieval husbands in Les Quinze joyes are too asinine to
realize or to verbalize their state, either because
marriage has brutalized them or because they choose to
blind themselves to reality, a complacency which
attracts the whip of the author's ire. Lest any man
among his readers be too prompt to assert his superi-
ority to this daunted and domesticated species, the
author concludes his diatribe by warning that "whoever
believes that [i.e., that he is in fact superior], the
better he is bridled" (QJ, lines 34-35, p. 115).

Ironically, although married men stampede into marriage like bewildered bovines, once married, they are
completely cut off from the herd, isolated by their own
egotism or the machinations of their wives. For the
medieval married man--if not for his modern counter-
part--fear of cuckoldry is enough to make any other man,
even one's best friend, suspect as a possible seducer.
Thus, the wife in the Seventh Joy is able to turn the
tables on a well-intentioned masculine friend of her
husband who has revealed her numerous indiscretions by
accusing him of being one of them (QJ, pp. 61-64)! In
other instances, a cunning wife will do anything in her
power to isolate her husband from the guidance and coun-
sel of his peers. Thus, in the Sixth Joy, the wife pur-
posefully makes a visit to her home by four important

guests of her husband an unforgettable experience.
Denied towels (they are all in the wash), sheets (they
are locked in a chest whose key is lost), and even hot
food (the fire has been out for hours), the guests vow
never to return and leave their erstwhile friend to his
solitary confinement. They sum up his plight in an
inspired comic litotes, observing that "whatever the
lord orders is not an act of parliament" (OJ, lines
94-95, p. 51), that is, his wife countermands his
slightest wish.

As the preceding discussion indicates, the husband
is the primary victim of the comic verve of the author
of Les Quinze joyes. In terms of comic of character, a
married man is credulous, doting, fearful of cuckoldry,
but most importantly in terms of the comic strategy of
this narrative, he is as pliable as putty in his wife's
hands. If his primary comic trait is submissiveness,
the medieval caricaturist posits that the wife's is
assertiveness. Her main motivation is the will to
dominate and domesticate her mate, to break his spirit
by a steady diet of manipulation, based on browbeating
and blackmail in bed.

Anticipating Simone de Beauvoir by 500 years, the
author of Les Quinze joyes might well have formulated
her famous dictum, "One is not born, but rather becomes
a woman."10 He would have altered only the word
"woman," replacing it with the word wife. For, according
to his comic categorical thought, if marriage isolates a
husband from his peers, it unites a callow young wife
with a bevy of wily women who will spare no effort to
initiate her into the secrets of the superior species.
The clever cleric presents a diabolical mirror image of
the ideal for older women found in Titus 2:3-5: "The
aged women likewise, that they be in behaviour as

becometh holiness, not false accusers, not given to much
wine, teachers of good things; That they may teach the
young women to be sober, to love their husbands, to love
their children, To be discreet, chaste, keepers at home,
good, obedient to their own husbands, that the word of
God be not blasphemed." In the risible Realpolitik of
Les Quinze joyes women train women, then women train
men. Evidently, in the menagerie of marriage, there can
be only one trainer. Hence, older women, as in the case
of the Old Woman in Le Roman de la Rose, have a "duty"
to disabuse younger members of the sisterhood, to unmask
men and marriage in the earliest stages of the connubial
relationship. They must share their compendium of
cunning. Thus, the author presents such role models as
the wily woman in the Eleventh Joy who succeeds in
foisting a very pregnant "maiden" on an unsuspecting
male, stressing this beldame's encyclopedic experience
in such matters, vaster than "all the Old Testament and
the New" (QJ, lines 63-64, pp. 83-84)! Once they have
entered the cage, all married women, unlike their
lackadaisical spouses, are quick to establish that they
will be the mistress in all senses. It is in this sense
that the "bait" ironically becomes the "baiter." Thus,
in the Third Joy, the author presents a "hen party" in
graphic detail, unmasking the female unmasking of men,
as it were, so that male readers can better appreciate
the predicament into which their fictional peers persist
in plunging. Called in as experts following a first
labor and delivery, a bevy of dissolute "matrons" read
the riot act to their recuperating hostess concerning
her husband: "'He's a hard man'," says one of them.
'As all my girl friends here now, when I was married to
my husband, people told me he was so mean that he would
kill me. But, by God, my dear he is now well tamed,

thank God, for he would rather break an arm than think of doing or saying anything to upset me'" (OJ, lines 66-72, p. 20). She goes on to explain that, after having taken "the bit in her teeth," she is now in a position where she always has the last word. Needless to say, the indoctrinated new mother emulates this exploit by putting her own husband through his paces upon his return. She insists, for example, that only he can prepare chicken broth in such a way that she can stomach it in her weakened state. The new father predictably makes a hash in the kitchen, and his wife crowns the comedy by claiming that she is eating the consomme only to give him pleasure.

Les Quinze joyes is rife with such ridiculous examples of "breaking in" new husbands. In each instance, the most important point is that the wife-trainer ensure that the husband-trainee understand that he can never win. Thus, after the return from the pyrrhic pilgrimage of the Eighth Joy, a spoiled wife takes sadistic pleasure in putting her exhausted husband in the wrong: "The woman, who is tired, will not do a thing for two weeks except talk with her girl friends and cousins about the mountains and all the beautiful things she has seen and everything which has happened to her, and most of all, she complains about her husband, saying that he did not do a thing for her and that she is all tired out from it. And the husband finds everything upside down at home and takes great pains to fix what is wrong. In short, he has all the trouble, and if any good comes from it, she will say that it is due to her and her careful housekeeping, and if things do not go well, she will scold and say that it is his fault" (OJ, lines 149-61, p. 70).

When intimidation alone is insufficient to create a comic inversion, the women characters of Les Quinze joyes usurp the prerogative of Renart the fox and turn to mendacity. Like the folkloric animal hero, they are incarnations of the trickster, enslaved to their bellies and lusts, and nothing loath to use lying as an obvious stratagem in dealing with husbands as credulous and doltish as Ysengrin the wolf. One lie in particular resonates throughout the narrative when a wife wants to be winning or when she has been lubricious: in the First, Fifth and Seventh Joys, one finds variants of the following repeated shameless falsehood concerning kissing: "'Truly,' said she, 'As God helps me, never did my mouth touch a man's except yours and your cousins' and mine, when they come here and you order me to kiss them'" (QJ, lines 217-21, p. 39). Such effrontery might make even Renart blush! The wives of Les Quinze joyes resemble the vulpine villain in another striking way: they love to laugh at their victims, to gloat over the gullibility of their spouses. Repeatedly, in the First, Fifth, and Fifteenth Joys, wives rejoice over victory in the battlefield where they always fare best, the bed. To stifle their snickering, they have to stuff their mouths with the sheets (QJ, pp. 11, 37 and 102).

If marriage fosters women's tendency toward trickery and teaches them to be trainers of their husbands, it is nevertheless not responsible for the main source of incompatibility between the sexes. This, asserts the author of Les Quinze joyes, true to the misogynistic medical mythology of the time, lies in women's sexual insatiability and sophistication. Female sexual frustration is the principal theme of several of the most important of the work's divisions, specifically the

Fifth, Seventh and Fifteenth Joys. The Seventh Joy, for
example, is a treatise on the mutual unhappiness caused
by women's sexual appetites and curiosity. It begins
with an unflattering but perhaps not entirely false
axiom: "Of whatever estate she may be, whether of noble
extraction or not, there is a general rule in marriage,
that each wife believes and insists that her husband is
the worst and the weakest--when it comes to the secret
business--of all the others in the world" (QJ, lines
6-11, p. 57). Even if a man begins well in this respect
during his flaming youth, he wears out faster, and hence
the "rations" he furnishes his wife diminish in quality
and quantity. At this point, female curiosity and
instinct prevail: "And sometimes some [wives] run the
risk of trying whether other men are as impotent as
their husbands . . ." (QJ, lines 66-68, p. 59). The
narrator implies that once a wife has varied the menu,
she will never return to rations, and since present
pleasures are always more vivid than past ones, she will
believe in her theory all the more, because, as the
cynical cleric concludes, "experience is the best judge"
(QJ, lines 75-78, p. 59). In the earlier Fifth Joy, the
author presents wives as being better connoisseurs than
their spouses in amatory matters by using a protracted
metaphor based on oenology: "When the woman has a lover
to her liking and they can have a tryst, particularly
after a long separation, they give each other so much
pleasure that nobody could describe it, so that the
husband's prowess is prized as nothing. After the afore-
mentioned pleasures, the woman takes as much delight in
her husband's caresses as a wine taster gets from a
drink of the dregs from others' glasses after having
sampled a good mulled wine or fine vintage . . ." (QJ,
lines 97-104, pp. 35-36). In Les Quinze joyes, as in

the _fabliaux_, sex is a comic commodity which no husband
can successfully purvey.

Thus, united by training and taste, married women
face their isolated and brutish opponents with equa-
nimity, using words as whips to keep their spouses in
the traces. As the tricksters in the marriage relationship, wives receive the reader's approbation. Bergson
says that everyone loves to control situations in the
same way children enjoy pulling a dancing-jack or puppet
on a string: "Instinctively, and because one would
rather be a cheat than be cheated, in imagination at all
events, the spectator sides with the knaves . . ."
(_Comedy_, p. 111). Furthermore, when the "dancing-jacks"
stubbornly refuse to acknowledge the strings, as is the
case in _Les Quinze joyes_, it is difficult to resist
laughing at the husbands' plights. It is clear that
they are puppets, not people marionettes which merit our
mirth.

As this discussion has shown, one of the most
original features of the comic in _Les Quinze joyes_ is
the author's refusal to resort to the lame resolution of
connubial conflict by a stock reversal. Instead, he
retains the "woman on top" inversion throughout his
narrative, repeating it in fifteen principal treatments
with almost unlimited permutations. Physical violence,
the trump card of otherwise inept males in other medieval comic genres like the _fabliau_ and the _farce_, is
eliminated in the tamed-tamer paradigm which the author
establishes. He presents marriage as a type of Hobson's
choice for men, a no-win situation. His unabashedly
hostile but humorous unmasking of marriage, husbands,
and wives, lends itself to explanation by Bergsonian
analysis. _Les Quinze joyes_ makes us laugh because, in
it, caricature, repetition and inversion expose the very
clockwork of connubiality.

NOTES

[1]See among others: P. Fal, "La Charade des _Quinze joies de mariage_," _Studia Neophilologica_, 20 (1948), 3-13; P. Louys, _Une Enigme d'histoire littéraire: l'auteur des Quinze joyes de mariage_ (Paris: 1903); and J. Misrahi, "L'Enigme des _Quinze joyes de mariage_," _Romance Philology_, 9 (1955-56), 177-87.

[2]See particularly _Les .XV. Joies de mariage_, ed. Jean Rychner (Genève: Librairie Droz, 1967), pp. vii-xix and 141-69. Future references to this work will be abbreviated as _QJ_ and included parenthetically in the text. All translations into English of _Les Quinze joyes de mariage_ are those of the author of this study.

[3]See W. Söderhjelm, _La Nouvelle française au XVe siècle_ (Paris: 1910), pp. 29-72; and Per Nykrog, "Playing Games with Fiction: _Les Quinze joyes de mariage, Il Corbaccio, El Arcipreste de Talavera_," in _The Craft of Fiction: Essays in Medieval Poetics_, ed. Leigh A. Arrathoon (Rochester, MI: Solaris Press, 1984), pp. 423-51. Other modern discussions of the work include: Franz-Josef Albersmeier, "_Les Quinze joyes de mariage_ und der réalisme bourgeois in der französischen Prosa des 15. Jahrhunderts, _Fifteenth-Century Studies_, 8 (1983), 1-13; Nazli Rizk, "Didactisme et contestation dans _Les Quinze joyes de mariage_," _Le Moyen Français_, 1 (1977), 33-89; and M. Santucci, "Pour une interprétation des _Quinze joyes de mariage_," in _Le Récit bref au Moyen-Age_, ed. D. Buschinger (Amiens: Université de Picardie, 1980), pp. 153-73.

[4]Henri Bergson, "Laughter," in _Comedy_, ed. Wylie Sypher (Baltimore: The Johns Hopkins University Press, 1984), pp. 61-190. Future references to this work will be abbreviated as _Comedy_ and included parenthetically in the text.

[5]Guillaume de Lorris and Jean de Meung, _Le Roman de la Rose_, ed. Félix Lecoy (Paris: Librairie Honoré Champion, 1970), Vol. 2, verses 13937-13976, pp. 174-75.

[6]As Rychner mentions (p. 144), the image of _la nasse_ is also found in the _Lamentations_ of Matheolus. However, nowhere else does the image attain the same stature; it is mentioned at least once in each Joy and often repeatedly: for example, five times in the First Joy, five times in the Tenth Joy, etc.

[7]Sigmund Freud, "Jokes and the Comic," in _Comedy: Meaning and Form_, ed. Robert W. Corrigan (San Francisco: Chandler Publishing Company, 1965), p. 256.

[8]As Bergson points out, "A comic effect is obtained whenever we pretend to take literally an expression which was used figuratively" (_Comedy_, p. 135). A hilarious battle for the actual pants (_les braies_) occurs in the _fabliau_ "De sire Hain et de dame Anieuse," in _Fabliaux et contes_, ed. Robert Guiette (Paris: Editions Stock, 1981), pp. 77-90.

[9]Molière, _George Dandin_, in _Oeuvres Complètes_, ed. Georges Mongrédien (Paris: Garnier-Flammarion, 1965), Vol. 3, p. 291. The English translation is that of the author of this study.

[10]Simone de Beauvoir, _The Second Sex_, trans. H. M. Parsley (New York: Vintage Books, 1974), p. 301.

CLANDESTINE MARRIAGES IN THE LATE MIDDLE AGES*

by Zacharias P. Thundy

There was widespread use and abuse of the practice
of clandestine marriages--marriages performed outside
the church without the benefit of the clergy, without
public bans, and/or without witnesses--in medieval
Europe. This was primarily due to disagreements among
canon lawyers on the nature of marital consent, the
teaching of Pope Alexander III, and the different Church
practices in force in different parts of Europe.
Literary evidence of clandestine marriages can be seen
in Gottfried's Tristan (thirteenth century), Aucassin
and Nicolete (thirteenth century), Chaucer's Troilus
and Criseyde (fourteenth century), Shakespeare's Romeo
and Juliet (sixteenth century), and John Webster's
Duchess of Malfi (seventeenth century). In real life,
the most remarkable cases of late medieval clandestine
marriages were the marriages of Thomas Cranmer (1489-
1556) and of Ulrich Zwingli (1484-1531)--even though the
Reformers preached against the Catholic practice of
clandestine marriages, they themselves practiced it. A
study of clandestine marriages will throw considerable
light on our understanding of marriages in the Middle

*An earlier form of this article appeared in Fifteenth-
Century Studies, XI (1985), pp. 121-36.

Ages. The following fictional case study of a clandestine marriage--this particular case, though it could
take place in the fifteenth century as well, is placed
in the twelfth century for bringing together the three
great canonists (Gratian, Peter Lombard, and Pope
Alexander III) under one roof--describes vividly the
medieval phenomenon of the clandestine marriage.

The year was 1160. Two young people, Robert (16)
and Marie (14), lived in the same neighborhood in the
city of Avignon in Provence. Robert's parents were the
Count and countess of Avignon, and they arranged a
marriage for Robert with Sigrid, the daughter of Duke
Otto of Ratisbonne. The parents on both sides performed
the betrothal (*promissa foedera*) of Robert and Sigrid
without seeking the consent of the couple; they also
performed *desponsatio* in which wedding pledges (*arrhae*),
including the bride's ring, were exchanged. Three more
steps for the completion of the marriage remained: the
traditio or the handing over of the girl by her father
or *mundoaldus* to the husband, the nuptial Mass in which
the spouses received the Church's blessing, and the
departure of the bride from the church for her new home
(*domum ductio*) led or carried by the groom.1 However,
the night before all these three ceremonies were to take
place, Robert and Marie tried to escape to Paris, but by
some misfortune joined the wrong caravan of merchants
and ended up in Bologna, Italy. The young couple pri-
vately exchanged marriage vows one evening in the cathedral church of Bologna. But before they could live
together and consummate their marriage, they were discovered by the agents of the dukes of Ratisbonne and
Avignon and were brought before the Bishop of Bologna
who was asked to declare the union of Robert and Marie
null and void. The Bishop convened the *iuris periti*

(lawyers of canon law) of the Bologna Marriage Tri-
bunal. At that time a canon law convention attended by
professors and canon lawyers from Paris, Bologna, and
Rome was being held at Bologna University. The bishop
presented the case before the canon lawyers.

The bishop explained: "Robert (16) and Marie (14)
claim that they are validly married. Robert's parents,
on the other hand, argue that the young people are not
validly married even though they claim that they have
exchanged marriage vows. It is easy for me to resolve
the issue if you, lawyers, agree on the answer to the
following simple question: 'What human act or sequences
of acts create or constitute a marriage?' I don't have
the time to do my own research; the young people are
eager to have the issue settled in their favor so that
they can go on their honeymoon. The Count of Avignon is
also in a hurry: he wants to complete all the ceremonies of the marriage of Robert to Sigrid of Ratisbonne. I am in a hurry to go and say good-bye to my
dying father in Vincenza."

The canonists at the meeting split into three
groups: the Paris School, the Bologna School and the
Roman Curia. They agreed to give their expert opinion
the next day at nine in the morning.

The bishop, the defendants, the bailiffs, and the
lawyers assembled the next day at the diocesan chancery
office. The Bishop of Bologna started the proceedings
with the invocation of the Holy Ghost: "Come, Holy
Ghost, fill the hearts of they faithful . . ." He
continued:

> Dear Reverend Fathers, the issue to be
> decided by this court is not what a mar-
> riage is. The classic Roman Law enshrined

in the sixth-century Emperor Justinian's
Digesta (23,2,1) has already defined it
for us: "Nuptiae sunt coniunctio maris et
feminae et consortium omnis vitae, divini
et humani iuris communicatio: [Marriage
is a union of a man and a woman, and a
community (or sharing) of the whole life,
a participation in human and divine law].
Of course, this definition comes from the
jurist Herennius Modestinus who died three
centuries earlier (c. 244). Justinian's
Instituta (1,9,1) also gives the definition developed by Modestinus' contemporary, Domitius Ulpianus (d. c. 228):
"Nuptiae autem sive matrimonium est viri
et mulieris coniunctio, individuam consue-
tudinem vitae continens" [Marriage, or
matrimony, is a union of a man and a woman
involving an undivided (exclusive, permanent) sharing of life].

Your discussion and verdict on the
issue must be based on these definitions
of marriage which are based on Natural Law
enshrined in the classical legal codes and
the Revealed Law manifested by the Holy
Scriptures.

Further, be reminded that there are different elements that make up the process
of marrying: the betrothal (consensus de
futuro, i.e., agreement or engagement to
marry at a future date), handing over of
the girl with mundium (endowment or dowry)
by her father or guardian to the groom,
the couple's consent to marry here and now

by accepting each other as husband and
wife (consensus de praesenti), the
solemnisation of marriage which includes
the nuptial Mass or at least the priest's
blessing, the leading of the bride to her
new home (domum ductio), and the act of
sexual intercourse which consummates
marriage.

In the year 1160 there is general agreement among canon lawyers that intercourse
with a casual intention to marry does not
constitute a marriage, that solemnisation
is not essential to marriage's validity,
and that the handing over of the bride and
domum ductio are likewise not absolutely
necessary to the validity of marriage.
The issues for you to decide in this case
are the following: Is consent de praesenti sufficient by itself to create a
marriage? Must consent necessarily be
followed by sexual intercourse? If intercourse is required for a valid marriage,
is a marriage made up exclusively of consent de praesenti indissoluble?

Gratian, the Master of the School of Bologna and the
illustrious author of Concordantia Discordantium Canonum
(A Concordance of Discordant Canons),--Pope Innocent II
would later call this work Corpus Decretorum and it
would later be known by its abbreviated title
Decretum--spoke:

I believe you are all aware of my work: I
have made a collection of all the known

authentic canons and have tried to har-
monize all the major texts on marriage.
With the ancient Roman law I agree that
consent creates marriage and not just
carnal intercourse (Nuptias non concubitus
sed [affectus] facit (Codex Justiniani,
Digesta, 17, 20); that is, without mutual
consent there is no marriage. Consent
involves the will to be married (maritalis
affectio). Now, if the young people
eloped to a territory where the Roman law
of mutual consent de praesenti for marriage validity is held in force, they are
married validly even in the absence of
parental consent,[2] which is what Robert
and Marie have done in this case. However, I should add the distinction between
matrimonium initiatum (the inchoate marriage) and matrimonium ratum (the ratified
or completed marriage), which means that a
marriage is only begun in betrothal (desponsatio) and that it is completed only
with sexual intercourse. This is to be
understood in the following way: intercourse without the intent to contract a
marriage, and the deflowering of a virgin
without the exchange of consent do not
create a marriage. But an antecedent
intent to contract marriage and the exchange of consent has this effect, that in
the losing of her virginity, or in her
intercourse, a woman is said to marry her
husband, or "to celebrate her marriage"

[Decretum, c. 27, q.7, d.45]. As a consequence, an inchoate marriage initiated by
desponsatio or simple mutual consent can
be dissolved; only a marriage ratified and
completed by subsequent intercourse cannot
be dissolved [Dictum c. 27, q.2, c. 34; c.
27, q.2, c.35-39; PL 187:1406-08], which
means that the indissoluble sacrament of
matrimony exists only when consent is
followed by sexual intercourse. Therefore, the marriage of Robert and Marie can
be dissolved since they have not had any
sexual union after their clandestine marriage.

Next, it was the turn of the Parisian School to
present its position. They chose Peter Lombard, the
compiler of the four famous Libri Sententiarum at the
University of Paris during the years 1155 to 1158;
though his books recorded mainly the sayings of eminent
Christian scholars of the past, he also set forth his
own interpretations and conclusions especially on the
act or acts that constitute a marriage. He started out
by insisting that all of the traditional conditions like
mundium and domum ductio and nuptial blessing are not
essential to marriage even though they may be mandated
by local or tribal custom and law; he confirmed the view
of his eminent predecessor at Paris, Hugh of St. Victor,
that marriage is constituted by consensus de praesenti
which creates a marriage before and separately from
intercourse. Peter Lombard continued:

Hic quaeritur, 'cum consensus de praesenti
matrimonium faciat, cuius rei consensus

sit ille, an carnalis copulae, an cohabitationis, an utriusque. Si cohabitationis
consensus matrimonium facit, tunc frater
cum sorore potest contrahere matrimonium;
si carnalis copulae, tunc inter Mariam et
Joseph non fuit coniugium . . . Dicamus,
igitur quod consensus cohabitationis, vel
carnalis copulae non facit coniugium, sed
consensus coniugalis societatis . . . Cum
igitur sic conveniunt, ut dicat vir:
Accipio te in meum coniugem, et dicat
mulier: Accipio te in meum virum; his
verbis vel aliis idem significantibus
exprimitur consensus non carnalis copulae,
vel cohabitationis corporalis, sed con-
jugalis societatis; ex qua oportet eos
cohabitare, nisi forte causae religionis
pari voto corporaliter separentur, vel ad
tempus, vel usque ad finem (<u>Libri</u> <u>IV</u>
<u>Sententiarum</u>, dist. 28, cc. 3-4; PL 192:
915-16). [Here the question is this:
"Since consent <u>de</u> <u>praesenti</u> effects
marriage, what is the object of that
consent, carnal copula, cohabitation, or
both?" If consent to cohabitation makes
marriage, then brother can contract
marriage with sister; if it is carnal
copula, then there was no marriage between
Mary and Joseph . . . Let us say, then,
that neither consent to cohabitation nor
to carnal copula, effects marriage, but
consent to married life . . . Therefore,
when man and woman agree to say "I take
you for wife" and "I take you for

husband," in these words or in others signifying the same thing, there is expressed
consent not to carnal copula, nor to
bodily cohabitation, but to married life;
for this reason it is their duty to live
together, unless perchance by a mutual vow
for religious purposes they are bodily
separated, for a time or permanently.]3

Peter Lombard concluded: "I make the careful distinction, which Gratian has not, between consensus de
futuro and consensus de praesenti: the former establishes marriage before and separately from intercourse;
this means that, after making a consensus de praesenti,
which includes affectio maritalis, the parties cannot
contract another marriage even when there was no intercourse; this means that the clandestine marriage between
Robert and Marie is valid and no dissolution of the
marriage is permissible."

The Bishop of Bologna then stood up and made this
statement: "We recognize the authority of the Decretals
of Gratian and also the authority of the writings of
Peter Lombard as many of us do in Italy. Our Italian
ecclesiastical courts dissolve marriages on grounds of
sexual non-consummation though such marriages have been
declared to be indissoluble by the Gallic marriage
tribunals. Therefore, unless a higher authority inter-
venes, we do not see any reason why we may not dissolve
the marriage of Robert and Marie. Therefore, by virtue
of the apostolic power invested in me, I declare . . ."

"Stop all court proceedings," a Roman canonist
spoke. "We have a higher authority here. We have His
Holiness Alexander III (1159-81), the great canonist
Orlando Bandinelli, in our midst today. He will give

his judgment, the last word, on the validity of the
marriage of Robert and Marie. Let me first give the
academic background of His Holiness:

Orlando Bandinelli earlier in his Summa
Rolandi (F. Thaner, ed. Summar Magistri
Rolandi [Innsbruck, 1874] sided with
Gratian; later in his Sententiae, compiled
between 1150 and 1158, switched over to
Peter Lombard's view that mutual consent
of the parties is sufficient to create a
marriage provided it is accompanied by
official witnessing by a priest or notary;
on the other hand, before consummation,
the apostolic authority of the Pope can
dissolve the marriage by dispensation.
However, his final thoughts as Pope on
what constitutes a marriage are found in
the Decretal Veniens ad Nos (X, 4.1.15):
(1) Present consent (consensus de praesenti of the Parisian School) freely given
between parties who are free from diriment
impediments like a prior marriage or
priesthood creates a valid marriage. (2)
Future consent (consensus de futuro)
freely given by the parties makes an
indissoluble marriage if that consent is
followed by sexual intercourse. (3) A
non-consummated marriage can be dissolved
by papal authority, for example, if one of
the parties wishes to take monastic vows.
Alexander III's decisions confirm these
principles. As Pope he was given the case
of a woman who had made her consent de

praesenti to marry a man without the
ecclesiastical formalities; later, she
made a consent _de futuro_ with another man
accompanied by sexual intercourse with
him; the Pope judged the case in favor of
consent _de praesenti_ (Mackin, p. 168). In
another case he ruled that betrothal, if
followed by intercourse even in the
absence of consent _de praesenti_, creates a
valid marriage because consent _de prae-
senti_ is presumed in the case (Mackin, p.
169). In a letter to the bishop of
Norwich, Alexander ruled that a valid
marriage is made by the simple consent _de
praesenti_ even in the absence of solemni-
ties and witnesses (Mackin, p. 169). All
this means is that he adopted neither the
Bologna- nor the Paris-resolution in full;
he rejected the Roman, Germanic, and
Eastern traditions which required some
solemnity for the validity of marriage; he
also rejected the requirement of the permission of the feudal lord, master, or
family for the validity of marriages (Donahue, p. 256).4

Alexander III now stood up and gave his irrevocable
decision on the marriage of Robert and Marie: "This
clandestine marriage of Robert and Marie is a valid
marriage--though I do not approve of clandestine mar-
riages--because there is a mutual consent _de praesenti_
here."

Robert and Marie were happy with the decision; both
the Paris and the Bologna canonists were pleased because

the Pope, a canonist, did not condemn them but rather
praised their efforts; the Bishop of Bologna was relieved because his decision was made easy by the Pope.

The impact of Alexander's definitive resolution of
the canonical dispute on what constitutes a valid marriage can be seen in the subsequent actions of the later
Popes. Pope Urban II (1185-87) confirmed Alexander's
judgment of the dissolubility of a non-consummated
marriage (Mackin, p. 169). Pope Innocent III (1189-
1216) followed Alexander's ruling and ordered in the
case of sponsa duorum--woman with two spouses--that the
first marital consent de praesenti alone makes the
marriage and supersedes any promise de futuro or de
praesenti followed by intercourse (Mackin, p. 170).
Finally, Book IV of Gregory IX's (1227-41) Decretals,
which appeared in 1234, proclaimed unequivocally the
Roman consensual position or the Alexandrine view that
it is consent de praesenti alone that creates a valid
marriage. The intention of the Alexandrine rules was to
ensure the freedom of the parties from external coercion; however, they made clandestine marriages available
to parties who were desperate and who could not hope to
secure the consent of their families or their feudal
lords.

One major by-product of Alexander's decision was the
necessary toleration of clandestine marriages, which
were valid on account of the presence of consent de
praesenti. Of course, authorities consistently deemed
clandestine marriages as illegal and condemned them
vigorously; for instance, the Fourth Council of Lateran
(1215), summoned by Innocent III, categorically forbade
clandestine marriages. Also, various provincial councils such as the councils of Cologne (1280), Padua
(1351), Prague (1355), Magdeburg (1370), and Salzburg

(1420), made attempts to legislate against secret marriages.

The force of the Alexandrine rules is also reflected
in the large proportion of marriage cases brought before
diocesan courts in the fourteenth and the fifteenth centuries; most of these cases were filed not for divorce
but for the enforcement of marriages, for the declaration of the validity of marriages, and for the restor-
ation of conjugal rights.[5] After examining the
evidence of medieval marriage cases, Charles Donahue
concludes:

> First, the Alexandrine rules were being
> applied in practice . . . Second, the core
> rule of the Alexandrine synthesis--present
> consent freely given between parties of
> proper age, even _absente_ solemnity or the
> consent of family or lord, makes a mar-
> riage which bars all others while both
> parties live--is what is at stake in the
> vast majority of these cases . . . Third
> . . . clandestine marriages, or at least
> unsolemnized marriages, were very common
> . . . Finally . . . there are some cases
> in which we may conclude that the parties
> chose informal marriage in order to escape
> pressure from their families or lords (pp.
> 267-68).

The controversy on the nature of marital consent
between the canonists of the Paris School and the Roman
Curia continued to rage even after Alexander III tried
to impose a resolution on the dispute; the issue was far
from being settled. Clandestine marriages were roundly

condemned, but many medieval people who knew that consent *de praesenti* constituted marriage continued to contract such unlawful but valid marriages; many parents,
however, still held on to the ancient Germanic law that
agreement to marry in the future (*consensus de futuro* or
engagement initiated by guardians) followed by intercourse constituted a valid marriage; canonists continued
to rely on the authority and intention of Gratian to
argue that parental consent was necessary not only for
the legitimacy but also for the validity of marriage.[6]

Since clandestine marriages continued to be contracted creating legal and moral chaos in the society,
the Council of Trent (1547-49, 1551-52, 1562-63) enacted
a universal law in its famous decree *Tametsi* in its 24th
Session on November 11, 1563, making clandestine marriages not only illegal but also invalid. *Tametsi*
(although) is the opening word of the decree which
states that juridical form is essential for the validity
of marriage:

> Although it is not to be doubted that
> clandestine marriages made with the free
> consent of the contracting parties are
> valid and true marriages, so long as the
> Church has not rendered them invalid; and
> consequently that those persons are justly
> to be condemned, as the Holy Synod does
> condemn them with anathema who deny that
> such marriages are true and valid . . .
> nevertheless the holy Church of God has
> for reasons most just, at all times de-
> tested and prohibited such marriages . . .
> Those who shall attempt to contract mar-
> riage otherwise than in the presence of

the parish priest, or of some other priest
by the permission of the said parish
priest or of the Ordinary, and in the
presence of two or three witnesses; the
Holy Synod renders such wholly incapable
of thus contracting and declares such
contracts invalid and null, as by the
present decree it invalidates and annuls
them.[7]

During the debate on the decree, the delegates of
the King of France stipulated that the decree include
the provision that the consent of the parents of the
marrying parties be a necessary element for the validity
of the marriage. The earlier drafts of the decree contained this requirement, but the final draft of _Tametsi_
returned to the spirit of the Alexandrine rules by not
even requiring the publication of the bans when there
was reason to fear force.[8] It is important to note
that _Tametsi_ was not implemented immediately in most of
Western Christendom. This situation was due to the
manner of the promulgation of the decree. According to
Tametsi, the decree would take effect in every parish at
the expiration of thirty days reckoned from the day of
its first publication in that church. The decree was
actually never published in many nations until the end
of the nineteenth century. The _Ne Temere_ decree of
August 2, 1907 issued by Pope Pius X (1903-1914) was
necessary to settle the numerous doubts resulting from
the _Tametsi_.[9]

My intention in citing these various legal positions, customs, canonical opinions, and papal decrees
has been to show that the problem of what constitutes a
valid marriage was not once and for all settled by the

Old Testament, New Testament, St. Augustine, Gratian,
Hugh of St. Victor, Peter Lombard, or Pope Alexander
III; there was still legal room for maneuvering for
parents, children, and ecclesiastical authorities. Real
people and fictional characters made various uses of
these different positions to suit their needs and purposes. In future studies I shall show that a better
understanding of medieval canon laws and theological
discussions on marriage is necessary to appreciate
medieval romances and troubadour poetry.

NOTES

[1]See Edward Schillebeeckx, Marriage: Human Reality
and Saving Mystery (London: Sheed and Ward, 1980),
256-58; II Cnute, c. 74 in F. Liebermann, Die Gesetze
der Angelsachsen (Halle: M. Niemeyer, 1903), I: 360-
61; H. Conrad, Deutsche Rechtsgeschichte (Karlsruhe: C.
F. Müller, 1962), I: 154.

[2]Gratian, Concordantia Discordantium Canonum, Causa
32, quaestio 2, caput 12: "Paternus consensus desidera-
tur in nuptiis, nec sine eo legitimae nuptiae habeantur,
iuxta illud Evaristi Papae: Aliter non fit legitimum
coniugium, nisi a parentibus tradatur." It is con-
troversial whether Gratian's text may be regarded as
requiring parental consent for the validity of marriage. See Charles Donahue, "The Policy of Alexander
the Third's Consent Theory of Marriage," in Proceedings
of the Fourth International Congress of Medieval Canon
Law, Toronto, 21-25 August 1972, ed. Stephan Kuttner
(Vatican: Bibliotheca, 1976), 271-72. All translations
are mine.

[3]See Theodore Mackin, What Is Marriage? (New York:
Paulist Press, 1982), 168-70; Donahue, 251-81; I am
indebted to Donahue's article for what follows in this
study on Pope Alexander's impact on the ecclesiastical
policy on marriage.

[4]Donahue, 256; W. Holdsworth, A History of English
Law, fifth edition (London: Methuen, 1942), III: 31,
201; F. Pollock and F. W. Maitland, The History of
English Law, second edition (Cambridge: The University
Press, 1968), II: 368-69; H. S. Bennett, Life on the
English Manor, 1150-1400 (Cambridge: The University
Press, 1937), 240-48; Donahue, 257: "In many parts of
England the daughter (and in some cases the son) of a
man who held by unfree tenure could not be married
without the tenant's making a payment, known as merchet,
to his lord . . . He could give in marriage . . . an
infant heir or heiress, and . . . he had to consent to
the marriage of any female tenant."

[5]See Michael Sheehan, "The Formation and Stability of
Marriage in the Fourteenth Century: Evidence of an Ely
Register," Mediaeval Studies, 33 (1971), 228-63; F. J.
Furnivall, ed., Child Marriages, Divorces, and Ratifica-
tions, EETS, 108, o.s. (London: Oxford University
Press, 1897).

[6] See Donahue, 271-72; John Noonan, "Power to Choose," *Viator* 4 (1973): 419-34; Raymond G. Decker, "Institutional Authority versus Personal Responsibility in the Marriage Sections of Gratian's *A Concordance of Discordant Canons*," *The Jurist*, 32 (1972): 51-65. There are passages in Gratian especially c. 36, q. 2, dictum post c. 11: "Legitime igitur post peractam penitenciam raptor poterit sibi copulare quam rapuit, *nisi pater puellae illam raptori detrahere voluerit*" and c. 30.1.5, dictum post c. 6: "His omnibus auctoritatibus occultae nuptiae prohibentur, atque ideo, cum contra auctoritatem fiunt nuptiae, *pro infectis* haberi debent," which seem to indicate that parental consent is needed for the validity of marriage. Such a line of thinking was perfectly consonant with Justinian's classic text *si patre cogente*: "Si patre cogente, ducit uxorem, quamnon duceret, si sui arbitrii esset, contraxit tamen matrimonium, quod inter invitos non contrahitur, maluisse enim hoc videtur." [If, at a father's compulsion, a son marries a wife he would not marry if he were able to follow his own decision, he has nonetheless contracted marriage; it is not contracted between the unwilling, (but) he appears to have married her.] See *Digest*, 23.2.22.

[7] See H. Denzinger, *Enchiridion Symbolorum, Definitionum et Declarationum* (Freiburg: Herder, 1937), 990-991.

[8] Denzinger, 991.

[9] Denzinger, 2066-70.

INDEX

326

CONTRIBUTORS

JUDITH BRUSKIN DINER earned a Ph.D. from New York University's Department of French and Italian in 1984. She is the author of an article, "The Courtly-Comic Style of Les Cent nouvelles nouvelles" (to be published by Romance Philology), and is currently translating Les Cent nouvelles nouvelles for the Garland Library of Medieval Literature (Series B).

ELIZABETH D. HARVEY, assistant professor of English at the University of Western Ontario, has published articles on medieval and Renaissance literature and is currently completing a book on Ovid and the feminine voice.

LYNNE HUFFER, doctoral candidate in French at the University of Michigan, has written on nineteenth- and twentieth-century literature and French women writers. She has published one article, "'Aurelia': Une intimite illusoire," Iris 2 (1986-87), and is currently completing a study of textuality and gender in the works of Colette.

WILLIAM E. JACKSON, associate professor of German at the University of Virginia, is the author of Reinmar's Women: A Study of the Woman's Song of Reinmar der Alte, and of articles on medieval German poetry and short fiction.

KATHLEEN ELIZABETH KELLS, a member of the faculty at Seneca College in Toronto, is currently on leave at The University of Western Ontario in London, Canada where she is completing a doctoral thesis in French-Canadian Literature on the poetry of Anne Hebert.

EVELYN S. NEWLYN, associate professor of English and director of Women's Studies at Virginia Polytechnic Institute and State University, has edited The Medieval Cornish Drama: A Bibliography, and is the author of articles on medieval literature for, among others, Nottingham Medieval Studies, The Journal of Popular Culture, and Studies in Scottish Literature.

JOHN A. NICHOLS, professor of history at Slippery Rock University, has published a number of articles on religious women, among them "Medieval English Cistercian Nunneries: Their Art and Physical Remains" in Melanges Anselme Dimier (1982). He is co-editor of a multi-volume work on Medieval Religious Women, the first two volumes of which, <u>Distant Echoes</u> (1984) and <u>Peaceweavers</u> (1987), have been published.

DIANE G. SCILLIA, assistant professor of Art History, Kent State University, is the author of several articles on Netherlandish art of the fifteenth century.

MARTIN B. SHICHTMAN, assistant professor of English at Eastern Michigan University, is co-editor (with Laurie A. Finke) of <u>Medieval Texts and Contemporary Readers</u>, a collection of twelve essays which considers the Middle Ages in the light of contemporary critical theory. He has also written articles on Layamon and Wace, Malory, <u>Sir Gawain and the Green Knight</u>, and portrayals of the Grail legend in film.

JAMES R. STAMM, associate professor of Spanish and Portuguese at New York University, is the author of <u>A Short History of Spanish Literature</u>, a text edition of two novels of Miguel de Unamuno, and numerous articles on subjects ranging from the medieval <u>Libro de buen amor</u> to the early Spanish novel, <u>Celestina</u>, Cervantes, and the picaresque novel.

STEVEN M. TAYLOR, associate professor of French at Marquette University (Milwaukee, Wisconsin), has contributed articles on medieval French literature to journals including <u>Fifteenth-Century Studies</u>, <u>Allegorica</u>, <u>Neophiloolgus</u> and <u>Le Moyen Francais</u>.

ZACHARIAS P. THUNDY, professor of English at Northern Michigan University, is the author of <u>Covenant in Anglo-Saxon Thought</u>; <u>English Poetry: An Introduction</u>; <u>Stories from the East and West</u>, and <u>The Folktales of the South Indian Kadar</u>. He is also the editor of several books including <u>Chaucerian Problems and Perspectives</u>.

MEDIAEVAL STUDIES